Australia Under Construction

nation-building – past, present and future

Australia Under Construction

nation-building – past, present and future

Edited by John Butcher

THE AUSTRALIAN NATIONAL UNIVERSITY

E PRESS

ANU
E PRESS

the Australia and New Zealand
School of Government

Published by ANU E Press
The Australian National University
Canberra ACT 0200, Australia
Email: anuepress@anu.edu.au
This title is also available online at: http://epress.anu.edu.au/auc_citation.html

National Library of Australia
Cataloguing-in-Publication entry

Title: Australia under construction : nation-building : past,
                present and future / editor, John Butcher.

ISBN: 9781921313776 (pbk.)
                9781921313783 (online)

Series: ANZSOG series

Subjects: Federal government--Australia.
                Politics and culture--Australia.
                Australia--Social conditions.
                Australia--Economic conditions.
                Australia--Politics and government.

Other Authors/Contributors:
                Butcher, John.
                Australia and New Zealand School of Government.

Dewey Number: 320.994

Cover design by John Butcher.

Funding for this monograph series has been provided by the Australia and New
Zealand School of Government Research Program.

John Wanna, *Series Editor*

Professor John Wanna is the Sir John Bunting Chair of Public Administration at the Research School of Social Sciences at The Australian National University. He is the director of research for the Australian and New Zealand School of Government (ANZSOG). He is also a joint appointment with the Department of Politics and Public Policy at Griffith University and a principal researcher with two research centres: the Governance and Public Policy Research Centre and the nationally-funded Key Centre in Ethics, Law, Justice and Governance at Griffith University. Professor Wanna has produced around 17 books including two national text books on policy and public management. He has produced a number of research-based studies on budgeting and financial management including: *Budgetary Management and Control* (1990); *Managing Public Expenditure* (2000), *From Accounting to Accountability* (2001) and, most recently, *Controlling Public Expenditure* (2003). He has just completed a study of state level leadership covering all the state and territory leaders — entitled *Yes Premier: Labor leadership in Australia's states and territories* — and has edited a book on Westminster Legacies in Asia and the Pacific — *Westminster Legacies: Democracy and responsible government in Asia and the Pacific*. He was a chief investigator in a major Australian Research Council funded study of the Future of Governance in Australia (1999-2001) involving Griffith and the ANU. His research interests include Australian and comparative politics, public expenditure and budgeting, and government-business relations. He also writes on Australian politics in newspapers such as *The Australian*, *Courier-Mail* and *The Canberra Times* and has been a regular state political commentator on ABC radio and TV.

Table of Contents

Contributors

Dr Fred Argy AM OBE

Fred Argy, a former high level policy adviser to several Federal governments, has written extensively on the interaction between social and economic issues. His focus in recent articles has been on the efficiency and distributional dimensions of equality of opportunity, employment policy and economic freedom. His most recent papers are 'Equality of opportunity in Australia — myth and reality' (Discussion paper no. 85, April 2006); 'Employment Policy and the clash of values' (*Journal of Public Policy*, volume 1, number 2, 2006); 'Distribution effects of labour deregulation' (*Agenda, Volume 14, Number 2, 2007, pages 141-155*) and 'Economic Freedom — the good and the ugly', (*Australian Quarterly*, v.79, no.5, Sept-Oct 2007: 33-39).

John Butcher, Research Associate, Australia and New Zealand School of Government, The Australian National University

John Butcher is a research associate with the Australia and New Zealand School of Government in the Research School of Social Sciences at The Australian National University. He coordinates the production of the ANZSOG Monograph series published by the ANU E Press. He has worked as a policy analyst for Commonwealth and State central and line agencies and as a performance analyst for the Australian National Audit Office.

Dr Anna Clark, Postdoctoral Research Fellow, Education, Monash University

Anna Clark is an Australian Postdoctoral Fellow in history education at Monash University. With Stuart Macintyre, she wrote the *History Wars* in 2003, published by Melbourne University Press, and in 2005 published *Convicted!*, a history book for children, published by Pan MacMillan. Her PhD thesis, *Teaching the Nation*, was published by Melbourne University Press in 2006 and examines debates about teaching Australian history in schools. Her latest book *History's Children: History Wars in the Classroom* (UNSW Press, 2008), is based on her postdoctoral research and uses interviews with 250 history teachers, students and curriculum officials from around Australia. Anna hopes to continue researching areas of history and national identity in the future.

Michael de Percy, Lecturer, Government Discipline, School of Business and Government, University of Canberra

Michael de Percy is a lecturer in government-business relations at the University of Canberra where he is also a doctoral candidate. His thesis focuses on the impact of the government-business relationship in deploying broadband infrastructure in Canada and Australia. Michael is a graduate of the Royal Military College

Duntroon and was previously the principal of a Canberra-based consulting firm specialising in government financial management. Before taking his current appointment, he consulted on strategic management issues with small-medium enterprises in the telecommunications industry.

Dr Richard Evans

Richard Evans is a journalist and an academic. He has worked on newspapers and legal magazines, and was a lecturer in journalism at Royal Melbourne Institute of Technology (RMIT). His work has appeared in *HQ*, *Quadrant*, the *Age*, *Overland* and *The Republican*, and been broadcast on ABC Radio National. His book, *Constructing Australia,* published by Melbourne University Press in 2007, tells the dramatic story of political turmoil, private tragedy and conflict that lie at the heart of three epic engineering events in Australia's history: the building of the Sydney Harbour Bridge, the Perth-Kalgoorlie Pipeline and the Overland Telegraph.

Professor Ian Marsh, ANZSOG Chair of Public Management, Graduate School of Government, The University of Sydney

Ian Marsh holds the ANZSOG Chair of Public Management at the University of Sydney. Professor Marsh, a former Senior Fellow of the Research School of Social Sciences, The Australian National University, took up his chair at Sydney in early 2005. A graduate of the Kennedy School of Government, and the Graduate School of Arts and Sciences, Harvard University, Professor Marsh was formerly an Associate Professor of the Australian Graduate School of Management, Research Director of the Liberal Party of Australia, and Associate of McKinsey & Co, and Private Secretary to the Minister for Defence. Professor Marsh is author of several books, including *Beyond the Two Party System: Political Representation, Economic Competitiveness and Australian Politics* (Cambridge University Press, 1995), *Into the Future: The Neglect of the Long Term in Australian Politics* (with David Yencken, Black Inc. 2005) and three edited collections: *Australian Political Parties in Transition?* (Federation Press, 2006), *Democracy Governance and Regionalism in East and Southeast Asia* (Routledge, 2006) and *Globalisation and the People* (with Jean Blondel, Takashi Inoguchi and Richard Sinnott, Routledge, 2006).

Professor Lyndsay Neilson, Director, Neilson Associates Pty Limited

Professor Lyndsay Neilson is currently on leave from the Victorian Government, advising the government of Dubai on the future management of urban Dubai, and the government of Saudi Arabia on the future development of Riyadh, the national capital city. Professor Neilson holds the position of Under-Secretary of the Department of Premier and Cabinet in Victoria, and was Secretary of the Victorian Department of Sustainability and Environment from 2002 to 2006 and

Secretary of the Department of Infrastructure from 2000 to 2002. He was previously Director of the Centre for Developing Cities at the University of Canberra and Deputy Secretary in the Commonwealth Department of Housing and Regional Development. At the time of the initiation of the Better Cities Program he was Chief Executive of the National Capital Planning Authority in Canberra. He has extensive experience in Australia and internationally in urban research, planning and management consultancy, public policy development and public administration.

Professor Michael Pusey, Professor of Sociology, School of Sociology, University of New South Wales

Michael is a Professor of Sociology at UNSW and a Fellow of the Academy of Social Sciences in Australia. Michael left school at 15 and worked in Tasmania as a photographer, a farm labourer and a shop assistant before studying at the Sorbonne and later at the University of Melbourne. He was a school teacher in Tasmania before moving to The United States where he completed his doctoral studies in sociology at Harvard University. Over the last 20 years at the University of New South Wales Michael has taught on social theory, the media and the public sphere, economic ideas, and, most recently, on quality of life in Australia. He was listed in 2005 by the *Sydney Morning Herald* as one of Australia's top 100 public intellectuals. His theoretical and research interests have focussed on quality of life, on the experience of time, on trust and civil society, and the changing nature of political and economic culture in Australia. In the early 1990s Michael Pusey's book *Economic Rationalism in Canberra: A Nation-Building State Changes its Mind*, started a national debate on economic rationalism and brought the term into public usage. It showed how Canberra had been taken over by 'economic rationalists' and warned of the economic and social costs of free market economic reform. Since then he has been studying how Australians experience markets and economic structures. His most recent book, *The Experience of Middle Australia*, examines the impact of economic restructuring on incomes, jobs, families, communities, politics and Australian culture.

Anthony Shepherd, Chairman, Board of Directors, Transfield Services Limited

Anthony Shepherd is Chairman of the Board of Directors, Transfield Services, a leading international provider of operations, maintenance, asset management and project management services. He was first appointed a Director in March 2001. He is also Chairman of the ConnectEast Group, the public company which is developing the $3.8bn EastLink Tollroad in Melbourne. Anthony began his career in the Public Service in 1963, when he joined the Federal Department of Supply. In 1974 he started with the Pipeline Authority, eventually moving to the position of Assistant Secretary before joining Transfield Group in 1979. He was Bid Manager for the successful bid for the ANZAC Warships Project in 1988/1989 and in 1989 became the inaugural Chief Executive Officer of the Infrastructure Development Corporation Pty Limited (IDC). IDC was established by the then State Authorities Superannuation Board, State Bank of NSW and Perry Development Finance Group as a company which advised and assisted the private sector in developing public infrastructure. He was an executive of the Transfield Holdings Group and Chief Executive Officer of its Project Development Division until 2000. Anthony was responsible for the Sydney Harbour Tunnel Project, Melbourne CityLink Project, as well as a number of other build-own-operate transfer (BOOT) projects and the redevelopment of Walsh Bay. He chaired the consortium which won the Lane Cove Tunnel Project and was an inaugural Director of Transurban Limited. He is a Trustee of The Sydney Cricket Ground and a member of the Premier's (NSW) Business Roundtable.

Professor John Wanna, Sir John Bunting Professor of Public Administration, Australia and New Zealand School of Government, The Australian National University

John Wanna is the Sir John Bunting Chair of Public Administration at the Research School of Social Sciences at The Australian National University. He is the director of research for the Australian and New Zealand School of Government (ANZSOG). The author or editor of 17 books, John Wanna has produced a number of research-based studies on budgeting and financial management including: *Budgetary Management and Control* (1990); *Managing Public Expenditure* (2000), *From Accounting to Accountability* (2001), and most recently *Controlling Public Expenditure* (2003). His most recent books include *Yes Premier: Labor Leadership in Australia's State and Territories*, and *Westminster Legacies: Democracy and Responsible Government in Asia and the Pacific*. He was a chief investigator in a major Australian Research Council (ARC) funded study of the 'Future of Governance in Australia' (1999-2001) and is currently chief investigator of the ARC funded project 'Improving Decision Making in Government Service Delivery'. His research interests include Australian and comparative politics, public expenditure and budgeting, and government-business relations.

Dr Robert Wooding, Honorary Research Associate in the School of History and Classics at the University of Tasmania

Dr Robert Wooding is an Honorary Research Associate in the School of History and Classics at the University of Tasmania. He has been working on a book about the history, society and governance of inland Australia, with a particular emphasis on the West Darling region. Previously, he had a career of close to two decades in the Australian Public Service in Canberra, mostly at the senior executive level in the departments of Health and Ageing, Immigration and

Multicultural Affairs and the Prime Minister and Cabinet. Dr Wooding has a PhD in History from the University of Sydney on the politics of re-planning the Indian city under colonial rule. Dr Wooding has recently taken up a senior advisor position within the Commonwealth Department of the Environment and Water Resources in Canberra.

Acknowledgements

This monograph arose from the special workshop, 'Nation-building in Australia: Past, Present and Future', offered as part of the *Governing by Looking Back* conference held at The Australian National University from 12-14 December 2007. I am indebted to Professors John Wanna, Paul 't Hart and Tim Rowse without whose encouragement, support and guidance the workshop would not have been possible. I am grateful to each of the speakers, discussants and contributors whose work appears in this monograph and to Professor Don Aitkin and Dr Andrew Leigh for their individual — and insightful — contributions to the workshop sessions. I also wish to offer special thanks to Mary Hapel and Helen Walker for their valuable assistance in making it all work.

John Butcher
April 2008

1. Nation-building in Australia: a discourse, iconic project or tradition of resonance?

John Wanna

Canada's national cultural museum, the Canadian Museum of Civilisation, located on the Ottawa River in Hull, Quebec, looking back over the capital Ottawa, is a national tribute to the history of Canada — or at least to the way modern Canadians would like their past to be remembered. It is perhaps one of the most 'politically correct' places in the world — with no hint of oppression of First Nation peoples, and nothing but cordial relations between the Anglo and French settlers. The curators can afford to upset no one. It is myth founded on myth. Two main themes stand out in its collections and stunning recreations of the past: the native Indian cultures, especially around the initial decades of white contact; and fabricated stories of European settlement.

The museum includes collections of huge native totem-poles, elaborate and laced with spiritual meaning and reincarnation. It displays Indian carvings, items of Chief Sitting Bull's clothing and west coast war canoes. It presents a simulated forest, settler huts and farms, village centres and seashore settlements. It also chronicles the rapid exploration by the explorers and fur-trappers, Arcadian peasant farmers, the coastal cod fishing and whaling settlements, early French townships, mid-west grain silos astride the rail tracks. It also contains the main national symbols: the Canadian Pacific Railway linking east and west (the 'ribbons of steel'), and the Canadian postal service. These are the contemporary representations of Canadian nation-building across an unforgiving expansive continent.

Australia has no real equivalent. Our National Museum of Australia, on an equally impressive site overlooking Lake Burley Griffin in Canberra, has a far more limited collection and little sense of our nation-building project(s). It carries the occasional iconic implements of traditional Australiana, such as Victa lawn mowers, Hill's hoists for backyard washing, a garish 1950s kitchen, and buffalo-catching jeeps from the Northern Territory outback. But it does not really disentangle a set of nation-building stories or celebrate nationhood. It has a small, anodyne section devoted to Federation in 1901, complete with polystyrene arches and photos of celebrating crowds. The National Museum is more a commemoration of incidentalism than a celebration of nationhood (however understood or from whichever narrative). Its Indigenous collection reflects a history of struggle and marginalisation — including biographies of individuals of the 'stolen generation'.

But, what do these recent representations tell us — encapsulated as they are in their respective cultural institutions? Both the Canadian and Australian institutions are keen to propound their own views of their nation's pasts. Both offer a sanitised reconstruction of the past — with historical resonances viewed through the lens of modern sensibilities. Canada celebrates the contributions of its various peoples but with the deep-seated conflicts airbrushed out of the picture; Australia assembles items that shaped the Australian consciousness, iconic but inherently random. Canada uses poetic licence to heighten dramatic effect; Australia uses pragmatism and practical inventions to record our occupancy of the continent.

Yet, these are both settler societies that formed federal nations as an answer to geographic scale and regional differences. They both have 'long' histories (of ancient peoples) and 'recent' histories (of settler colonisation). If colonisation is problematic and difficult to recount or take any discernable pride in, popular symbols of nation identity are a much more safe topic attracting less controversy. But how *do* nations capture and construct their past. What do they include and exclude? How they capture their past is itself an important 'nation-building' narrative and gives indications about the national psyche looking both forwards and backwards.

From the early days of white settlement, the Australian polity has had to contend with adversity. Governments had to deal with a large dry continent, vast distances, a harsh climate, and a scattered but mobile population. Everything appeared to be in short supply. After the 'British Invasion' the notion of an empty continent (as opposed to terra nullius) took on two different meanings: the Indigenous people had a very low population density and were expected to be bred out or die out; and nothing was built or developed for the colonialists to use or rely upon.

Each state had its own various narratives about conquering and coping with the Australian emptiness. For some there was a belief in the notion that rain followed the plough, that the drive to settle marginal lands would temper the climate. Others believed that intrepid explorers would discover inland seas and rivers turning back to water the centre. Others felt that the gold rushes would provide the opportunistic means to develop secluded regions and relocate populations. Railways in the nineteenth century proved one of the more enduring forms of opening up the countryside and connecting the coastal capitals to emergent provincial towns and to the productive hinterlands. Every bush town and prospective hamlet wanted a rail artery. Occasionally, optimism triumphed over reality. Entire cities could be laid out in selected inland sites by planners and administrators anxious to populate the bush. Their follies would be pardoned by the fixation to build the nation.

Over time, Australia arguably developed a fascination with nation-building in an empty continent. It had to build from scratch. And the 'building' was literal. It consisted of connecting places by roads, by rail, and by sea through ports and jetties. It meant building palatial central railway stations and networks of regional stations, ornate classical parliament houses in each colony (the cost of which nearly drove some of the early colonies bankrupt). It meant building government administrative precincts and constructing local housing projects often with innovative statutory authority organisations and specialist government commissions. It was an engineer's state, often resourced by borrowed funds from UK banks.

But, how do we understand the nation-building discourse today? I suggest there are four possible interpretations we can derive from its usage.

First, nation-building is a 'new world' phenomenon and discourse. It resides in the huge landmasses of the Americas, Africa and Australasia. There is little equivalent discourse in the old world of Europe, China or Japan, although Communist Russia developed its own variety in its strenuous efforts to 'catch up with the west' from the 1920s onwards. In the 'new world' societies this discourse implies the taming of enormous wildernesses by colonialist regimes, usually through the provision of fundamental infrastructure. It extols the pioneering spirit — either collectively as in the case of Australia and occasionally Canada, or individually in the case of the United States. Baudrillard and Benedict Anderson often tried to capture the retrospective images of this discursive culture and its signifiers.

Second, nation-building can be used in connection with particular policy proposals. These become icon policies or icon projects. Such projects are treated differently than the norm. They are devised and formulated in non-standard ways, exceptions are made, and arguments in their favour are able to cut through. Iconic propositions seem able to gain institutional and popular support and projects emerge from the drawing board to construction. Iconic policies draw on popular emotions and rely on sentiment to get them through the normal policy process. Iconic policies that 'work' are lauded for their prescience and forward-thinking capabilities; iconic policies that 'fail' are ridiculed as white elephants with those involved left fighting the war of excuses. But, interestingly, the fact that white elephants repeatedly occur at regular intervals does not seem to shake the implacable faith of those interested in promulgating the next wave of nation-building projects. The iconic dreamers and fabricators appear immune to the risks or warnings of failure. They cut through.

Thirdly, nation-building can be regarded as a governance tradition that has great resonance at certain times. Such a tradition is something that waxes and wanes in and out of favour but holds a deep resonance in people's consciousness. Politicians and administrators feel a deep need to periodically do something 'to add to the building of the nation'. It is a set of beliefs within governance in the same way that Westminster, ministerial responsibility, or public service independence are resonance traditions. They are not always there and consciously prominent but are turned to periodically, to assist in periods of stress or turbulence. Resonance traditions suggest that there is the need every now and again to have a demonstration effect — returning to customary traditions of nation-building to help renegotiate our politics with the present.

Fourthly, the usage of the term is generally skewed towards the harder infrastructural meanings, but it does not have to be so. Nation-building carries a certain 'boys toy' ring. It means monuments, earthworks, big dams, suspension bridges, hydo-electric schemes. It does not usually mean, for instance, taxation collection — which is fundamentally a means of collective saving and investing in society both now and into the future. Indeed, taxation is usually considered as simply a drain on economic potential for some limited collective public goods. We tend to understand 'taxation' and compulsory saving from a liberal individualist position (on the assumption that people know how to spend their personal wealth better than the community does) rather than from a nation-building perspective — and yet taxation may have played a far greater role in Australia's nation-building than any iconic project or monument. Similarly, annual budgets of government can be seen as nation-building statements — but they are more conventionally regarded as simply recurrent spending plans. Taking this point a step further, the term nation-building is not much used to describe the routine administration of state so essential to good governance (although elements of this do appear in Michael Pusey's classic sociological study of the post-war administrative elite who were changing their minds from being nation-builders to economic rationalists). It is not used to describe the operation of the health or education system so essential to our productive life and standard of living. These 'invisible' forms of nation-building are subterranean but foundational. They are the 'excluded voices' from the discourse but which we need to acknowledge in a more complete assessment of the nation-building exercise.

In the chapters that follow we canvass these various interpretations at greater length, while in particular exploring the various strictures or obsessions that have characterised our nation-building experiences. We ask questions about the Australian discourse over time — what has happened and what is happening to the discourse, is it alive and well, going underground, undergoing transformation or in need of renewal and re-imagining.

The chapters by John Butcher, Michael Pusey, Anna Clark and Ian Marsh all explore the dimensions of the changing discourse — providing their own assessments and suggestions for reinvention. Other authors are more interested in how ideologies and professional strictures have shaped or channelled nation-building into certain paths. So, Fred Argy discusses how economic doctrines accepted by the Australian state have produced a 'fiscal straitjacket' that has held back economic development. Anthony Shepherd discusses why the state lost interest in nation-building agendas, and what might rekindle greater interest today. Michael de Percy asks whether conformism, standardisation and central controls serve the interests of nation-building in policy sectors that rely more on vibrancy and collaborative innovation. He compares Australia's slow progress with the new icon of fast broadbanding to Canada's more entrepreneurial, community-based but also effective approach to policy development.

Others bring the discussion back to the unconventional dreaming and periodic subscription to bizarre projects that have existed over time and still retain some attraction to modern policy-makers (semblances of traditions of resonance). Robert Wooding wonders why so many otherwise sensible people have continued to dream of massive inland waterworks as a way of filling the empty continent. The dream of castles in the air still finds its adherents especially when tough times such as extended droughts hit the continent. Richard Evans reminds us of our penchant for the white elephant — where conceptualisation was often more important than the social outcomes achieved. Lyndsay Neilson recounts how the Building Better Cities urban infrastructure program of the Hawke and Keating era was put together (a white elephant in some quarters but a planning renaissance in others). He looks at the legacy of such an ambitious program over a decade after it was aborted by the Howard government.

This monograph reminds the contemporary policy debate about the resonances of nation-building. It stresses the importance of the tradition in historical context but also probes its limitations and shortcomings. Together these essays suggest the need for reinvention and recasting in our beliefs about nation-building as we negotiate a more complex policy future.

2. The unfinished business of nation-building

John Butcher

Abstract

The rhetoric, mythology and practical consequences of nation-building are inextricably bound in the Australian story. Iconic infrastructure projects such as the Snowy Mountains Hydro-Electric Scheme are embedded in the collective national memory because of their audacity, scale and impact upon the shaping of the nation. However, it can be argued that other national institutions, from the ABC, to the CSIRO to the Australian Parliament also had nation-building as a primary *raison d'etre*. In a decidedly post-Keynesian age, however, the ascendancy of economic rationalism as the dominant public policy framework appeared to have consigned nation-building to an historical footnote. It has for some time been out of fashion to expect governments to intervene to correct market failure, other than through the reduction of regulatory or policy barriers to market participation. The nation was largely 'finished': the market largely 'mature' and the private sector could be leveraged to fill any gaps in the national patchwork using a mixture of deregulation and public private partnerships. This chapter asks the following questions: Has nation-building really been abandoned as a policy frame, or has it simply gone underground? Are today's major infrastructure projects the natural descendents of Keynesian era nation-building? What are the new frontiers of nation-building in the information age?

Why 'Nation-Building'?

In the months leading to the 2007 Australian general election, 'nation-building' re-entered the national political debate in spectacular fashion. The major political parties vied with one another to prove their nation-building credentials. The then Opposition Leader, Kevin Rudd, former Opposition Leader, Kim Beasley, then Prime Minister John Howard and then Deputy Prime Minister and Leader of the National Party, Mark Vaile — among others — invoked the term at various times during the federal election campaign. Even State Premiers like the former Premier of Queensland, Peter Beattie, weighed in on the nation-building angle. In so doing, each evoked a paradigm of nation-building as a policy framework for meeting the long term social and economic obligations of government.

The election campaign embedded the term in the consciousness of politicians, the electorate and the media. 'Industry welcomes nation-building Budget', or so-said the headline for Tony Jones' May 2008 Budget night interview with Australian Industry Group Chief, Heather Ridout on ABC TV's flagship program *The 7:30 Report*.[1] Was this merely a rhetorical 'hook' for a newspaper storyline or a media 'grab' or did it signal a genuine shift in the policy focus of governments? For his part, the then Opposition Shadow Treasurer, Wayne Swan (now Treasurer), declared that the Howard Government's Budget 'fails the *future test*'. This, of course, begs the question about what 'tests' might reasonably be applied to putative nation-building initiatives.[2]

A contested term

In Australia the term 'nation-building' is most often associated with the heroic efforts of Colonial and Australian visionaries who recognised that the potential of the continent could be unleashed only through the direct financial and policy intervention of government. However, the term also carries different meanings and emphases in different contexts. For example, nation-building can refer to the re-building or establishment of the institutions of civil society in 'failed states' or even the reconstructing nations in the wake of 'regime change'.

In this context, it might be said that, in a sense, Australia has in recent years shifted its nation-building efforts 'off-shore' to developing countries within its sphere of influence, such as the Solomon Islands or Papua New Guinea, where it is engaged in restoring or establishing civil society institutions, or as part of its commitments to post-war/post regime-change reconstruction in East Timor, Afghanistan and Iraq.

Social historians might approach the subject of nation-building as a form of national or cultural narrative in which the nation — or, more pertinently, the national identity — is the cumulative product of social, political and economic relations, relations between settlers and indigenous peoples, changing gender roles, the emergence of social movements or the experience of war.

Although each of these offers a legitimate and valuable lens onto our national identity, it is generally accepted in the Australian context that 'nation-building' refers to a deliberate policy framework whose aim is to construct the social and economic infrastructure of the nation state. For the purposes of this chapter, nation-building will be addressed as a policy frame which is, in part, an extrapolation of a 'settler narrative'.

Nation-building and the settler narrative

Nation-building in 'new world' nation-states of Australia, New Zealand, Canada and the USA, is a 'settler' narrative. It is a narrative concerned with taming the landscape, carving a country from the wilderness, conquering the 'tyranny of distance' and harnessing the land's bounty for productive purpose.

In some ways the Australian narrative differs from that of other settler societies. For example, whereas Australia's nation-building story is concerned with the struggle against a hostile landscape, physical isolation and remoteness from the 'mother country', the story in Canada is, in essence, about the geopolitical imperative of establishing a nation in a race against a powerful, ambitious and expansionist neighbour, the United States. The settler narrative of the United States, by contrast, is imbued with the notion of *manifest destiny* — the right, sanctioned by Divine Providence, to claim the continent for *republican democracy*.

Often, the nation-building story is a 'retrospective narrative': a lens for interpreting the past rather than a framework for charting a prospective future. As a retrospective narrative, there is, of course, a tendency to enlarge, embellish and emboss past events and even imbue them with almost mythic status.

An Australian story

In Australia, the nation-building story has traditionally centred on 'iconic' infrastructure projects. This is the imagery most often invoked by politicians when trying to tap into a transcendent national story. Commonly cited examples include the Snowy Mountains hydroelectric scheme (the 'Snowy') or even the Sydney Harbour Bridge.[3] Thus, the story of Australia is that of a fledgling nation fighting above its weight. It is also, in part, a story about 'visionary' projects whose scale, audacity and symbolism transcended mere function.

Past investment by government in strategic national infrastructure was a response to perceived market failure — the incapacity of markets then prevailing to deliver public goods. Governments felt they had to step in because only government could command the resources to deliver nationally strategic projects.

Despite the importance of nation-building in the national historical narrative, however, Michael Pusey argued in his 1992 book, *Economic Rationalism in Canberra: A Nation-Building State Changes its Mind,* [4] that the contemporary Australian state had largely turned its back on the federation era visionaries and post war Keynesian re-constructionists in favour of an *instrumentalist* economic rationalism in which the market is king, government is small, and government's role in constructing the *nation* is largely finished.

Should we accept that the nation is 'finished' and, if not, what does 'nation-building' *mean* today? Importantly, what do politicians and the public generally understand by it? Is nation-building — like 'mateship' or the 'fair go' — just a symbolic feel-good catchphrase (whose meaning is, nevertheless, vigorously contested) or does it describe a genuine policy frontier with a broadly agreed framework and preferred policy instruments?

More than bricks and mortar

Although the popular consciousness in Australia links nation-building with physical infrastructure: with roads, railways,[5] reservoirs and dams, in reality nation-building is about more that just bricks and mortar. Frequently overlooked is the contribution to nation-building of core civic, cultural or social institutions. It can be argued that nation-building was a driving force in the establishment of institutions such as the Post Master General (now Australia Post), the Australian Broadcasting Corporation (the ABC) or the Commonwealth Scientific and Industrial Research Organisation (the CSIRO) — or, for that matter, the Commonwealth Bank or Telecom (now Telstra) which, unlike their privatised descendants, were not initially concerned solely with maximising financial returns to their shareholders. Even Australia's Parliament, our body of law and our democratic system of government, are essential components of ongoing nation-building.

It can also be said that past investment in public health, education and the arts had the broader purpose of creating a particular kind of society embodying those values held by broad consensus to be quintessentially 'Australian'. If we accept that proposition, what then can we say about the contemporary attitude towards these institutions? Does privatisation or disinvestment in public health and education, for example, signal a diminishing attachment to these values?

Certainly, a number of commentators on contemporary Australian affairs (Pusey 1992, 2003; Mackay 1993, 2007; and Aitkin 2005) have expressed concern that the diffusion to Australia of neo-conservative precepts of government (see Mishra 1990:69-95; Gould 1993: 129-130; Glennerster 1989:108-128) have threatened to seriously undermine public confidence in the capacity of public institutions to address societal needs.

It is possible that future nation-building enterprises will have 'soft ' and 'hard' elements. Examples of soft nation-building might include such things as reconciliation between indigenous and non-indigenous Australia or achieving an Australian republic. Hard nation-building — as ever — will focus on delivering physical infrastructure to support the nation's productive capacities. In all likelihood, nation-building enterprises deserving of the name will embody soft and hard elements — structural reforms to health or education, for example, will require major investments in social, human and physical capital.

A nation-building doldrums

During the 1980s and 1990s it became almost an article of faith for Australian governments — Commonwealth and State, Labor or Coalition — that governments needed to refocus and align their efforts with their 'core business'. Nation-building, it seemed, was not core business, at least not in the traditional sense of iconic infrastructure projects or the creation of new institutions. Policy mixes emphasising deregulation, commercialisation, corporatisation, downsizing and privatisation suggested that, as far as Australian governments were concerned, the time for active nation-building has passed.

Even so, the Hawke and Keating Labor governments made policy forays that might, retrospectively, be seen as broadly nation-building in their intent. For example, the Hawke Labor government's monetary and fiscal reforms of the early 1980s could be characterised as having established a new frontier for nation-building in which policy instruments and structural reforms take the place of bricks and mortar. These were durable reforms that transformed the national economy and provided the bedrock for Australia's strong economic performance to the present day.

In 1991, the Hawke Labor Government allocated $816 million over five years to the *Building Better Cities Program* under which the Commonwealth, State and Territory Governments would work co-operatively to improve urban development processes and the quality of urban life through improvements to urban planning, service delivery and co-ordination within and between the various levels of government. By the mid 1990s the Keating Labor government was making largely symbolic nation-building gestures in the form of grand policy statements, such as *One Nation*, *Working Nation* or *Creative Nation*. Although these employed the *rhetoric* of nation-building, they mainly amounted to a 're-branding' of existing programs without significant new investment.

Although these latter efforts might be legitimately cast as attempts to weave or strengthen the fabric of contemporary Australia, it might be said that they failed somehow to capture the public's imagination — possibly because they lacked the audacity and vision of past efforts. Apart from the significant structural reforms of the Hawke era, these initiatives did not survive the election of the Howard Coalition government in 1996. Not only had they failed to achieve the political or institutional momentum that would see them continue under a new administration, they had become inextricably associated with the Australian Labor Party's 'brand' and so, could be jettisoned without a backwards look by the incoming Howard administration.

From back burner to front burner

Politicians, academics and commentators are once again talking about the need for governments to intervene in significant ways to provide for the security of our water supply or to provide sustainable, clean energy. Achieving these goals is increasingly regarded by large parts of the electorate as essential for our national survival. Furthermore, it can be argued that such goals are, at present, far beyond the capability and capacity of the market to achieve on its own.

John Howard, in a 2001 address to the Centenary Conference of the Institute of Public Administration, acknowledged a nation-building past when he lauded:

[t]he great national issues of the past century — the turning of the dream of Federation into reality, post war reconstruction and repatriation, the peaceful settlement of millions of migrants, the vast nation-building projects like the Snowy and our rail and road networks to name just a few...[6]

As the leader of a government with, at the time, avowed 'small government' credentials, the Prime Minister's remarks fell short of acknowledging a nation-building *future*. The nation, now 'built', needed only ongoing maintenance.

By 2005, however, the Howard government appeared to have re-discovered nation-building as a policy framework. For instance, John Howard, in an interview on Channel Seven's *Sunrise* program, portrayed the Darwin to Alice Springs railway as an exercise in contemporary nation-building.[7] Built as a public private partnership with $1.3 billion in financial assistance from the Commonwealth, Northern Territory and South Australian governments, the line is the fruition of a promise first made by the Commonwealth in 1911.[8] The press, however, characterised the Commonwealth's $191 million contribution to the railway (opened by the Prime Minister in January 2004) as an attempt to shore up beleaguered conservative governments in the Territory and South Australia: nation-building *lite*, perhaps.[9]

Despite misgivings about the economic rationale for the Alice to Darwin link, it has proved popular with the public — it has even been dubbed 'the Steel Snowy' in an evocation of the nation-building spirit.[10] Indeed, a strong residual public affection for some of Australia's more iconic nation-building projects was demonstrated when in 2006 a public outcry over plans by the Commonwealth to divest itself of the government's remaining shares in Snowy Hydro resulted in the Commonwealth reversing its decision.[11] This reversal, according to the Prime Minister, reflected a recognition of the 'overwhelming feeling in the community that the Snowy is an icon. It's part of the great saga of post-World War II development in Australia.'[12]

In part, the Snowy Hydro story suggests a degree of 'privatisation fatigue' in the community and a degree of public unease about the transfer of public assets into private hands under the pretext of improving efficiency and promoting 'choice'. It may also signal a revival of a belief in the potential of government to use its legislative and financial muscle to meet the challenge of national survival.

Both the Alice to Darwin Railway and the reversal of the Snowy Hydro privatisation demonstrate that nation-building is inextricably linked to the political currents of the day. For that matter, recourse to the rhetoric and symbolism of nation-building is a natural and useful response in the face of internal and exogenous political threats.

The Rudd ascendancy

The rhetoric — if not the substance — of 'nation-building' is beginning to define the boundaries of contemporary national political debate. In January 2007, then Prime Minister, John Howard, seemed to allude to something approaching a nation-building agenda when he spoke in the following terms to the National Press Club about his plan to secure Australia's 'water future':

> By getting the big things right — by reforming and retooling our economy — we can afford to do the bold things — like saving the Murray-Darling Basin from economic and environmental decline, like securing our nation in a time of threat and uncertainty, like positioning Australia as a twenty-first century energy superpower, like meeting the challenge of climate change in a way that supports our competitiveness and plays to Australia's strengths. Water scarcity is a major national challenge. And there will be other challenges we must confront in the years to come. But with the resilience, adaptability and boldness Australians have shown in the past, they can be overcome.[13]

For his part, then Opposition Leader, Kevin Rudd, remarked when he spoke to the Australia Industry Group in February 2007:

> Building the infrastructure for a modern, dynamic economy is a major priority for Labor ... Rather than leave it entirely to the States or to the private sector, I want to see the Australian government return to its true nation-building role by investing in the nation's infrastructure.[14]

Kevin Rudd's announcement on 21 March 2007 that, if elected, Labor would roll out a $4.7 billion national high-speed broadband network, effectively threw down the nation-building gauntlet. In his 10 May Budget Reply Speech, Rudd made the following comparison:

> In the nineteenth century, governments laid out railway networks as the arteries of the economy. In the twenty-first century, governments around the world are ensuring that high speed broadband networks are laid out — as the arteries of the new economy ... This is the nation-building that the nation needs.[15]

Of course, these announcements are consistent with long-standing ALP policy to pursue nation-building. Indeed, Chapter 6 of the Australian Labor Party's *National Platform and Constitution 2007* is dedicated to the question of nation-building.[16] Since taking office, the Rudd Labor Government has established a Ministry of Infrastructure, Transport and Regional Development together with a new statutory advisory council, *Infrastructure Australia*, to:

... provide advice to Australian governments about infrastructure gaps and bottlenecks that hinder economic growth and prosperity. It will also identify investment priorities and policy and regulatory reforms that will be necessary to enable timely and coordinated delivery of national infrastructure investment.[17]

Infrastructure Australia is portrayed as a 'key driver in the Rudd Government's plan to fight inflation'. This it will do, according to the government, 'by boosting the economy's productive capacity [and] unlocking infrastructure bottlenecks like clogged ports and congested roads'. The government has also pledged to 'develop a strategic blueprint for Australia's infrastructure needs and ensure future projects are determined by economic, social, and environmental needs — not short-term political interests'.[18]

Nation-building — a revival?

Until recently, nation-building has seldom featured in the utterances of politicians or public commentators except when extolling (or lamenting) the halcyon days of grand public infrastructure schemes of such a scale that they could only be underwritten by government: schemes designed to harness the potential of our natural bounty and, in so doing, create a new society. Indeed, one might have been justified in concluding that nation-building had been consigned to the status of an historical footnote.

Every now and then, when someone promotes a grand — and sometimes silly — scheme to reverse the nation's rivers, water its deserts or in some way profoundly transform its productive heartland, Australians sit up and take notice. Somehow nation-building is inextricably bound up with the 'idea' of Australia and still resonates in the popular consciousness. With the froth and bubble of a long election campaign now behind us it is prudent to ask whether nation-building is set to 're-surface' as a contemporary policy and political discourse.

Nation-building appears set to undergo a renaissance as the Australian national 'idea' is re-forged in the cauldron of drought and climate change. The 2008 federal election demonstrated a clear recognition on the part of policy-makers and the electorate that the emerging challenges of climate change and water security will require concerted government action and that 'the market' has neither the capability or capacity to meet these challenges without the backing and muscle of governments.

The content and direction of nation-building may also be shaped by other factors such as the resources boom, an unprecedented budgetary surplus, the new Federal government's resolve to address key capacity bottlenecks and, perhaps not least, public weariness with the excesses of *new public management*.

Globalisation too may define a new policy frontier for nation-building — both as a consequence of the economic stimulus it provides as well as the threats it poses to national identity and national institutions. In this light, policies mandating the transition from analogue to digital communications, or policies opening up of the telecommunications market (through — ironically — the corporatisation of Telecom and the subsequent sale of its successor, Telstra) might be seen as exemplars of late twentieth century nation-building.

This will not be comfortable territory for politicians, institutions and a public obsessed with tax cuts, interest rates and budget surpluses, not to mention a horror of public borrowing. The battlelines drawn around Labor's ambitious plans for national broadband illustrate the tension between values of fiscal rectitude and visionary risk-taking. It has ever been thus in the business of nation-building.

Confronting these and other challenges may stir governments and the electorate from the 'comfortable and relaxed' complacency into which the nation seems to have lapsed. We may yet realise that the nation is not 'finished' by a long shot and governments will re-discover a mandate for big, bold initiatives.

References

Aitkin, Don. 2005. *What was it all for? The re-shaping of Australia*. Allen & Unwin.

Glennerster, Howard. 1989. 'Swimming against the tide: the prospects for social policy'. Chapter 5 in Martin Bulmer, Jane Lewis and David Piachaud (eds) *The Goals of Social Policy*. Unwin Hyman. pp 108-128.

Gould, Arthur. 1993. *Capitalist Welfare Systems: A comparison of Japan, Britain and Sweden*. Longman.

Mackay, Hugh. 1993. *Reinventing Australia: The Mind and the Mood of Australia in the 90s*. Angus & Robertson.

Mackay, Hugh. 2007. *Advance Australia Where?* Hachette Australia.

Mishra, Ramesh. 1990. *The Welfare State in Capitalist Society*. Harvester Wheatsheaf.

Pusey, Michael. 2003. *The Experience of Middle Australia: The Dark Side of Economic Reform*. Cambridge University Press.

ENDNOTES

[1] Australian Broadcasting Corporation, The 7:30 Report, Broadcast: 08/05/2007, accessed at http://www.abc.net.au/7.30/content/2007/s1917924.htm

[2] Australian Broadcasting Corporation, The 7:30 Report, Broadcast: 08/05/2007, accessed at http://www.abc.net.au/7.30/content/2007/s1917892.htm

[3] Although calling the latter an exercise in nation-building rather stretches the notion, it does serve to demonstrate the propensity to selectively re-interpret our nation-building past.

[4] Michael Pusey, *Economic Rationalism in Canberra: A Nation-Building State Changes its Mind*, Cambridge University Press, 1992.

[5] Of course, the history of failed attempts to create a national standard gauge railway system in the first part of the twentieth century offers a salutary lesson in the perils of nation-building within a federal system of government.

[6] *The Australian Public Service,* speech given by the Prime Minister, John Howard, to the Centenary Conference of the Institute of Public Administration, 19 June, 2001, accessed at http://australianpolitics.com/executive/publicservice/01-06-19howard.shtml

[7] John Riley interview with John Howard on Sunday Sunrise, 6 March 2005, accessed at http://seven.com.au/sundaysunrise/politics/19343

[8] *Alice Springs-Darwin Railway*, accessed at http://www.infrastructure.gov.au/transport/programs/rail/alice.aspx

[9] Mary Gearin, *Alice to Darwin railway go ahead surprises many*, Landline, First Published 3/12/2000, accessed at http://www.abc.net.au/landline/stories/s217515.htm

[10] See Northern Land Council, *Doing Business on Aboriginal Land*, at http://www.nlc.org.au/html/busi_infra_case_1.html

[11] *Lateline*, Australian Broadcasting Corporation, TV Program Transcript, Broadcast: 02/06/2006, accessed at http://www.abc.net.au/lateline/content/2006/s1654370.htm

[12] *The Snowy Mountains Scheme*, accessed at http://www.cultureandrecreation.gov.au/articles/snowyscheme/

[13] 'John Howard outlines visionary $10 billion programme to secure Australia's water future',

Thursday, 25 January 2007, accessed at http://www.malcolmturnbull.com.au/Pages/Article.aspx?ID=642

[14] 'Prosperity Beyond the Mining Boom', Speech to The Australian Industry Group, Canberra, 27 February 2007, accessed at http://pdf.aigroup.asn.au/representation/events_and_speeches/Kevin_Rudd_Speech_270207.pdf

[15] Federal Opposition Leader, Kevin Rudd, 'Budget Reply speech to the House of Representatives', 10 May 2007, accessed at http://australianpolitics.com/2007/05/10/2007-budget-reply-speech-kevin-rudd.shtml

[16] *ALP National Platform and Constitution 2007*, Chapter 6: Nation Building, pp 72-99, accessed at http://www.alp.org.au/download/now/2007_platform_chapter6.pdf

[17] http://www.infrastructure.gov.au/department/infrastructureaustralia/index.aspx

[18] Rudd Government to Dramatically Overhaul National Infrastructure Policy, Joint Media Statement, 21 January 2008 AA004/2008 Joint, accessed at http://www.minister.infrastructure.gov.au/aa/releases/2008/January/AA004_2008.htm

3. In the wake of economic reform … new prospects for nation-building?

Michael Pusey

Abstract

Has economic reform run its course? What potential remains for the resumption of nation-building progress? Contrary to expectations, Canberra is emerging from 20 years of neo-liberalism with disciplined government, ample revenues, an effective regulative apparatus and — perhaps — the capacity for government to steer the economy towards a brighter future. These prospects are weighed against the negative impacts of neo-liberalism on our institutions and then examined from the three viewpoints of: (1) our national political experience; (2) the administrative apparatus; and, (3) popular expectations. This chapter then considers the dynamic energies inherent in the challenges, respectively, of climate change, infrastructure development, and economic policies based on the enhancement of quality of life.

Introduction

I am best known for a book sub-titled '*A Nation-building State Changes its Mind*' in which I argued that the state apparatus had given up on the nation and decided to build the economy instead.[1] In the wake of a quarter century of root and branch neo-liberal economic re-engineering of a whole society it is useful to now reflect on the prospects for a renewal of nation-building.

A few comments at the outset will save time. We Australians do have a somewhat unique charter myth. Australia is a Benthamite society with a very secular, unromantic and down-to-earth utilitarian idea of itself.[2] For Britons today evocations of national identity will play on 'our British heritage'. Americans will use well-developed moral vocabularies to talk about their founding rights and freedoms. Old European nations evoke their own notions of national destiny with appeals to myths of origin, to communities of descent, and to millenarian and heroic histories. Here in Australia we pushed the Aborigines aside and quickly set about constructing a nation geared to something like the delivery of the greatest good to the greatest number. Our foundation population was 'born modern' committed to Enlightenment ideas of progress and steeped in the view that society could be improved through the application of reason and industry.[3]

This was never a romantic and giddy metaphysic but it did carry its own kind of unifying symbolism. Progress understood as security, as freedom from war and strife and, above all, as prosperity for all is — or was — our own quasi-utopian ideal. It shaped our national imagination and, right up until the early 1980s, it served to sustain and to integrate what was then a centrist two party political consensus and a full gamut of public policies aimed at building a still new nation. To catch the flavour and the meaning think to those brochures we used to attract migrants to Australia in the 1940s and 50s. All the key bits of our story are there: massive infrastructure developments (the Snowy Mountains Scheme and the like), a relaxed lifestyle, the absence of old class antagonisms, vistas of new suburban dwellings priced within the reach of the 'common man', free education for all, a vast sunny continent with unlimited potential offering improving quality of life for all. This was the Australian post-war dream. Construed in this way, nation-building may be the 'white-fella' version of The Dreaming; in short the idea of ourselves that we go on reconstructing and projecting into the future to lead our understanding of who we are.

Neo-liberalism (and the attendant phenomena of globalisation or economic rationalism) has imposed its own strictures on states and governments everywhere. But are we the only society that has surrendered its charter myths, and its images of its own future, to the dull compulsions of the markets? Or could it be that there is once again a potential for a positive, constructive, re-emergence of nation-building governance. Is there a potential to stop the tail from wagging the dog and to once again draw the markets into the service of the people? Perhaps the time is right for such questions: in Europe globalisation tends to dissolve and subsume the idea of national purpose into the larger framework of the European Economic Community. Here, by contrast, we find ourselves thrown onto our resources. We are not threatened with any national emergency or with belligerent neighbours. Not withstanding the plight of Aboriginal Australia we have no serious ethnic, religious, or social divisions. A strong national economy sustained by a resource boom offers the best prospects in a long while for mid to long-term economic stability. The Treasury is as, I heard one senior Treasury official recently say in public, 'awash with money. We hardly know what to do with it'.

So what potential might there be for nation-building to wake from 25 years of amnesia? To answer that question I want to examine the prospects for a resumption of constructive nation-building from three viewpoints: national politics; national administration; and national political culture.

1. National politics

First of all, we should note that we have grown accustomed to radicalism. The Whitlam government was a radical government. The Fraser government was not. But the Hawke and Keating Governments were radical in much the same way that the four Howard governments have been. As with the Thatcher governments, radical governments want to 'crash through' and if necessary destroy existing institutions to get their way and overcome what the reformers love to call 'institutional inertia'. And here I am reminded of a 1996 speech by Paul Keating about economic reform and institutional change in which he made a very revealing comment about his government's attitude to institutional change.[4] His words were, 'If you stop pedalling the bike falls over'. He was speaking explicitly about the dynamics of change as an advocate for top-down, 'crash-through' economic functionalism. He might just as easily have said that the only way to maintain the momentum of reform is to keep the whole national population reeling on the back foot. What I heard in this justification for a general strategy were two admissions. First, he was admitting that there was no consensus for economic reform and, implicitly, that public policy deliberations are futile and a waste of political time and economic opportunity. The second presumption was that strong leaders must keep up the momentum so that all normative questions about what the people really want are always left behind, subordinated in advance to economic functions, so that they cannot effectively mobilise resistance to economic reform. How times have changed!

Libertarian, free market, laissez faire economics, economic reform, structural change, economic rationalism — call it what you will — was developed in the 1970s and early 1980s and pressed upon the developed Trilateral democracies (of North America, Western Europe and Japan) as a remedy for what was touted as a general systemic problem. These democracies were held to be drifting, rudderless, in the grip of a 'New Class' of self-serving drones, paralysed by bureaucracy, and weighed down with an overload of mutually contradictory decisions. In the words of the 1975 report to the Trilateral Commission, the problem was that these democracies had become ungovernable.[5] My point is that, at least in its own terms, the Australian version of crash-through reform has done its job with a vengeance. Over a quarter of a century two ruling parties — the ALP and the Coalition — and their ministers, have demonstrated, dramatically, that they can call up massive reserves of organised power to transform a whole nation society.

Second, contemporary politics and contemporary politicians have entirely changed. In a recent article Bob Brown, leader of the Greens, ventured the view that most politicians still come to this demanding and thankless work because they want to make a difference. Yes, maybe, but if we put their values to one side for the moment I think we can see the result of a generational transformation in our career politicians — at least at the national level. The terrible work of intra-party politics, of committee work, of selling the Government's, or the Opposition's line on a whole range of policies weighs so heavily on these overworked people that they scarcely think about their constituents — except at election time when they feel a little more vulnerable. The branch party members have vanished. But there is something more: politicians no longer recognise themselves or understand what they do in received notions of Millean representative democracy and popular sovereignty. Collectively at least, as members of a Party, an Opposition or a Government, they no longer believe that sovereignty lies with the people. That notion has been stood on its head. For them professional, grown-up, big-league, politics is about aggregating and managing big interests. For the most part they no longer believe that it is their duty to obey public opinion but rather that it is their job — with the help of an army of media advisers and spin doctors — to bend, cajole, and manage the public into an acceptance of whatever the system can deliver within whatever parameters are set by big interests operating in an increasingly globalised economy. Grassroots, face-to-face, town-hall, and party branch-based democracy of the post-war and later Whitlam times is now eclipsed as a motive force for big politics. Political communication is done through the Media. My point then is that nation-building could only make sense to this generation of professional politicians as a tightly managed top-down process.

Third, for a quarter of a century both major parties have been wedded to a politics that sits in outright contradiction with our national history. Our tradition is one in which the state led and private capital followed in close partnership. Butlin reminds us that from our very beginnings a pattern of reliance on public investments as the driver for development 'became so entrenched that it was not until the 1930s that private capital investments exceeded public capital outlays — and they still accounted for just over one third of total capital formation in the 1970s'.[6] From the time of Prime Minister Hawke's 'trilogy' commitment of 1984 we have been subject to an aggressive application of a doctrine that John Braithwaite has so exquisitely labelled the 'hydraulic model'.[7] It proceeds from the same libertarian American ideology that drives neo-liberal free market economic reform and assumes that to have strong markets you must have weak states. Our two major parties seem committed to this renunciation of our past with the application of policies that are deeply averse to public spending and which assume — in the face of all the contrary evidence — that the state sector is a national burden, a hindrance to development, and that a dollar spent in the private economy is a productive dollar and worth more than a dollar spent in the public sector. Our politicians do not wish to recognise that the libertarian Anglophone variant of modern capitalism shows up poorly even on conventional economic criteria of comparative economic performance.[8] I can think of no other developed nation whose politicians have so completely abandoned their institutional inheritance to a foreign ideology.

Fourth, in the wake of a now defeated Australian settlement both major parties believe that they must accede to the demands of a corporate business sector that operates in a changed relationship to the Nation. The destroyed Accord between the Labor government and the unions marked the end of a century of what the political scientists called 'corporatism': namely government through a cooperative three sided partnership, brokered by the State, between Capital and Labour. Now faced with a globalised multi-national corporate sector, politicians no longer believe that they can do much to moderate the raw elements of the broader economic dispensation within which the people must live their lives. The comparative evidence so clearly shows that different nations adapt to the same global economic forces in very different ways — in many cases with strongly positive outcomes for their national populations.[9] Yet our politicians have decided that governments of either persuasion must first of all serve a Business Council (the CEOs of the top 100 corporations) that always makes the same demands: namely, for a predictable environment for investment; for the minimum attainable price for labour; and for the minimum attainable level of corporate taxation. The national accounts tell the story. Over the 20 years from 1980 to the year 2000 the total wages share fell from 60% to 54% as the profit share rose from 17% to just on 24%. The government share stayed at about the same low level. And the trend continues. The point is that nation-building in any form that costs a lot of money cannot happen unless the Business Council will allow it to happen.

Through this window into national politics we see mixed prospects for a resumption constructive nation-building. On the one hand, there is clear evidence that national governments can govern strongly and effectively. Yet this was done in the name of neo-liberal economic restructuring of a whole nation society. Could this newfound strength be used over the longer term to re-build our infrastructure and to draw the markets and major corporate interests into the service of a more progressive and inclusive future for 'the Nation'? Is that what a Rudd government will try to do? We don't know.

2. The Canberra bureaucracy and the federal structure

The first point I want to make is that the top Canberra public service has turned its back on nation-building. This is so important because we have known since the early '70s that, in developed nations, top public servants are typically, with their ministers, the co-authors or even the originators of national policy. Now the neo-liberal economic rationalists dominate Canberra. We are a light year away from the Coombs 1976 *Royal Commission on Government Administration* which recommended that Treasury should be stripped of much of its power and that economic policy-making be largely devolved to the line or spending departments in order to gear it more closely to the real, coal-face, economic and social priorities of nation-building. In 1991 the findings reported in *Economic Rationalism in Canberra* showed that power was instead concentrating in the central agencies of the Department of the Prime Minister and Cabinet, The Treasury and the Department of Finance and Administration.[10] An older generation of broadly experienced and more broadly educated small L liberal and Fabian intellectuals — most of them with degrees in humanities, social science and the law — were losing out to a new elite of younger, dry, narrowly-trained, neo-liberal economists who were, from the early 1980s, being reeled up into the central agencies through the mechanism of accelerated promotion. From the first Hawke-Keating years, the Public Service Board quickly lost its independence. The very idea of a Career Service charged with giving advice 'without fear or favour' was put to the sword as top public servants were brought to heel, put on short-term contracts, told to perform and to do the ministers' bidding or risk losing their performance pay and all hopes of further advancement.

As they say 'the rest is history'. The post-war generation of committed centrists and progressively minded improvers and nation-builders with longer time horizons were overwhelmed in an ideological restructuring, a political re-education if you prefer, of the top federal public service. In 1992 Coombs, himself a former Governor of the Reserve Bank of Australia, was not shy in venturing the judgement that 'the intellectual and moral basis of Australian society is being corrupted' and that 'the driving force behind [these reforms] is a view of the economy as a machine independent of social purposes'. Today public policy is set within an ideological mould that is, at least in principle, averse to public expenditure, to public borrowing, to what we used to call the 'mixed economy', to planning *per se* and to the deployment of state power to steer the national economy into any kind of mid and long-term nation-building initiatives. Not surprising then that John Wanna and his colleagues should conclude that, after 20 and some years of these reforms, Australia has a system of public expenditure that is averse to capacity building and for which 'budget rationing rather than budget maximising has become the Australian creed'.[11] This is a culture that is likely to prejudge nation-building initiatives as reckless adventures and to shun large publicly funded infrastructure projects and capacity building.

My second point is that we have a demonstrably efficient and professional bureaucracy. Despite occasional lapses into the overt politicisation of elements of public administration, there is no evidence of systemic corruption. The streamlining of the forward estimates, accrual accounting, new information technologies and the increasing sophistication of Department of Finance and Administration controls on expenditure have all contributed to huge gains in the efficiency of a Canberra public service that is half the size of 20 years ago.[12] The forced mobility of senior public servants across different program and policy areas has, with strong central agency coordination, produced a loss of corporate memory and of hands-on experience in dealing with specific program areas. At one point in the early 1990s there were at most one or two Senior Executive Officers in the then Department of Education with any expert knowledge of schools and education. Most of them were drop-in economists, accountants and managers from other areas focussed only on coordination and efficiency. On the other side of the coin these reforms have given the lie to the 'new right' dogma that bureaucracies and governments are inherently unable to cope with the complexity of coordinating national affairs. The bureaucracy has proven that it can forecast and control expenditures accurately, that it can respond flexibly to changed funding priorities and that it can, *perhaps*, effectively coordinate policies across and between departments rationally and efficiently.[13] Although the experience of nation-building has been long forgotten, the capacity to coordinate major initiatives over time and perhaps across several departments is probably much stronger that it ever was.

Thirdly, we have new tools for pro-active nation-building. Let me briefly mention three of them. John Braithwaite explains that tax collection from multi-national corporations has increased at about three times the growth in GDP and that this is largely the result of new information technologies. It is clear that IT systems and our experience in learning how to use them have greatly augmented the capacity of government to plan and monitor programs and initiatives. Another cause for optimism appears when we look past the shibboleths about deregulation to the real story. True, the deregulation of the financial sector led to profiteering by the banks and contributed to unsustainable levels of private indebtedness and an artificial inflation of house prices. The partial deregulation of the labour market and, most egregiously, 'WorkChoices', has produced another type of sponsored exploitation. In other areas, however, we see not free-for-all laissez-faire deregulation but, instead, the emergence of what Braithwaite calls a 'regulatory capitalism' that is extending and deepening regulatory supervision across a range of public and private industries with amazing speed.[14]

In the interests of creating a more predictable future, business is more often inclined to accede to public calls for governments to provide sound publicly enforceable safety, prudential, environmental and ethical standards for corporate activity. Improved regulation also has the demonstrated potential to turn privatisation into a good news story. For example if the government can impose suitable standards for telephony and broadband spectrum usage on a fully privatised Telstra then the revenues from the sales of government equity in such enterprises can be used for other purposes.

It is worth noting that some 25 years ago we had scarcely heard about accountability or about targeted or performance based funding. We are now much more able to make public administrative and financial systems deliver on their promises. For example, ongoing British reforms of the National Health Service under Blair have used targeted funding and improved efficiencies in the delivery of health care to eliminate queues for elective surgery in British hospitals. In short the available instruments for the delivery of nation-building have vastly improved from the days of post war reconstruction and the Whitlam governments.

Fourthly and more worrying are the challenges to nation-building that accrue from our creaking federal system. The year 2007 should be remembered as an example of an especially glaring dissociation and imbalance between the state and federal levels of governments. On the one hand, the 2007 election gave us a picture of a national government awash with revenues as our two major political parties were forced into a perverse and ideologically sponsored competition to see which would better squander a once-in-a-lifetime opportunity to build a modern national infrastructure by handing back tax revenues in electoral bribes. On the other side of this canvass we find a NSW Labor government selling off precious coastal forest land to pay for improvements to a rail and public transport system that is in ruins from decades of neglect, incompetent management and chronic under-funding. Similarly we have seen the Queensland and NSW governments locked in competition to grant unsustainable water licences to their own up-stream water users at levels that are seriously endangering our principal national river system.

Three observations will suffice to point to the magnitude of these problems. In the first place, and in contrast with other federations like Canada, we suffer from a mighty fiscal imbalance between a federal state that collects some 75% of all revenues and a state sector that is still constitutionally responsible for the lion's share of service delivery and public works. Secondly and less obviously we see that the national press gallery of some 200 and more Canberra based journalists does a reasonably good job in scrutinising the actions of the federal government. By contrast, at the state level, which carries the major share of constitutionally assigned responsibility for public works and service delivery, there is so little scrutiny that successive NSW government have been allowed to get away with such egregious blunders as the bungled funding of the Sydney Cross City Tunnel, the desecration of east Circular Quay, the commissioning of unserviceable train rolling stock and, most recently — and in the face of the best advice — the go-ahead for the Sydney Water desalination plant. What is more, in this environment regional policies that involve still more problematic inter-government cooperation are virtually impossible. Thirdly we hear many experienced administrators telling us that divided state/federal responsibility for the delivery of services nearly always results in buck-passing and failures of coordination. The provision of pharmaceuticals in public hospitals and most recently the fraught attempts of federal government to intervene in Northern Territory Aboriginal policy are but two examples of these failures. Divided responsibility generally fails and it greatly impairs our capacity to mount nation-building initiatives that mostly intrude into state jurisdictions and require a concerted whole-of-government approach.

In conclusion (to this second section) it would seem that in the wake of 20 and more years of neo-liberal re-engineering of the machinery of government we have a more technocratic and managerially oriented top federal public service with an ingrained ideological aversion to nation-building and a much reduced capacity for delivering fearless and independent advice to ministers. On the other side of the coin there have been huge gains in efficiency, budget management and coordination. Yet, even in the face of an increasingly dysfunctional imbalance between federal and state levels of government, we find some encouragement in the observations of Wanna and others that the federal government has shown itself increasingly capable of directing and monitoring expenditures, even in areas that are outside its formal jurisdiction.[15]

3. Our national political culture

What has happened to our memory of nation-building post-war government? How does an earlier history of nation-building shape the norms and standards that we apply to contemporary politics and to our assessments of a 25-year-long experience of economic reform?

We have not given up our expectations of what good government can achieve. First there was the floating of the Australian dollar and then the deregulation of the capital markets. Then privatisation, labour market reform, micro economic reform, user pays, cutting government spending, competition policy, more labour market reform (WorkChoices) and the push for the privatisation of Medicare. All of these reforms were pressed on us with the same unrelenting message. Government is a blunt instrument and for the most part the enemy of progress and prosperity. Taxation is a form of theft. We should rid ourselves of the Nanny State, expect less of governments, become a shareholder society, and rely instead on the creative energies of private enterprise and free market capitalism. Australians were urged to accept the new doctrine 'that economies, markets and money would always, at least in principle, deliver better outcomes than states, governments and the law'.[16]

Have we bought this message? The evidence shows that we value efficiency and want a well functioning economy but that we do *not* want economic considerations to one-sidedly redefine or restrict the role of government. Take a glimpse at the evidence. My *Middle Australia* interview surveys of 1996 and 2000 included a question asking whether respondents thought that governments, of whichever party, could do 'quite a bit' or 'very little' to effect change in 13 domains labelled as follows: 'to keep prices down', 'to reduce unemployment', 'to improve general standards of living', 'to improve health and social services', 'to reduce poverty', 'to cut crime', 'to make business pay fair wages', 'to create more job security', 'to support families, to reduce the gap between rich and poor', 'to control economic change', 'to hold society together', and 'to support communities'. The results show that an average of about 70% of middle Australians believe that governments can do 'quite a bit' across this broad range of functions. We are not, and never have been, gung-ho libertarians. Clearly

Australians have resisted the new doctrines and still expect effective proactive governments to steer economic development.

Australia has not accepted institutional reform. In the midst of the economic boom and in the wake of relentless attempts to persuade them to the contrary the Middle Australia respondents believe that the nation was better served by the older post-war 1945 to 1985 institutional order than it is by the newer, reformed, institutional order that has been foisted upon them with economic reform. While not denying the need for change, over half of the respondents believed that the older economic institutions including industrial awards and national wage fixation, had brought 'only benefits' or 'more benefits than harm'. Our review of the data from the much larger 2003 Australian Survey of Social Attitudes (AuSSA) showed that two thirds of us believe that 'awards and wages are the best way of paying workers and setting conditions'. Only 29% of Middle Australians expressed support for economic reform defined as 'the deregulation of business, competition and privatisation'. Again these findings are consistent with the 2003 AuSSA survey showing that only about 10% of respondents approved selling off major services to private interests. What we see revealed in these several findings is are our own preferences for an older institutional order that has defined the nation virtually since federation and which has shown itself to be remarkably resilient even in the face of saturating elite attempts to win credibility and legitimacy for the new neo-liberal dispensation.

We have clung steadfastly to our inherited belief that states, business and trade unions should work together, collectively, to build a fair, secure and prosperous future. My own *Middle Australia* data accords with the findings of numerous surveys, including the comprehensive *Australian Electoral Studies (AES),* showing that nearly three quarters of us believe big business has too much power.[17] Conversely the AES survey shows that the number of people believing that trade unions have too much power has been falling steadily for 30 years to a minority today of only 41%. Interestingly, in the 2005 *Australian Survey of Social Attitudes* we hear a huge 76% of respondents agreeing with the proposition that 'when big businesses break the law they go unpunished'. About 60% thought that the federal government is run not for 'the benefit of the people' but entirely, or mostly, 'for the benefit of a few big interests looking out for themselves'. The AES survey put the number at 67% in 2004. My Middle Australia study shows that middle Australia is interested in politics and cares about 'the Nation'.

Australians think about the distribution of power from within a normative framework that is linked to their perceptions and concerns about the distribution of income. An ever-larger proportion of Australians also want to see a more equitable distribution of income and wealth. The Middle Australia survey asked whether respondents thought that 'the incomes and job prospects of middle Australians were rising or falling'. In 1996 two-thirds of our respondents said that income and job prospects were falling and, strikingly, as the economy settled further into boom conditions, the number of people saying that wage and salary earners were the *losers* from economic reform rose by some 13 percentage points to 70% in the year 2000. My own and several other studies show that people do not think this distribution is fair and that those judgements are quite tightly related to differences in income. Successive national surveys show the proportion of Australians who thought that income differences were too large has grown from 62% in 1984 to 84% in 2003.[18] In reviewing these and other findings in the light of the AuSSA 2003 survey Nick Turnbull and I were struck by the unwavering two thirds majority support that Australians give to the Award and Arbitration system which they see as the fairest way of setting levels of pay. Here, specifically with respect to the distribution of power and income, we see manifest a re-affirmation of an enduring, historically conditioned preference for the same bedrock structure of power and income distribution that was set in place at Federation and which has ever since defined the political economy of our nation.

Preliminary conclusions

Now to some preliminary conclusion on the prospects for a resumption of nation-building. First of all there is the obvious point that nothing can happen unless governments make it happen. And here the news is probably good. Canberra has demonstrated that it can call up massive reserves of power to change the course of national development. In the wake of these changes it is likely that government has less leverage over wages and monetary policy and less room in which to moderate the demands of the corporate sector. But we do have ample revenues and, probably, a hugely more efficient Canberra administrative apparatus with a freshly demonstrated capacity to deal coherently with the immense complexity of modern government.

The aim of a 25-year-long, top-down, neo-liberal re-engineering of a whole nation society was always to drive the market ever more deeply into the grain of daily life as a denominator of value and an automated code for all significant life decisions. The market was meant to bury deliberative politics, to reduce popular expectations of government, to redefine politics as economic management *tout court* and to neutralise normative culture. To use Francis Fukuyamas' phrase, it was meant to bring us to the end of history and even to kill the shaping influences of memory and history in national politics. Had it succeeded Australia would feel more like Singapore and 'the Nation' would be dead as a motive force in our lives. But thankfully it has not succeeded. A certain pragmatic utilitarianism is still actively shaping our imagined future, our intuitions and value judgements about fairness, and about what progress and national development should mean: and we care about it. Our own 'Whitefella Dreaming' might still be working on our collective will and imagination.

With four final points I hope to persuade you that the changed nature of the challenges we face in the future may come to the rescue of our nation-building past.

Firstly, it is likely that *a constructive adaptation to global warming* will give rise to structural and cultural changes of a kind that we last saw in the aftermath of World War II. Economic history teaches us that War transforms the relations between economy, political culture and the state. In our case World War II brought on a permanent concentration of income tax powers at the national level, a still ongoing program of mass emigration of new settlers to our shores, and a spate of iconic nation-building programs like the Snowy River scheme. These are iconic elements in our own version of the 'Dreaming' that keep alive our hopes for nation-building.[19] Facing up to global warming has the potential to resuscitate our national imagination in a similar way. It presents us with challenges that obviously call, not only for incremental changes at the household level, but also for whole-of-government action at the national level. Here we need think only of what will be required to bring the Murray Darling river system back to life in a future of reduced and more variable rainfall. This challenge alone has the potential to break up much of the rusted, stalemated, framework of current federal-state relations: think of the implications, not just for allocation and the pricing of water, but also for a whole clutch of related and interconnected changes that will redefine water conservation, forest management, primary industry, farming practice and rural and regional development. It even has the potential to heal the tragic gulf that now divides urban from rural Australia.[20]

Changes on this scale are likely to burst the limits of routine pragmatic political accommodation. They force appeals to a latent collective national imagination and so take on an iconic force that can change motivations and bring people together with an enlarged sense of collective agency and identity. With this could come a restored sense of sovereignty and political agency. So also global warming might give us an opportunity to mobilise power in a way that brings vested interests to heel. More fundamentally, it has the potential to restore the legitimacy of state intervention and to generate the needed cultural energy for nation-building government — those very resources that our economic reformers have tried so hard to erode! It creates spaces in which strangers can more easily recognise each other as citizens of the nation joined in mutual responsibility for the longer-term future that they will bequeath to their own children. Of course all this could be so easily sidelined. My point is simply that the challenge of global warming has the potential to produce some very powerful nation-building proteins.

A second creative challenge has to do with *the re-building of our infrastructure*. We are members of the OECD with a per capita national income that is about the same as France. France has a first-world national transport and rail network: ours is not much better than India or, at best, Malaysia. We have some of the world's most liveable cities that are being stressed by bad public transport and the absence of all coherent planning. The same is true at every level of our run-down education system. Ditto for our broadband capability and for our investments in research and development in new technologies and value-added quality niche manufacturing. Look out from the breakwater at Newcastle harbour and you will see (on my last visit there) up to 52 ships waiting to load coal from our hopelessly outdated loading terminals. The point is, simply, that our infrastructure deficits are huge, glaringly incommensurate with our aspirations as a first world nation — and, that, now, for once in a lifetime, we have both the revenue and compelling economic justifications for doing something about it. Huge reconstructions change expectations, create opportunities and fire up the national imagination.

Third, it is a commonplace of political sociology that progressive and modernising social movements — of which the women's movement, the peace movement, and environmental and conservation movements are the most notable instances — can only make way in the face of organised political power when entrenched opposing interests are in disarray. The point is that, *in Australia today, at the level of ideas, the neo-liberal opposition to constructive governance and nation-building is eclipsed or even exhausted*. No one is listening anymore to the worn out ideological catch calls for more privatisation, user pays, cutting government spending, smaller government, and more competition: and perhaps likewise, thankfully, labour market reform. For the moment at least the vested interests have lost their voice. It takes a lot of energy and a long time — maybe 20 or 30 years — for selfish power to persuade national populations to accept policies that are opposed to their larger national interests. And even then it can take a comparatively short time for the ideologies to come undone and for the people to come to their senses. There is a good chance that even blind ideological objections to public borrowing could be swept away by renewed political calls for constructive nation-building.

With the fourth and last point I come to the prospect about which I care most. My survey of middle Australian attitudes showed that even 10 years ago there was no consensus for economic reform and, more to the point, that the broad middle was waking up to the realisation that more economic reform meant more pressure on families, run down public health and education services, less job security, more stressful workplaces, urban degradation, uncertain retirement incomes, and probably declining whole-of-life incomes. Later national survey numbers confirm that an increasing proportion of us are seeing, for the first time, that more economic reform also brings reduced standards of living for our children. It is a perfect example of what some people call 'social learning'. Intuitively, and ever more consciously, a national population may just be waking up to the truth that a booming economy and increasing GDP means environmental degradation, endangered futures and *falling quality of life*. And with that awareness comes a recognition that 'the Economy' is not animal mineral or vegetable, not a thing in itself, but a symbolic construction that comes out of society itself as a *political* artefact and something that we have the power to change.

As that understanding sinks in a nation can more easily understand for itself that economic rationalism is a perfect irrationality, an ideological concoction, and a form of systematically distorted communication. We see then that we must again understand and use the economy in exactly the same way as our great 'Nugget Coombs' generation of nation-builders did, namely as a set of practical instruments for improving the lives of a national and now global population. What is the use of money if it makes you poorer? That unsettling question has the potential to change the meaning of money. I think I hear that bit of the story coming at us like a steam train in a tunnel.

Here we are at the end. Of course, there are no metaphysical or historical guarantees. Still, I put it to you that the prospects for a resumption of constructive nation-building are better than they have been in a long while.

Acknowledgements

In preparing this chapter I have been greatly helped by several friends and dialogue partners. My thanks go to John Braithwaite, Tim Rouse, John Wanna, John Butcher, Adrian Fordham and Ian McAllister, among others.

ENDNOTES

[1] Michael Pusey, *Economic Rationalism in Canberra. A Nation Building State Changes its Mind*, Cambridge University Press, 1991.

[2] Hugh Collins, 'Political ideology in Australia: The distinctiveness of a Benthamite society' in *Australia: The Daedalus Symposium*, ed. Stephen Graubard, Angus and Robertson, Sydney, 1985.

[3] John Gascoingne, *The Enlightenment and the Origins of European Settlement in Australia*, Cambridge University Press, 2002

[4] Paul Keating speaking on Social Policy at the University of New South Wales, 11 November, 1996

[5] Michel Crozier, Samuel P. Huntington and Joji Watanuki, *The Crisis of Democracy*, Task Force Report no. 8, New York University Press, New York, 1975.

[6] N.G. Butlin, A. Barnard and J.J. Pincus, *Government and Capitalism: public and private choice in twentieth century Australia*, Allen & Unwin Sydney 1982 p 320-322

[7] J. Braithwaite, 'Institutionalising trust: Enculturating distrust', in V. Braithwaite and M. Levi eds, *Trust and Governance*, Russell Sage, New York, 1998.

[8] L. Mishel, J. Bernstein, S. Allegretto, *The State of Working America 2004/2005*, Economic Policy Institute, Cornell University, 2005.

[9] Francis G. Castles, *The Working Class and Welfare: Reflections on the Political Development of the Welfare State in Australia and New Zealand, 1890-1980*, Allen & Unwin. 1985.

[10] Michael Pusey, *Economic Rationalism in Canberra. A Nation Building State Changes its Mind*, Cambridge University Press, 1991.

[11] John Wanna, Joanne Kelley and John Forster, *Managing Public Expenditure in Australia*, Allen and Unwin, 2000, chapter 12.

[12] Andrew Leigh, 'Reinvigorating the Australian Project', Garran Oration, RSSS, ANU, Canberra, *Australian Journal of Public Administration*, 64(1) 3-7. March 2005.

[13] John Wanna and his colleagues seem to say that horizontal coordination across different departments is working more efficiently while other reports — *CAEPR Working Paper No. 36*, CAEPR, CASS, ANU, Canberra — suggest, for example, that coordination across departments in the area of indigenous affairs has generally failed.

[14] My thanks to John Braithwaite for sharing with me a chapter, entitled 'Neo-liberalism or regulatory capitalism?' of his forthcoming book on this subject.

[15] See Wanna et al.

[16] This is one of two definitions of 'economic rationalism' that I put forward in the so-called 'economic rationalism debate' that exploded with the publication of *Economic Rationalism in Canberra in the early 1990s*. The other is that 'economic rationalism is a doctrine which says that, 'the market is, at least in principle, the only means of setting values on anything'.

[17] *Trends in Australian Political Opinion; Results from the Australian Electoral Study*, 1987-2004 Ian McAllister and Julliet Clark.

[18] M. Pusey and N. Turnbull, 'Have Australians Embraced Economic Reform?' chapter 10 in *Australian Social Attitudes. The First Report*, (eds.) S Wilson et al, University of New South Wales Press, 2005.

[19] My friend John Carroll, a conservative cultural theorist, says that the Aboriginal idea of 'The Dreaming' is our best theory of culture. It certainly solves a problem that I have never known how to handle. With every historical reference to a remembered past I am accused of being a 'Golden Age' apologist who wants to turn the clock back to 1950s — an accusation that I vehemently reject. So how to speak of the past without opening yourself to accusations that you are 'essentialising' it?

[20] Kenneth Wiltshire, *Tenterfield Revisited, Reforming Australia's system of government for 2001*, Queensland University Press, 1991, p14.

4. The challenge of teaching Australian history

Anna Clark

Abstract

When Prime Minister John Howard gave his speech to the National Press Club on the eve of Australia Day in 2006 he called for a 'root and branch renewal' of history teaching in our schools. 'In the end,' he said, 'young people are at risk of being disinherited from their community if that community lacks the courage and confidence to teach its history.' Nation-building is often conceived in very tangible forms — engineering marvels, wars, and even national institutions can claim credit for helping to define the nation's legacy. Teaching the nation's history in schools also raises questions of national definition. But what story of Australia do we want to teach in schools? This chapter examines recent public debates over Australian history teaching and argues that meaningful nation-building will not arise from a simplistic promotion of Australian nationalism, but by encouraging genuine critical engagement with the past.

Introduction

On the eve of Australia Day in 2006, then Prime Minister John Howard spoke at the National Press Club in Canberra with a 'state of the nation' style address celebrating Australia's democracy, economy and national identity — the 'Australian Achievement', in his words. The speech was also a call to protect that achievement: more than ever, Howard maintained, Australia required greater national cohesion and identification.

One of the keys to that cohesion would come from a more consistent national history education. Howard lamented the state of historical knowledge and national connection among Australian schoolchildren. Australian history had become lost in a stew of 'themes' and 'issues', he said, and required a 'root and branch renewal' to restore its proper place in the curriculum.[1] It was hard to disagree with his sentiment: Australian history education is largely inconsistent and uncoordinated. With the possible exception of New South Wales, students around the country learn patchy, repetitive versions of the nation's past that chop and change between topics. Often they just learn the same things again and again. They are indeed alienated from their nation's past.

Yet this wasn't simply a call for curriculum restructure. Howard wanted a renewal of history education to promote 'Australianness' to the nation's youngest citizens — 'our children'. The Prime Minister regretted that the subject had 'succumbed to a post-modern culture of relativism where any objective record of achievement is questioned or repudiated'.[2] What was needed, he said, was a stronger, more positive national story for Australian schools. Such a position isn't surprising. Many Australians share the view that a nationally affirming history education is essential for national cohesion and identity — essential for nation-building, in fact. My concern is that any understanding of history education as 'nation-building' actually reduces the capacity for critical reflection and understanding among students; and that these are the very qualities of citizenship that we should be fostering in a democracy.

History for the future

In his 2006 Australia Day address, the then Prime Minister, John Howard, explained how teaching the nation's past was key to any effort to sustain Australia's identity and national ethos. 'Part of preparing young Australians to be informed and active citizens is to teach them the central currents of our nation's development,' he insisted. In other words, not teaching this national story could threaten the future of the nation itself: 'young people are at risk of being disinherited from their community if that community lacks the courage and confidence to teach its history'.[3]

Coming so soon after the Cronulla riots in December 2005, the timing and tone of Howard's speech was pointed: social cohesion was not the product of good fortune but conscientious and collective efforts. A number of influential commentators also picked up on Howard's reference to the riots a couple of months earlier, and connected his call for a more systematic and nationally affirming history education with these divisive demonstrations.[4] The Cronulla riots embroiled hundreds of young Australians in disturbing scenes of violence, drunkenness and racism masquerading as patriotism. They also confirmed an apparently fractured national identity that many Australians, including the Prime Minister himself, found worrying and extreme.[5]

Howard's Australia Day speech responded directly to these divisions in Australia, and suggested that they threatened the fabric of the nation's future. While he acknowledged that 'Australia's ethnic diversity is one of the enduring strengths of our nation', he offered the following caution: 'our celebration of diversity must not be at the expense of the common values that bind us together'.[6] Those common values had to be deliberately cultivated, he reasoned, and the history curriculum was a natural place for promoting Australia's shared identity and heritage. While the Prime Minister shied away from advocating an overly celebratory history education, he believed in the fundamental importance of a distinct national narrative for schools that was ultimately affirming: teaching the nation's story was critical to ensuring its strength and identity.

References to nation-building conjure up images of bridges, irrigation projects and even institutions — those building blocks that are tangible tributes to national strength and prosperity. And taken together, they form a sort of narrative of nation-building, if you like, documenting its triumphs and contributions over time. In Howard's Australia Day speech we had another sort of nation-building narrative — less tangible, perhaps, but no less real. This was the nation-building potential of 'history' itself. For nations are built on stories that their peoples collectively believe in and aspire to as an 'imagined community', to use Benedict Anderson's famous phrase.[7] And there was a strong underlying message in Howard's speech that without this story of the 'Australian Achievement', young people risked being nationally illiterate.

He had plenty of supporters. The historian Gregory Melleuish applauded the Prime Minister's 'vision for a new style of Australian history'. For too long the subject has often 'had as its main objective the indoctrination of students into a set of narrow dogmas,' he cautioned, but Howard 'has provided the outline of an Australian history that is humane and open-minded in approach, and which will enlarge the outlook of our young people. Let us hope that a 'coalition of the willing' emerges to make this vision a reality.'[8] In another article for *The Australian*, Janet Albrechtsen was similarly unequivocal: 'there is much work to be done in undoing the progressive curriculum foisted on Australian schoolchildren'.[9]

Members of the public also supported the Prime Minister's announcement as evidenced in correspondence to major Australian dailies and weblog postings. In a letter to the *Adelaide Advertiser* Grattan Wheaton agreed 'with everything Mr Howard said about the teaching of history/geography subjects in schools'.[10] Contributing to Andrew West's weblog in the online edition of the *Sydney Morning Herald*, some eager bloggers also backed the Prime Minister's history initiative. 'In my opinion, history should be a mandatory subject during a person's education,' offered 'Lexa'. 'With all the "Aussie Pride" of Australia Day and the togetherness that is being touted around, perhaps it would be easier to implement if people KNEW what they had to be proud of.'[11]

Comments like these were by no means isolated. There is a powerful popular sentiment that the role of national history is to strengthen the nation itself. Correspondingly, the role of history education is commonly held to bolster that national story by passing it on to the next generation.[12] So when the former Education Minister, Julie Bishop, announced a national history summit a few months after Howard's Australia Day address, there were similar messages of support published in newspapers, online journals and discussions around the country. Comprising eminent historians and public commentators from around the country, the Australian History Summit was proposed to develop a new national approach to teaching the nation's past. 'The time has come for a renaissance in the teaching of Australian history in our schools,' Bishop insisted. 'By the time students finish their secondary schooling, they must have a thorough understanding of their nation's past.'[13]

In a letter to *The Australian,* Jenny Hammett commended the minister's summit initiative: 'I am frequently staggered by how little people know of our history. Australia has a richness of history full of the drama, tragedy and joy of human experience. It is a unique tapestry that for too long has been hijacked by the self-interest of those who seek to force a dominant view and have stifled argument by controlling the education of our children.'[14] Another correspondent to *The Australian,* Miranda Kelly, expressed similar concern: 'How can we, as a nation, possibly expect to compete on the world stage if Australian history — warts and all — is not taught as a compulsory subject in our schools?' she asked. 'If not, we face the tragic reality that our future leaders will have no idea how our nation developed.'[15]

Such support was hardly unexpected. The urge to teach the 'Australian Achievement' in schools is a position that many Australians of varying political persuasions actively share. They see the role of history education is precisely to educate 'tomorrow's citizens' about their national heritage and identity. It is the conduit for developing knowledge and pride in the nation and its past and any failure to connect with our national story is seen as a threat to the identity, strength and future of the nation itself.

It is not my intention to dismiss these popular understandings of history's national importance, for this belief in the nation-building potential of history education is widely and deeply held across the political spectrum. I also think it is misleading to suggest that 'mainstream Australia' has been manipulated by some sort of conservative political campaign to redefine Australian values. Like Judith Brett, I sense that 'ordinary Australians' have helped shape the past decade in Australian political life, as much as they have been defined by it.[16]

But I remain concerned if Australian history teaching is coopted to promote or instil any national affiliation that is automatic, rather than reflective. History education is uniquely placed in the culture wars over 'Australianness' because it is the only place that citizens are formally presented with their nation's past. Despite the obvious inconsistencies in the delivery of history education, in one form or another, students learn about their national heritage and identity in thousands of schools around the country — that is why claims to define approaches to Australian history education generate such heated public debate. Nevertheless, I argue that the current problems of history teaching around the country must not be met with a narrowly 'national' curriculum response.

When Howard concluded his 2006 Australia day speech with some words from history, he was laying out what he hoped would be a return to the nation-building hopes and beliefs of previous generations: 'we should also affirm the sentiment that propelled our nation to Federation 105 years ago — one People, One Destiny', he pledged.[17]   But there are significant pedagogical problems with such expressions of history's national potential and importance: while I agree that understanding the nation's past is essential for all students, I also want them to learn about history as a discipline — above and beyond any 'Australian story' or core national knowledge. I'm aware that this desire for a more complex approach to the subject rubs uneasily against the widespread belief in teaching an Australian history that strengthens the nation rather than critiques it. But it is clear that historical understanding and awareness do not come from parochial national knowledge. Indeed, the term 'historical literacy' does not mean demonising or demolishing the national past, but it does require a capacity to reflect upon it.

Historical literacy

The problem with any nationally affirming approach to history education is that it fails to encompass the disciplinary components of the subject: why do people disagree over Australian history, for example? And how do we deal with these contrasting historical interpretations? Such questions go beyond any specific national role for history teaching to consider deeper questions about the nature of history itself — and that means encouraging students to think about history beyond their national past. History is much more than an account of 'what happened'. It offers a deeper understanding of national values and identity rather than simply confirming them in class.

While most responses to Howard's Australia Day speech agreed that Australian history was in urgent need of curriculum support and renewal, a number of historians and educators qualified their support by emphasising a more complex approach to the discipline. Speaking on the ABC's *7.30 Report*, historian, Stuart Macintyre, acknowledged the need for a stronger national history curriculum, so long as that was not at the expense of critical engagement in the classroom. 'I think we would all agree that we need to do more to restore history,' he acknowledged, 'but we need to make sure that that is open to diverse viewpoints and that it is not simply an exercise in indoctrination.'[18] Historian Graeme Davison went one further and insisted that any national benefit from the subject in fact depended on history's capacity to generate engaged discussion and debate among students. History's worth in a liberal democracy lies in its capacity to develop critical thinking: 'We cannot inculcate democratic values in the polity unless we encourage critical and independent judgement in the classroom.'[19] Annabel Astbury, professional services manager at the History Teachers' Association of Victoria, similarly hoped that history's complexity would not be overlooked by any emphasis on the Australian story. 'A history class free from question and repudiation therefore does not augur well in producing "good citizens"', she warned.[20]

Some public contributors to the discussion also questioned any emphasis on 'national facts' at the expense of more complex engagement. 'Certainly, it's a fact that Federation occurred in 1901,' wrote Daniel Berk in a letter to *The Australian*, 'but are the reasons behind this historic event 'facts' or opinions? That event was the product of a whole host of different opinions that motivated people to behave and interact in various ways, with Federation as the end result.'[21] Contributing to an online discussion hosted by the *Age* newspaper, 'Kim' posted this response: 'History is seen and told differently by the different sides and participants, so while facts are important and should be taught, theory, discussion, arguments and debates should also be encouraged.'[22]

Meanwhile, other commentators wondered about the potential parochialism of any national history emphasis. Robert Manne said he thought it was 'more important for historical literacy and for citizenship to have a rough working knowledge of what's happened in the world'.[23] The historian Clare Wright was similarly doubtful about any possible emphasis on prescribed facts in an Australian history education at the expense of skills: 'I'm all for the compulsory teaching of Australian history in schools,' she argued. 'But planting the seeds of ideas and learning means more than getting the facts straight.'[24]

Comments such as these begin to define an understanding of history that moves to a more complex consideration of national benefit *through* critical engagement. Such a view contends that history can help us understand why people disagree over the past, and why historical interpretations change over time. Indeed, it confirms that history is as much about contemporary values as it is about trying to understand events, ideas and beliefs from another time and place.

History educationists have attempted to codify these complex skills of historical understanding in a way that enables students to learn about the importance of the subject while retaining its complexity in the classroom. This doesn't mean the facts are not important, or that the national story should not be taught. Of course students need to know 'what happened' in Australia's past. But they should also engage with the discipline beyond that national knowledge. This is a call for 'historical literacy', a term I borrow from history educationists Tony Taylor and Carmel Young. They acknowledge that knowing the nation's story is essential — but so too is learning historical skills, reconciling different perspectives and developing students' own judgements and ideas about the past.[25]

The concept of historical literacy builds on research by North American scholars such as Peter Seixas and Sam Wineburg, who argue that the value of history education lies precisely in its complexity. Simplistic national affirmations actually cease to be 'history' because they forego the fundamental elements of the discipline such as critical engagement, understanding why historical interpretations differ, and reconciling the values of the past with the present. School history 'should provide students with the ability to approach historical narratives critically', Seixas explained. 'We need to teach students to think historically.'[26] Wineburg has similarly criticised what he termed the 'textbook mentality' of history education, which presumes national historical knowledge simply needs to be known rather than *understood*.[27]

These pedagogical approaches to the subject insist on teaching an approach to history that can accommodate contrasting opinions and shifting understandings. To that end, says Seixas, 'This is the promise of critical historical discourse: that it provides a rational way, on the basis of evidence and argument, to discuss the differing accounts that jostle with or contradict each other.' That means 'it would be self-defeating to attempt to resolve these arguments before we get into the classroom, in order to provide students with a finished truth,' he continued. 'Rather, we need to bring the arguments into the classroom.'[28]

The work of Peter Lee and Ros Ashby in the United Kingdom has also questioned any approach to history education limited to nation-building. Again, this doesn't mean national content is irrelevant, but for history education to have intellectual merit beyond national affiliation it must have an intellectual component. 'Students need to know about the past or the whole exercise becomes pointless,' Lee acknowledged. 'But understanding the discipline allows more serious engagement with the substantive history that students study, and enables them to *do* things with their historical knowledge.'[29]

By encouraging this deeper approach to the past, the nation-building potential of history education lies in its capacity to develop a national engagement that stems from students themselves. This is certainly the belief of American scholars Linda Levstik and Keith Barton, who both confirm the democratic potential of the subject, and insist that it is 'uniquely privileged to provide the shared sense of national identity necessary for democratic participation.'[30] Indeed a complex history education is needed to cope with a complexity of voices and perspectives in a liberal democracy.[31]

This is not to say I am unsupportive of a more consistent and coordinated national story for schools. Historical literacy demands that students need content and context to engage with the past, and knowing Australian history is fundamental to that context for Australian students. But they also need to be able to work with this history. Students and teachers deserve a subject that expands their historical understanding and analysis, rather than limits it to a project of patriotism — and it is to the classroom that I finally turn to consider their thoughts on history's place in Australia.

'Doing' history in the classroom

For the past two years I have been directing a large ARC funded research project about history teaching.[32] The research was developed in response to some of these national concerns over history teaching — generated in particular by a popular belief in the subject's nation-building potential.

In all, 246 high school students, history teachers and curriculum officials from each of the eight Australian States and Territories were interviewed for this research. (I have also interviewed around 80 respondents from four provinces in Canada as a part of comparative study.) This qualitative study did not set out to present yet another statistical survey of what students do not know about their national past. Rather, these classroom perspectives challenge assumptions that the national benefit of Australian history education lies in doing 'more of it' or returning to 'the basics' of an affirming national narrative. It is not that the students I spoke with question the importance of their nation's heritage — far from it — but they do have strong opinions about what it offers them and other young Australians.

Overwhelmingly, these students support the teaching of Australian history in school. When I asked a group of boys at an Islamic school in Western Sydney whether Australian history should be a compulsory subject, Oyuz thought it probably should, 'Because it's good to know what happened in the past'. His classmate Ahmed captured the sentiment even more strongly: 'It's not just good to know,' he said, 'we *should* know.'[33] Jill, a year nine student from a public school on the New South Wales Central Coast, thought that everyone should study Australian history. 'I can't understand why other states don't learn about it,' she said, 'because it's really important that we do'.[34]

Even those students who doubted the effectiveness of mandatory Australian history *per se* sensed the importance of the subject. Jill's classmate Les said that he didn't think the subject should be mandated, because 'I've always found from personal experience that if you try and make things compulsory it's the fastest way to make people *not* interested'. But he acknowledged that 'you have to Australian history' in some form.[35] Chen, a year 11 student at a public girls' school in Sydney was similarly ambivalent about the extent of any exclusively national historical education, but she thought it was nevertheless essential to teach: 'Yeah, I think it should be compulsory, like at one stage of your life, but not like throughout your primary school and throughout your high school.'[36]

Despite this widespread acknowledgement by students that Australian history should be taught, they didn't suggest its value comes from any parochial or chest-thumping patriotism. In fact, the opposite is almost certainly true: time and again, students described their understanding of the subject's importance in terms of learning about Australia in an international context, considering multiple perspectives, and engaging in more open-ended learning. At an independent girls' in Canberra, for example, Annie thought Australian history should be compulsory in school, but that a broader and more critical context would make it more engaging for students: 'I think that we need to move away from the Australian perspective because we are *not* the only country in the world, whatever they might have us believe. And maybe just [have] more discussions as well.'[37]

For so many of these students, history's worth stems from how it helps them to think, above and beyond any core national knowledge. When I spoke with a group of students from a girls' school in Brisbane, Lily thought history was 'different to a subject like maths and stuff, because you can look at it and *interpret* it'. That interpretation 'may not be the same as the person next to you,' she said, 'but it doesn't mean it's wrong'.[38] Jeff goes to a Catholic boys' school in Brisbane and also thinks the subject is more engaging 'with the student going out and being a proactive learner, rather than the teacher sort of feeding them information'.[39]

That's not to say students would prefer *laissez-faire* discussion-based lessons with no content at all. But they're critical of approaches to the subject that preclude any historical engagement from them. Maddison, a year 12 student from Perth, did not like learning history when the lessons were 'Entirely textbook focused. I mean, textbooks are important for a lot of it, but entirely textbook — especially the textbooks we get — is horrible.' 'Yeah,' said his classmate Eva, 'I don't like the kind of style where you just read and answer questions. It's okay if you're reading and kind of talking about it.'[40]

How do you learn history best?

Many Australians believe the purpose of Australian history teaching is essentially nation-building. Yet in classrooms around Australia students want a much more complex appreciation of the subject, where knowing the nation's past and critically engaging with it are not mutually exclusive. These year 12 students a public school in Darwin recognised the place for learning historical content, but they also wanted teaching methods that included and encouraged different points of view:

> Daniel: We've never really had anything other than classroom discussions.
>
> Natalie: We did a lot of debating last year, like arguing our different sides, and I think one of the really big components is having good teachers. I think what made that so interesting was that we had really good teachers who know their stuff and have like actively engaged us and they've questioned our opinions, and it's just been a really good experience.

Gabby: I think on the whole, I don't want to speak for everyone in our history class, but I get the feeling that we all *learn* better through the discussions.

Others: Yes.

Gabby: Through being able to ask those questions and that sort of thing, rather than just reading dates out of a textbook. Although that is helpful in some instances, I think as a whole a lot of our learning has been through discussion.[41]

Comments such as these are vital in the midst of these public and political debates over history teaching. Indeed, far from being challenged by the possibility of multiple perspectives, the students I spoke with overwhelmingly say that's how they learnt history best.

Teachers also understand the importance of learning both the content and skills of historical inquiry. And, like their students, they are not sure that teaching a more nationally-oriented curriculum is necessarily the answer. In Tasmania, Margaret thought that Australian history *should* be compulsory, but she wasn't convinced by the current public discussions about core national knowledge. 'There are basics about geography and history that kids need to understand who they are,' she insisted. 'But I never want to see a situation that says you'll teach this to this person on this day and in this way, because you have to come from where kids are at.' She was exasperated by the political pressure that had been generated following Howard's 2006 Australia Day speech: 'Oh look, you read in the paper all the time about the history the kids should know and I keep thinking, "Right, come into a classroom and teach it". It doesn't work.'[42]

By contrast, at a public school in Brisbane, Mary says the reward for teaching historical complexity is when her history classes really come alive: 'It's fun, it's good — you create critical kids,' she explained. 'The really bright ones will actually learn to challenge you as well as the texts and the sources and stuff.'[43] Stephen from Adelaide was similarly open about the skills of critical analysis he hoped to instil in his students: 'I like students to think, I like them to be critical thinkers. I like them to question what they're being fed, and even question what I might say to them as well.'[44] Such classroom perspectives provide a stark contrast to the public calls for an affirming and exclusive national approach to the subject.

These teachers and students acknowledge the importance of teaching Australian history, but they expressed real concern about implementing a narrowly national approach to the subject. The limitations of history teaching for nation-building certainly weren't lost on these students at a Catholic boys' school in Perth. In fact, they sensed the merits of the subject lay precisely *outside* any narrowly national appeal:

Q. Do you think Australian history should be a compulsory subject?

Adrian: I don't think it should be to the extent that American history has been taught. Like I think it should still be taught from the perspective that it's open to interpretation.

Brendan: Yeah, I think if it's compulsory, it shouldn't be inward-looking like America, and I think it should be the whole investigative sort of history. I don't like the idea of just learning facts, and then being told what to think.

Jeff: Because that would be boring.

At a public girls' school in Sydney, Andie also thought the subject's interest and importance depended on understanding its complexity and encouraging the questions it raised in class:

For me, it sort of puts everything into perspective, because in other subjects it's sort of like me, me, me, and sort of like thinking in a small scale, but in history you can think in a really broad scale. It's not that we're insignificant, but in a global scale we've lived for so many years and people have done so many great things, it's just really interesting to learn about it.[45]

Such comments reveal that discussions of history's value beyond any national appreciation are not restricted to the academy. The teachers and students I spoke with certainly understand the complexities of history education — what is more, they suggest, the subject is more interesting and engaging for it. And that means fostering history classes that not only connect students to Australia's past, but also help them become critical thinkers who can engage with challenging ideas and different points of view. When I asked the group of students from the New South Wales Central Coast whether they enjoyed studying history, Les was effusive: 'I love it', he said. 'I really like the flexibility in history because you can look at everything and there's no direct answer.' Added Ryan: 'And everyone's allowed to have their own opinions. Like, you're allowed to have yours — I don't care — as long as you can kind of back up your evidence.'[46] This critical capacity, I argue, is exactly the sort of 'nation-building' that Australian history education should encourage.

Conclusion

Many Australians believe history should be a source of pride, and that young people should have an affirming national story with appropriate values to aspire to. Yet we also require space for these national narratives to be critically discussed in class. While there is no doubt Australian history should be an essential component of young Australians' school education, we need to ensure their historical understanding is expanded rather than limited it to any simplistic or uncontested national narrative. And that means a fundamental reconsideration of history teaching away from the nation-building rhetoric of the 'Australian Achievement' to a more complex engagement with Australian history and identity. For it is with those skills of inquiry and analysis that any real nation-building potential of Australian history will be realised — and, perhaps surprisingly, many students say just that. So shouldn't we be offering a national history that students feel they are helping to define?

References

Albrechtsen, Janet. 2006. 'Textbook case of making our past a blame game.' *Australian*, 1 February.

Anderson, Benedict. 1991. *Imagined Communities: Reflections on the Origin and Spread of Nationalism*. 2nd ed. London, New York: Verso.

Astbury, Annabel. 2006. 'A lesson in history.' *Age*, 6 February.

Australian Broadcasting Corporation. '7.30 Report.' 26 January 2006. Available from: http://www.abc.net.au/7.30/content/2006/s1556052.htm (accessed 5 February 2006).

——. 'Lateline.' 18 August 2006. Available from: http://www.abc.net.au/lateline/content/2006/s1718847.htm (accessed 20 August 2006).

Barton, Keith C. and Linda S. Levstik. 2004. *Teaching History for the Common Good*. Mahwah, N.J.: Lawrence Erlbaum Associates, Inc.

Berk, Daniel. 2006. 'Letter.' *The Australian*, 19 August.

Bishop, Julie. 2006. 'Our classrooms need to make a date with the facts.' *The Australian*, 6 July.

Brett, Judith. 2005. 'Relaxed and Comfortable: The Liberal Party's Australia.' *Quarterly Essay*, no. 19.

Davison, Graeme. 2006. 'The New Politics of School History'. *Symposium*, no. 34 (October): 7.

Elder, Catriona. 2007. *Being Australian: Narratives of National Identity*. Sydney: Allen & Unwin.

Grattan, Michelle. 2006. 'PM claims victory in culture wars.' *The Age*, 26 January.

Hammett, Jenny. 2006. 'Letter.' *The Australian*, 21 August.

Harvey, Michael. 2006. 'PM wants new history.' *Herald-Sun*, 26 January.

Howard, John. 2006. Prime Minister John Howard's address to the National Press Club on January 25, 2006. Available from: http://theage.com.au/news/national/pms-speech/2006/01/25/1138066849045.html?page=fullpage#contentSwap1 (accessed 31 January 2006).

Kelly, Miranda. 2006. 'Letter.' *The Australian*, 19 August.

Lee, Peter. 2001. 'Understanding History.' Paper presented at the Canadian Historical Consciousness in an International Context: Theoretical Frameworks conference, Centre for the Study of Historical Consciousness, University of British Columbia, Vancouver, BC. Available from: http://www.cshc.ubc.ca/pwias/viewabstract.php?10 (accessed 29 November 2007).

Levstik, Linda S. 2000. 'Articulating the Silences: Teachers' and Adolescents' Conceptions of Historical Significance.' In *Knowing, Teaching and Learning History: National and International Perspectives*, edited by Peter N. Stearns, Peter Seixas, and Sam Wineburg, 284-305. New York and London: New York University Press.

Létourneau, Jocelyn. 2006. 'Remembering Our Past: An Examination of the Historical Memory of Young Québécois.' In *To the Past: History Education, Public Memory, and Citizenship in Canada*, edited by Ruth Sandwell, 70-82. Toronto: University of Toronto Press.

Melleuish, Gregory. 2006. 'A better way of looking at our past.' *The Australian*, 30 January.

Olick, Jeffrey K. 2003. 'Introduction.' In *States of Memory: Continuities, Conflicts, and Transformations in National Retrospection*, edited by Jeffrey K. Olick, 1-16. Durham; London: Duke University Press.

Seixas, Peter. 1997. 'The Place of History within Social Studies.' In *Trends and Issues in Canadian Social Studies*, edited by Ian and Alan Sears Wright, 116-29. Vancouver: Pacific Educational Press.

——. 2002. 'The Purposes of Teaching Canadian History.' *Canadian Social Studies* 36, no. 2. Available from: http://www.quasar.ualberta.ca/css/Css_36_2/Arpurposes_teaching_canadian_history.htm (accessed 15 July 2002).

——. 2006. 'What is Historical Consciousness.' In *To the Past: History Education, Public Memory, and Citizenship in Canada*, edited by Ruth Sandwell, 11-22. Toronto: University of Toronto Press.

Spillman, Lyn. 1997. *Nation and Commemoration: Creating National Identities in the United States and Australia*. Cambridge: Cambridge University Press.

Taylor, Tony and Carmel Young. 2003. 'Making History: A Guide for the Teaching and Learning of History in Australian Schools.' Canberra: Department of Education, Science and Training.

Wertsch, James V. 2002. *Voices of Collective Remembering*. Cambridge: Cambridge University Press.

West, Andrew. 2006. 'Bad history: blame John Howard.' *The Sydney Morning Herald*, 31 January 2006. Available from: http://blogs.smh.com.au/thecontrarian/archives/2006/01/bad_history_i_b.html (accessed 1 February 2006).

Wheaton, Grattan. 2006. 'Letter.' *The Advertiser*, 27 January.

Wineburg, Sam. 2001. *Historical Thinking and Other Unnatural Acts: Charting the Future of Teaching the Past*. Philadelphia: Temple University Press.

Wright, Clare. 2006. 'One story is rarely the whole story.' *The Age*, 24 July.

'Your Say: Facts or friction'. In *The Age*(online edition), 10 August 2006. Available from: http://blogs.theage.com.au/yoursay/archives/2006/08/whos_history.html (accessed 10 August 2006).

ENDNOTES

[1] John Howard, *Prime Minister John Howard's address to the National Press Club on 25 January, 2006* (available from http://theage.com.au/news/national/pms-speech/2006/01/25/1138066849045.html?page=fullpage#contentSwap1 [accessed 31 January 2006]).

[2] Ibid.

[3] Ibid.

[4] Michelle Grattan, 'PM claims victory in culture wars', *The Age*, 26 January 2006; Michael Harvey, 'PM wants new history', *Herald-Sun*, 26 January 2006.

[5] Catriona Elder, *Being Australian: Narratives of National Identity* (Sydney: Allen & Unwin, 2007), 303-7.

[6] Howard, *Prime Minister John Howard's address to the National Press Club on 25 January, 2006*.

[7] Benedict Anderson, *Imagined Communities: Reflections on the Origin and Spread of Nationalism*, 2nd ed. (London, New York: Verso, 1991).

[8] Gregory Melleuish, 'A better way of looking at our past', *The Australian*, 30 January 2006.

[9] Janet Albrechtsen, 'Textbook case of making our past a blame game', *The Australian*, 1 February.

[10] Grattan Wheaton, 'Letter', *The Advertiser*, 27 January 2006.

[11] cited in Andrew West, 'Bad history: blame John Howard', *The Sydney Morning Herald*, 31 January 2006 (available from: http://blogs.smh.com.au/thecontrarian/archives/2006/01/bad_history_i_b.html [accessed 1 February 2006]).

[12] See, for example: Jeffrey K. Olick, 'Introduction', in *States of Memory: Continuities, Conflicts, and Transformations in National Retrospection*, ed. Jeffrey K. Olick (Durham; London: Duke University Press, 2003); Lyn Spillman, *Nation and Commemoration: Creating National Identities in the United States and Australia* (Cambridge: Cambridge University Press, 1997); James V. Wertsch, *Voices of Collective Remembering* (Cambridge: Cambridge University Press, 2002).

[13] Julie Bishop, 'Our classrooms need to make a date with the facts', *The Australian*, 6 July 2006. The participants at the Summit were: Andrew Barnett, Geoffrey Blainey, Geoffrey Bolton, David Boon, Bob Carr, Inga Clendinnen, Kate Darian-Smith, Nick Ewbank, John Gascoigne, Jenny Gregory, Gerard Henderson, John Hirst, Jackie Huggins, Paul Kelly, Jennifer Lawless, Mark Lopez, Gregory Melleuish, Margo Neale, Geoffrey Partington, Lisa Paul, Peter Stanley, Tom Stannage and Tony Taylor.

[14] Jenny Hammett, 'Letter', *The Australian*, 21 August 2006.

[15] Miranda Kelly, 'Letter', *The Australian*, 19 August 2006.

[16] Judith Brett, 'Relaxed and Comfortable: The Liberal Party's Australia', *Quarterly Essay*, no. 19 (2005).

[17] Howard, *Prime Minister John Howard's address to the National Press Club on 25 January, 2006*.

[18] Australian Broadcasting Corporation, '7.30 Report', 26 January 2006 (available from: http://www.abc.net.au/7.30/content/2006/s1556052.htm [accessed 5 February 2006]).

[19] Graeme Davison, 'The new politics of school history', *Symposium*, no. 34 (October 2006): 7.

[20] Annabel Astbury, 'A lesson in history', *The Age*, 6 February 2006.

[21] Daniel Berk, 'Letter', *The Australian*, 19 August 2006.

[22] 'Your Say: Facts or friction', *The Age* (online edition), 10 August 2006 (available from: http://blogs.theage.com.au/yoursay/archives/2006/08/whos_history.html [accessed 10 August 2006]).

[23] Australian Broadcasting Corporation, 'Lateline', 18 August 2006 (available from: http://www.abc.net.au/lateline/content/2006/s1718847.htm [accessed 20 August 2006]).

[24] Clare Wright, 'One story is rarely the whole story', *The Age*, 24 July 2006.

[25] Tony and Carmel Young Taylor, 'Making History: A Guide for the Teaching and Learning of History in Australian Schools' (Canberra: Department of Education, Science and Training, 2003), 8.

[26] Peter Seixas, 'The Place of History within Social Studies', in *Trends and Issues in Canadian Social Studies*, ed. Ian Wright and Alan Sears (Vancouver: Pacific Educational Press, 1997), 116-17.

[27] Sam Wineburg, *Historical Thinking and Other Unnatural Acts: Charting the Future of Teaching the Past* (Philadelphia: Temple University Press, 2001), 79.

[28] Peter Seixas, 'The Purposes of Teaching Canadian History', *Canadian Social Studies,* 36, no. 2 (2002) (available from: http://www.quasar.ualberta.ca/css/Css_36_2/Arpurposes_teaching_canadian_history.htm [accessed 15 July 2002]). See also: Jocelyn Létourneau, 'Remembering Our Past: An Examination of the Historical Memory of Young Québécois', in *To the Past: History Education, Public Memory, and Citizenship in Canada*, ed. Ruth Sandwell (Toronto: University of Toronto Press, 2006); Peter Seixas, 'What is Historical Consciousness,' in *To the Past: History Education, Public Memory, and Citizenship in Canada*, ed. Ruth Sandwell (Toronto: University of Toronto Press, 2006), 14.

[29] Peter Lee, 'Understanding History' (paper presented at the Canadian Historical Consciousness in an International Context: Theoretical Frameworks conference, Centre for the Study of Historical Consciousness, University of British Columbia, Vancouver, BC, 2001) (available from: http://www.cshc.ubc.ca/pwias/viewabstract.php?10 [accessed 29 November 2007]).

[30] Keith C. Barton and Linda S. Levstik, *Teaching History for the Common Good* (Mahwah, N.J.: Lawrence Erlbaum Associates, Inc., 2004), 61.

[31] Linda S. Levstik, 'Articulating the Silences: Teachers' and Adolescents' Conceptions of Historical Significance', in *Knowing, Teaching and Learning History: National and International Perspectives*, ed. Peter N. Stearns, Peter Seixas, and Sam Wineburg (New York and London: New York University Press, 2000).

[32] This research project has been funded by a Discovery Grant from the Australian Research Council. The investigators are Tony Taylor and Anna Clark from Monash University, Stuart Macintyre from the University of Melbourne, and Carmel Young from the University of Sydney. The project began in September 2005 and is due to finish in 2008. The names of students and teachers have been changed.

[33] Interview with students, independent Islamic school, Sydney, 23 August 2006.

[34] 'Jill', public high school, New South Wales Central Coast, 22 August 2006.

[35] 'Les', public high school, New South Wales Central Coast, 22 August 2006.

[36] 'Chen', public girls' high school, Sydney, 21 August 2006.

[37] 'Annie', independent girls' school, Canberra, 17 August 2006.

[38] 'Lily', independent girls' school, Brisbane, 24 July 2006.

[39] 'Jeff', Catholic boys' school, Brisbane, 25 July 2006.

[40] Interview with students, public senior college, Perth, 24 May 2006.

[41] Interview with students, public high school, Darwin, 21 June 2006.

[42] 'Margaret', history teacher, public high school, Hobart, 4 May 2006.

[43] 'Mary', history teacher, public high school, Brisbane, 26 July 2006.

[44] 'Stephen', history teacher, Catholic boys' school, Adelaide, 15 June 2006.

[45] 'Andie', public girls' school, Sydney, 21 August 2006.

[46] Interview with students, public high school, New South Wales Central Coast, 22 August 2006.

5. A passion for white elephants: some lessons from Australia's experience of nation building

Dr Richard Evans

Abstract

A 'white elephant' is a magnificent, high-status possession that is not particularly productive, costs a lot to maintain, and which you cannot get rid of. Since colonial times, Australians have had a weakness for white elephants. Traditionally, these were massive, debt-funded public works schemes that were economically, environmentally or socially dubious. In recent years, our white elephants have taken on different guises, but the ruinous expense and misdirected effort remain the same. This paper explores some of the reasons for our society's historic enthusiasm for white elephants, and suggests some remedies.

Introduction

In the dark days that followed the tragic and unnecessary death of Humpty Dumpty, a crisis meeting was held at the Royal Palace. Surrounded by his most senior counsellors, the King thumped the desk in exasperation. 'What this shows,' he thundered, 'is that I need *more* horses and *more* men!' This joke hinges on a remarkable aspect of human nature. We are smart creatures, and a vital aspect of human intelligence is the ability to learn from experience. But we also *fail* to learn from experience: as individuals, as communities, and as nations.

Perhaps the bleakest example of the human capacity to ignore the lessons of experience was provided by the Allied military command on the Western Front during World War I. The supreme commander of the British forces, Sir Douglas Haig, believed that to win the war the German army had to be defeated, and that the best way to achieve this was by massive frontal assault. He attempted this in 1916, with the Battle of the Somme. The British offensive was a disaster: they took 60,000 casualties, nearly 20,000 of them killed, on the first day. Undaunted, Haig pressed on with the assault for four months. In what remains the bloodiest battle in history, the British failed to reach the targets that had been set for the first day of the offensive.[1]

As winter closed in, making military operations impossible, there was much soul-searching in the British government. What should the war strategy be for 1917? Certainly, not another Somme. An amphibious landing to outflank the Germans? Helping the Italians to attack Austria? Or just holding the line and waiting for the USA to enter the war?[2] Haig, however, had no doubts. He wrote in his diary that the solution was plain.

1. Send to France every possible man

2. ' ' ' ' ' ' aeroplane

3. ' ' ' ' ' ' gun.[3]

Here was the King, demanding more horses and more men. Haig got his way, and the result was ... another Somme. Though not as bloody as the previous year, the 1917 offensive similarly wrested a few miles of blasted quagmire from the German army at fearful cost in blood and treasure. Among the casualties were many thousands of young Australians.

'A capacity for independent judgment'

It is common for Australians to look back at World War I with pride and even some complacency. It was in the grim theatre of war that we first showed the world that we were different from the pompous, stupid, class-ridden English. The Diggers were first-rate soldiers, and their success was a reflection of the strengths of our national character.

In 1920, General Sir John Monash attempted to explain the remarkable fighting qualities of the men he had commanded:

> The democratic institutions under which he was reared, the advanced system of education by which he was trained — teaching him to think for himself and to apply what he had been taught to practical ends [meant that] ... mentally the Australian soldier was well endowed. In him there was a curious blend of capacity for independent judgement with a readiness to submit to self-effacement in a common cause ... He was always mentally alert to adopt new ideas and often to invent them.[4]

It is hard for an Australian not to feel proud and pleased at such words, and there is no reason to doubt Monash's assessment of his soldiers. However, the ANZAC myth, this belief in our own innate independent thinking and clarity of judgement is, when applied to Australian society more widely, a delusion. Worse it is a particularly dangerous delusion. If we are a hardy, cheerful, laconic and adaptable people, always ahead of the game, we have no need to critically assess ourselves. The very suggestion is ridiculous.

We do have our weaknesses, our blind spots. Among them is a weakness for white elephants.

'The nineteenth century equivalent of city walls'

The term 'white elephant' is one of those figures of speech which is almost always used by people unaware of its origins. It comes from a story told about the ancient Empire of Siam. There, albino elephants, because of their rarity and striking appearance, were considered sacred. They were symbols of the Emperor's power and semi-divine nature. One emperor devised an ingenious way to punish any courtier who annoyed him: he would present the man with one of the sacred imperial white elephants. The gift could not possibly be refused, nor could it be given to anyone else. And the Emperor knew that keeping the elephant in the magnificent style which custom demanded would financially ruin even the wealthiest of nobles.[5] Thus a 'white elephant' is any magnificent, high-status possession that is not particularly productive, costs a lot to maintain, and which you cannot get rid of.

Since colonial times, Australians have been suckers for white elephants. We ran up massive debts to fund the construction of railways, dams and bridges, schemes that were often motivated more by status than economy. Edward Shann, best remembered for his classic economic history of Australia published in 1930, was scathing of this tendency. 'They were building,' he said, 'in haste and on credit, the nineteenth century equivalent of city walls.'[6]

In 2007, I was commissioned to write the text of the book which would accompany the ABC TV documentary series *Constructing Australia*, which told the story of three great Australian engineering projects: the Sydney Harbour Bridge, the Kalgoorlie Pipeline, and the Overland Telegraph.[7] Throughout, I tried to keep some perspective, and make the story more than a celebration of Aussie ingenuity. I emphasised, for example, that the Sydney Harbour Bridge was a genuinely debatable proposition.

To criticise the Bridge now seems like shooting Skippy: unthinkable, if not un-Australian. The Bridge is our most distinctive man-made icon, the centre-piece of many a fireworks display and Qantas advertisement. If the Bridge had not been built, it would have retarded the development of Sydney; and perhaps that would not be such a bad thing. Had the Bridge not been built, perhaps Sydney today would be a smaller and more liveable city. Maybe other capital cities and other centres in New South Wales would be larger, our economy, government and culture less centralised. It is, at least, a question worth raising.

Unfortunately, I did not have the space to express my reservations about the Australia's single most iconic symbol of nation building: the Snowy Mountain Scheme.

Australia's Great White Elephant

The Great Depression put all thought of major capital works on hold in Australia for the best part of a decade, but even before the end of World War II, engineers and their political masters were again thinking big. The Snowy Mountain Scheme was one important result. Legislation for the project, which captured the water of the Snowy and Eucumbene rivers in massive dams and diverted it for electricity generation and irrigation, was passed in 1947. The project was not fully completed until 1974.

The Snowy was, no question, an epic engineering feat. Its combined storage capacity was equal to that of every dam and reservoir in Australia built before 1940: 160 km of tunnels and 130 km of aqueducts carried the water through a mountain range to the inland plains. The scheme became, and still is, an object of enormous national pride. It is somehow special, almost beyond criticism.[8]

But the Snowy is a white elephant — perhaps Australia's Great White Elephant. Economically, the scheme cannot be defended. As one analyst delicately put it:

> The assessments made in this discussion have been economic and in their light the Snowy Scheme can hardly be regarded as a 'paying prosposition' ... The primary worth of the Snowy is psychological ... Australians ... have proved that they do not live by bread alone, although had they realised at the outset that the price of this loaf could be so high they may have hesitated before buying it.[9]

The scheme has also been an environmental disaster. Much of the irrigation water was used unwisely — not least because the cost was massively subsidised — resulting in salinity and land degradation. So much water was diverted, too, that the Snowy River itself was all but destroyed.[10] And, as the governments of Australia, Victoria and New South Wales discovered in 2006 when they tried to flog it off, you can't even sell the bloody thing.

Australia is, as we all know, experiencing a catastrophic drought. It is not the worst ever in terms of rainfall and land area, but in terms of the numbers of people affected, it can perhaps be called the Great Drought. The water infrastructure of all our cities is under strain: the situation in many rural areas is disastrous. The issue of water, and how it should be managed, is a high national priority. In itself, this is a welcome development. But it is an indictment on our civic culture that the problem was allowed to become so serious.

Disaster and social change

Historically, Australian society has often faced up to important problems only when disaster –apocalyptic and undeniable disaster — forces us to face facts. I am currently seeking support for a history of the Black Friday bush fires of 1939. These fires were the most calamitous in the recorded history of Australia. More than 10% of the surface area of Victoria was burnt, scores of people were killed, and whole settlements reduced to ash, rubble and twisted metal. The disaster was of such magnitude that it forced Australian society — in rural areas, at any rate — to change its attitude to the natural environment and to fire, and to forge stronger and more civic-minded communities.[11] It took the fall of Singapore to make us realise that we could no longer place our trust in the British Empire. It took the calamitous road toll of 1970 in Victoria — the total was over 1000 — to change our attitudes to cars and how we use them. It took the AWB bribery scandal to make us realise the truth of an Adam Smith truism: that a privatised monopoly is the one thing worse than a state monopoly. There are many other examples.

That disaster should act as an agent of change is not surprising — but really it should not require disaster, not when we pride ourselves on our clear-eyed realism, and when there is plenty of warning. That Australia would face a water crisis in the early years of the twenty-first century was predictable — and was predicted. In 1968, C.H. Munro, a professor of civil engineering at the University of New South Wales, gave a public lecture on Australia's water future. Munro was scathing of our culture of waste, of how in our large cities 'the use of water for roses and lawns and car washing are taken for granted as essential human needs'.[12] He was thinking long-term, and saw trouble ahead:

> Planning authorities contemplate a population of five million people in Sydney by the year 2000. To some this is a horrible thought. Certainly it poses many problems to the engineer and town planner in regard to transport ... provision of water supply and sewerage and the like.[13]

We can't say that we were not warned; we just didn't listen.

In 1966, as a severe drought affected much of New South Wales and Queensland, a senior agricultural economist wrote:

> Government policies ... and skewed values which allow us to regard the failure of an electrical retailer as divine retribution but the bankruptcy of an under-capitalised and inefficient farmer as a blot on the social escutcheon, may well cause the cost of [future] droughts to be avoidably high.

> There is need for farmers and governments to confer in evaluating the lessons of past droughts and in planning for the future. All proposals, particularly those with a strong political bias such as for widespread irrigation development, should be judged by business criteria [and] ... in terms of ... the population generally, which has, in the end, to bear the cost.[14]

We can't say that we were not warned; we just didn't listen.

New white elephants

J.J.C. Bradfield, the driving force behind the creation of the Sydney Harbour Bridge and a prophet of diverting rivers to irrigate the Australian desert, was fond of quoting the great American engineer Daniel Burnham: 'Make Big Plans, for little plans have no magic to stir men's blood.'[15] Restoring damaged land and river systems, devising ways to make the water we have go further, managing our farmland, forests, cities and towns more efficiently and intelligently: these are projects which do not stir the blood. But that does not make them any the less important.

Certainly they are more important, more worthy of money, resources, discussion and effort than what has replaced dams, bridges and pipelines as the white elephants of our age. I am referring to the Major Event. I come from Melbourne, and in 2006 we hosted the Commonwealth Games. This privilege was secured after the only other city willing to do the job withdrew its bid. And so, at vast expense — how vast is hard to say because all the figures are very woolly, but their very wooliness suggests that it was a lot — Melbourne staged a largely meaningless sporting event organised around a largely meaningless group of countries. It was strange living through it — for months it seemed that some sort of cosmic mother-in-law was coming to visit, and that she mustn't see that the bedroom was untidy or the renovations were unfinished, and we simply *must* install a new patio, even though we can't afford it.

We do a lot of this sort of thing in Melbourne: the FINA World Swimming Championships of 2006 springs to mind, as does the F1 Grand Prix. Now *there* is bizarre event. It is the twenty-first century equivalent of a medieval tourney: a stupendous display of conspicuous and pointless consumption. It is Austin Powers-land, defiantly politically incorrect, complete with leggy pit girls and tobacco ads. It is worth visiting, once, to experience the roar and the smell, as someone once described it, of burning money. And yet this vast travelling festival global capital runs at a dreadful loss. Year after year, the circus flies in, loses money — our money, much if it — and then leaves.

The economic justification for Major Events is revealingly vague. There is talk of visitor numbers, turnover generated, money spent in secondary areas, growing the brand (Melbourne is a brand, apparently). It is much like the Snowy. If you point out that the power that is generated is too expensive, then you are told that it also provides irrigation water. If you argue that the water has been wasted, grossly subsidised, and that we have no business growing rice in Australia, then you are told that the same water generates power. And that anyway, there are flow-on benefits, and the whole thing was inspiring and made people proud, and that only mean-spirited bean counter of questionable patriotism would look too closely at the bottom line.

The nation-building challenges that face us now are not glamorous. They are to adapt our ways of living, working and travelling to the realities of the land that we inhabit. Among other things, this involves fostering some of the qualities which John Monash identified in the Australian soldier of 90 years ago: a high-quality education; an openness to new ideas; an independent but unselfish cast of mind; and — crucially — involvement with the institutions of civil society.

As an historian, I read a lot of old newspapers. Something which often strikes me is how many clubs and committees and associations there used to be, and how actively involved ordinary people were in the affairs of unions, political parties, local councils, churches, debating societies, and much else. Some people still do all these things, of course, but they are a small minority now: it used to be the common thing. Some of these civic groups achieved great things, such as female suffrage. Others did no more than run a tennis competition. And there were groups that were pernicious: dedicated to fostering racial and sectarian prejudice, for example. For all that, there was and still is value, in and of itself, in such civic participation.

Our political culture is becoming dangerously distanced from ordinary people. Our political parties are machines of power. Their membership bases are tiny, and democracy at branch level is a sober farce. At the same time, governments are increasingly interventionist, centralist and disdainful of due process. The recent change of federal government offers hope for reform, if only on the premise that a change is as good as a holiday. But it does concern me that the Rudd administration shows some of the managerialist, reflexively authoritarian tendencies that marked its predecessor.

If there is a weakness in our nation that needs repair, needs building, it is in the institutions of civic society, in empowering and encouraging participation. The process of decision-making may take longer. Internal dissent and discussion others may frustrate or embarrass those in executive authority. But if nothing else it might prove a protection against our weakness for white elephants.

ENDNOTES

[1] Lynne McDonald, *Somme*, Michael Joseph, London, 1983.

[2] Leon Wolff, *In Flanders Fields: The 1917 campaign*, (1958) Penguin, London, 2001.

[3] Ibid, p.105.

[4] General Sir John Monash, *The Australian Victories in France in 1918*, Lothian, Melbourne, 1920, p. 314.

[5] *OED*, 1st ed., vol III, p.85.

[6] E.O.G. Shann, *An Economic History of Australia*, Cambridge University Press, Cambridge, 1930, p. 126.

[7] Richard Evans and Alex West, *Constructing Australia*, Miegunyah Press, Melbourne, 2007.

[8] *Current Affairs Bulletin*, 'Murrumbidgee irrigation: A regional study', vol. 31, no. 10, 1 April 1963.

[9] *Current Affairs Bulletin*, 'The Snowy: An appraisal', vol. 31, no. 13, 13 May1963, pp. 207-8.

[10] Tim Flannery, 'Beautiful lies', *Quarterly Essay*, no. 9, 2003.

[11] Tom Griffiths, *Forests of Ash*, Cambridge University Press, Cambridge, 2001.

[12] C.H. Munro, *The Future Conservation of Australia's Water Resources*, University of Sydney, Sydney, 1969, p. 11.

[13] Ibid, p. 28.

[14] *Current Affairs Bulletin*, 'Drought', vol. 38, no. 4, 11 July 1966, p. 64.

[15] Richard Raxworthy, *The Unreasonable Man: The life and works of J.J.C. Bradfield*, Hale and Iremonger, Sydney, 1989, p. 94.

6. Populate, parch and panic: two centuries of dreaming about nation-building in inland Australia

Dr Robert Wooding

Abstract

In February 2007, then Queensland Premier, Peter Beattie, made reference to an old idea of diverting water from the upper reaches of some of the major coastal rivers of tropical North Queensland towards the drier parts of Western Queensland. This idea was most famously promoted in the late 1930s and early 1940s by the retired New South Wales Government engineer JJC Bradfield, who was the principal designer of the Sydney Harbour Bridge. The 'Bradfield Plan', inspired by major hydraulic engineering projects in the self-proclaimed 'modern economies' of the United States and the Soviet Union, represented the apotheosis of a century or more of misconceptions and imaginings about inland Australia. This paper will examine the Bradfield Plan and related proposals in the context of the history of the policies adopted by colonial, State and Federal governments towards inland Australia — particularly the western parts of the Darling Basin (or West Darling) — over the past two centuries, and will demonstrate that the intermittent revival of these ideas is a symptomatic of a pervasive policy-making climate of unrealistic optimism about nation-building and regional development which is interspersed by bouts of desperation and panic, typically triggered by external shocks such as droughts or falling export prices. The dream of an inland Australia with a strong population base continues to play a subtle, but critical role in shaping governmental thinking about key issues about the economy, environment, immigration policy and international relations.

Introduction

This chapter represents one facet of a more extensive research project on the historical development and future prospects of the Australian inland, especially the area that lies between the Great Dividing Range and the deserts of Central Australia. The question I will attempt to answer here is that of why a grandiose 'nation-building' solution to the perceived problems of the inland has retained a significant presence in public debate for more than seven decades, even though it has repeatedly and convincingly proved to be impractical and financially unviable.

My broader research project focuses principally on perceptions and understandings of the inland, both from those who have lived and continue to live there and from the overwhelming and growing majority of Australians who live along the coastal strip of the continent. I have also paid particular attention to the perceptions and policies of governments at all levels as they affect the inland.

Over much of the twentieth century and into the twenty-first, the inland and northern areas of Australia have been widely perceived as being in a state of 'decline' or, at the very least, as languishing due to our collective failure as a nation to take action to release their untapped potential. Federal, state and local governments have produced myriad plans for improving the lot of inland and northern Australia, including monumental, 'nation-building' solutions, some of which — such as the Snowy Mountains Scheme, the Ord River Scheme and the Alice Springs to Darwin railway — have been completed after many decades of deliberation, while others have never left the drawing board because they have been perceived to be overly expensive and/or impractical.

Of those monumental 'nation-building' projects that have not proceeded to an implementation stage, perhaps the most celebrated and controversial is that which is known as the Bradfield Scheme for diverting water from the rivers of the tropical north to those of western Queensland. While it has been subject to frequent and intensive criticism from scientists and other experts, the Bradfield Scheme has had an enduring appeal among some politicians and other public figures, and has had at least two major revivals in public debate since it was developed in its current form during the 1930s: most recently in 2007, as I will now discuss.

Part 1 — Raising the ghost of Bradfield

Queensland farmers were relatively late entrants into large-scale irrigation activity on the Murray-Darling Basin, with Queensland having played no part in the major intergovernmental agreements about the Basin prior to 1996, when it joined the Murray-Darling Basin Agreement. In the 1980s, Queensland irrigators were using less than 1% of the total water extracted from the Basin for human purposes, but this proportion was to rise rapidly to 5% by 2007. Although the use of Murray-Darling water by Queensland farmers remains low compared to the other states, this fivefold increase in their relative share has drawn considerable attention, and some criticism, from political leaders and the media, in light of a growing national concern about the long-term sustainability of the current level of irrigated farming taking place across the Basin.

In early 2007, against the background of this growing criticism and in the context of intergovernmental discussions about the Howard Government's newly announced $10 billion 'National Plan for Water Security', Queensland Premier Peter Beattie chose to revive the 'Bradfield Scheme': a nation-building proposal from 70 years earlier that was devised by John Jacob Crew ('Jack') Bradfield

(1867-1943), the Queensland-born chief engineer of the Sydney Harbour Bridge and Brisbane's Story Bridge. In the late 1930s and early 1940s, Bradfield had developed and promoted the idea of building a network of dams, pipes and channels to bring water from the Tully, Herbert and Burdekin rivers (which flow into the Pacific Ocean in tropical north Queensland) across the Great Dividing Range and south to the arid plains of western Queensland and NSW and north-eastern South Australia. Beattie's 2007 version of the Bradfield Scheme, which he presented in an 'open letter to all Australians', was tailored specifically to address growing national alarm about the long-term health of the Murray-Darling system. Beattie proposed to take the water further south than Bradfield envisaged; all the way to the Warrego River, a tributary of the Darling. He claimed that this would increase the flow through the Darling and Murray into western New South Wales and South Australia by up to 1000 gigalitres per annum: approximately the same amount drawn from the system by Queensland irrigators.[1]

Beattie's proposal gained widespread attention, and provided media outlets with an opportunity to display photos and archival footage of Jack Bradfield supervising the construction of the Sydney Harbour Bridge. However, within a few days, the proposal had faded from public debate. During its fleeting time in the spotlight, the Beattie version of the Bradfield Scheme was subjected to criticism from engineers, economists, environmental scientists and other experts on the basis of the same objections that had been repeatedly raised since it was first promoted by Bradfield in the late 1930s.[2]

It is not my intention here to explore in detail the various criticisms that have been made of the Bradfield Scheme over the past 70 years. Interested readers can access these in many other published works. Typically they have revolved around concerns that the massive costs of the Scheme would outweigh any conceivable benefits and that evaporation and other technical problems would mean that little of the water taken from the northern rivers would ever reach those further south and west.[3] Recently, Tom Griffiths and Tim Sherratt have produced an alternative 'what if' history in which the Commonwealth Government is imagined to have chosen to invest in the Bradfield Scheme rather than the Snowy Mountains Scheme as a centrepiece of post-World War II reconstruction. Griffiths and Sherratt have painted a fairly grim picture of both the environmental and economic consequences of such a decision, illustrating the spurious nature of many of the scientific claims underpinning Bradfield's proposals.[4]

Instead of criticising Bradfield's proposal, I will attempt to identify those aspects of the national psyche to which it most appealed. My thesis is that the short-lived resurrection of the Bradfield Scheme in political debate during 2007 is a symptom of a longstanding tendency for grand hydraulic engineering or land redistribution schemes to come to the forefront of public consciousness at times of major uncertainty about the long-term economic, social and environmental sustainability of our inland communities. Such periods of uncertainty have typically coincided with periods of drought and economic downturn in inland areas; as was the case in early 2007, when most parts of rural Australia were entering a sixth successive year of major drought, a drought which former Prime Minister Howard described as 'the worst in living memory' and which South Australian Premier Mike Rann claimed was a 'one in 1,000 year' event.[5]

There appears to be a longstanding tendency for Australians and those who govern them to panic about the future prosperity of inland Australia during periods of drought and economic uncertainty and to reach out for grandiose, expensive and unrealistic nation-building schemes which will allegedly secure that prosperity. Psychiatrists and psychologists describe a personality that veers between despair and unrealistic optimism as *labile*, and our shifting attitudes towards the inland over the past two centuries has warranted the use of this term.

For the most part we have perceived the inland areas of Australia as having almost unlimited potential as future sites for nation-building projects such as dams, irrigation areas, railways, roads, new towns and cities and vast mining and industrial projects. However, during times of drought or uncertainty, our optimism has rapidly dissipated and we have become haunted by apocalyptic visions of decline and despair which we have attributed to our own selfish and heedless actions in neglecting or unsustainably exploiting the environment. At these times, we have demonstrated an urge to reach for all-embracing solutions; the grander and more unrealistic they are, the better we seem to like them. As I will now discuss, the most popular of these possible solutions has always been that of building dams, channels and pipelines to bring water from where it is plentiful to where it is scarce.

Part 2 — Bradfield's 'hydraulic dreaming'

Advocacy on the part of politicians and enthusiasts of the idea of bringing water from the north of Australia to the inland, and of the related idea of permanently filling Lake Eyre by fresh or sea water, dates back to the 1870s and 1880s. Interest in such massive hydraulic projects appears to have been originally inspired by contemporary French proposals to using seawater to flood inland depressions in the Sahara desert. The proposal to build a canal from the Upper Spencer Gulf to flood Lake Eyre with seawater was seriously considered by South Australian Parliament in 1883 and was raised again in 1905, but was rejected on the basis of impracticality and cost.[6]

In this same period, a young engineer named Jack Bradfield was working for the New South Wales Government Engineer for Water Conservation, Hugh

McKinney, on a proposal to build a network of locks and weirs along the Barwon and Darling Rivers. An experimental, and rather leaky, wooden panel weir was constructed at Bourke in 1897, but the New South Wales Government eventually abandoned the scheme for a number of reasons: in particular, because it considered that the improvement in navigation on the rivers would benefit South Australian paddle steamer operators over the NSW Railways, and that the commercial prospects for irrigated farming in western NSW were slight, given the time and cost involved in transporting produce to major markets. Bradfield later claimed that he began to contemplate the broad outline of his inland water scheme while he was working on the Barwon-Darling project during the 1890s.[7]

Bradfield retained his enthusiasm for hydrological projects, and moved on to work on the construction of Burrinjuck Dam on the Murrumbidgee, which enabled the establishment of the Murrumbidgee Irrigation Area during the 1910s. He then left the field of water engineering to work on the Sydney underground railway, the Sydney Harbour Bridge and the Story Bridge across the Brisbane River. While working on the latter project in the late 1930s, he formed a friendship with John Douglas Story, the senior Queensland public servant after whom the bridge was later named.[8]

Through his friendship with Story, Bradfield was able to gain the ear of the Labor Premier, William Forgan Smith, and was given a brief to work clandestinely on a proposal to divert water from the northern coastal rivers to the inland. Bradfield's assistant, Jack Snowdon, later recalled a day in 1937 when Bradfield (who was now 70) was enjoying his normal post-lunch nap at his desk when he suddenly jumped out of his chair and said:

> Snowdon, I want you to drop everything and work on this water scheme for Queensland! He produced a map that he had drawn on in blue pencil. There was a ring around the watershed of the Herbert River in the north linked to Wairana on the Burdekin and the Clarke rivers, through the Great Dividing Range to the Flinders, under the railway line at Jardine Valley railway station and into the Thompson River which ran into Lake Eyre. This was Bradfield's inland water scheme.[9]

Snowdon was required to travel incognito across the entire region that would be affected by the proposed scheme; a task which he completed through a combination of rail travel, hitchhiking and on foot. In February 1938, Bradfield presented Story with a ten page paper entitled 'Queensland, The Conservation and Utilisation of her Water Resources' for the Premier's perusal. Forgan Smith was then in the middle of an election campaign but, once this was concluded, he arranged a face-to-face meeting with Bradfield. According to Jack Snowdon, Forgan Smith's first question to Bradfield was 'How much?'

Bradfield did a double shuffle and said '£30,000,000'. That was the end of the inland water scheme from an official standpoint.[10]

Bradfield continued to push his ideas for watering the inland through all the public and private avenues available to him, which — given his celebrity status as the chief engineer of the Sydney Harbour Bridge — were many and varied. In 1938 he gained the ear of Treasurer Robert Casey, who opened the way for him to present his plans to Prime Minister Joseph Lyons. However, following Lyons's death in April 1939, his successor Robert Menzies politely dismissed both Bradfield and his Scheme. Bradfield pressed on, devising ever grander versions of his Scheme, which incorporated not only the waters of tropical north Queensland, but also those of most central and northern Australian rivers, in order to create a network of water-filled gorges leading south to a permanently-filled Lake Eyre.[11]

Bradfield gained support for his Scheme from other public figures, most notably Ion 'Jack' Idriess, the journalist and bestselling author who is now best remembered as the author of a number of overwritten but entertaining semi-histories of inland Australia such as *The Red Chief* and *Lassiter's Last Ride*. Idriess had devised his own plan for watering the inland which he presented in a national lecture tour, a newspaper and magazine articles, and in a book entitled *The Great Boomerang* (the title of which refers to the shape of the large inland area which Idriess believed would be 'made bloom' by the diversion of the water.) Another supporter of both Bradfield and Idriess was Fred Timbury, then Mayor of Roma in South-West Queensland, who — like both Idriess and, most recently, Peter Beattie — wished to extend the Bradfield Scheme further south to bring the water not just to the Thompson river but into the Murray-Darling system. Two further contemporaries, Brisbane engineer LBS Reid and his advocate, former policeman Alfred Noakes — proposed a rival version of the Bradfield Scheme in which water would be drawn, not from the east coast of tropical Queensland, but from rivers flowing north and west into the Gulf of Carpentaria.[12]

These advocates received significant publicity in the press and other public forums during the 1940s, and Idriess's *The Great Boomerang* reached a large readership. Bradfield's plan, along with the rival Ord River Scheme proposed for the Kimberleys, even gained the attention of British Government officials, who saw it as a possible mechanism for opening up hitherto unoccupied territory for the resettlement of the Jewish population of central Europe.[13]

After Bradfield's death, the scheme was given serious consideration on a number of occasions both by the Queensland and Commonwealth governments. In 1945 it was examined by the Chifley Government in the course of its intensive policy deliberations on post-war reconstruction, but was found to be inferior to two other proposals; the Snowy Mountains Scheme and the Ord River Scheme.[14]

In 1947, intoxicated by visions of rapid post-war development, the Queensland Government directed a reluctant bureaucracy to re-examine the Bradfield Scheme in the light of the results of surveying and mapping work undertaken by defence forces in North Queensland during World War II. Once again, the Scheme was found to be overwhelmingly expensive and unlikely to provide anywhere near as much water for irrigation as Bradfield had claimed.[15]

In the early 1980s, the Bjelke-Petersen Government in Queensland proposed a revised version of the Bradfield Scheme as a potential Bicentennial project, and Malcolm Fraser's Federal Government pledged $5 million to support a feasibility study, a pledge which was not fulfilled due to Fraser's defeat in the 1983 election. Preparatory work undertaken by a consultant for the Queensland Government, which was not released at the time, found that the Scheme was viable in engineering terms at a cost of over $3.5 billion in current prices; however, the consultant made no recommendations as to the extent to the project could ever be expected to provide an adequate return on such an investment. The then Queensland Minister — and now independent Federal Member for Kennedy — who commissioned the consultant's report in 1982, R. F. Katter Jnr, continues to promote the Bradfield Scheme: calling for it as recently as mid-February 2008, in a speech to the Federal House of Representatives.[16]

The Bradfield Scheme was also briefly examined by the New South Wales Government in the late 1930s, and by the South Australian Government in the late 1980s as a potential solution to Adelaide's water supply problems. During the 1990s and 2000s, it has been propounded by prominent broadcaster Alan Jones, Melbourne businessman Richard Pratt, former National Party Leader Ian Sinclair and various Coalition backbenchers in Federal Parliament, by remnant elements of the One Nation Party and — as we noted at the beginning of this chapter — by former Queensland Premier, Peter Beattie.[17]

It would seem that, despite the periodic floating of the Bradfield Scheme by politicians and other opinion leaders, its massive fiscal weight inevitably causes it to founder among the shoals of bureaucratic resistance. Its fundamental problem is its enormous up-front cost, as appears to have been immediately obvious to Premier Forgan Smith when he rejected Bradfield's first proposal in 1938. The huge investment of taxpayers money in the Scheme could only be recovered over many years through direct charges to water users and indirect economic benefits arising from population growth and increased economic activity in inland areas. Most reliable estimates indicate that these returns would almost certainly fail ever to cover the enormous expense required to implement the Bradfield Scheme.

Bradfield himself recognised this drawback, and consequently sought to justify his scheme not just as a means of bringing additional irrigation water to inland areas, but also as a mechanism for promoting favourable climate change across a vast area of the inland. Bradfield, drawing on the 1920s work of E.T. Quayle, a former employee of the Commonwealth Meteorological Bureau, claimed that a permanent increase in the area of the interior covered by surface water — possibly including a permanently filled Lake Eyre — would raise the humidity of the atmosphere through evaporation, leading to a higher average rainfall across the inland. Quayle's work purported to show that farms lying to the south-west of large bodies of water receive, on average, three inches more rain per annum than other parts of the same regions, and Bradfield used these findings to contend that his Scheme would bring greater fertility to vast areas of the inland that were not directly watered by his proposed river diversions.

Quayle's theories were derived from those that had underpinned the nineteenth century proposals to flood the Sahara and Lake Eyre, which I have already discussed. Such ideas were also put forward in relation to the plan to lock and weir the Barwon and Darling Rivers in the 1890s, when they were debunked by the esteemed NSW Government Astronomer, Henry Chamberlaine Russell, who observed that — as the upper atmosphere shifts at the rate of hundreds of miles a day — any water evaporating from inland lakes and pools is over the Pacific Ocean by the time it might develop into rainfall. Quayle's theories, as they were re-presented by Bradfield, were comprehensively dismissed by other prominent meteorologists in the 1940s. A recent study looking specifically at Lake Eyre has suggested that its permanent filling may slightly raise the average level of precipitation directly above the lake itself, but would have little or no effect on rainfall levels across the surrounding region.[18]

Wherein lies the explanation for the continuing support for the Bradfield Scheme, in spite of the strong criticisms that have been made by scientists, economists and other experts? Historians and other writers have generally interpreted the ongoing interest in the Scheme in the manifestation of a longstanding tendency for Australians to identify the idea of 'nation-building' with major hydraulic engineering schemes such as dams and irrigation works: the Mulwala Canal, the Snowy Mountains Scheme, the Ord River Scheme and so forth. This 'water dreaming', as Tom Griffiths and Tim Sherratt have termed it, has led Australians to have faith that hydraulic engineering schemes will return a form of psychic income over and above any tangible commercial and economic benefits. This attitude was perhaps typified in the comments made by New South Wales parliamentarian E.W. O'Sullivan in the early 1900s in relation to the proposal to construct Burrinjuck (then 'Barren Jack') Dam:

> I would like to say that I consider it is a terrible mistake to attempt to reduce land settlement to a commercial basis. You have something far more important than the obtaining of profit out of the people to consider when promoting land settlement. You are making homes for them, and adding to the resources of the country, and incidentally to the revenue

of the country, and above all you are giving the people something which they can cherish as their own, whether it is theirs by leasehold or freehold.[19]

Historians have identified this attitude towards economic development as lying at the heart of many of the major irrigation and water supply schemes constructed in twentieth century Australia. The Bradfield Scheme is seen as having a particularly romantic appeal due to its evocation of the 'quest for the inland sea' that helped to inspire the nineteenth-century exploratory expeditions across the Murray-Darling Basin and northwest into Central Australia led by John Oxley, Thomas Mitchell and Charles Sturt. It has been suggested that the emotional legacy of the quest for the inland sea influenced the post-World War I flowering of the 'Australia Unlimited' school of writing that promoted the rapid development of the 'red centre' (a term used in preference to the more negative 'dead heart') and the tropical north.[20]

By the 1930s and 1940s, it has been argued, the idea of 'opening up' and irrigating the dry interior of Australia had gained further inspiration from major 'nation-building' hydrological schemes in the emerging world superpowers, the United States of America and the Soviet Union: in particular, Franklin Roosevelt's Tennessee Valley Scheme and Stalin's Dnieper River project. The intellectual climate underpinning the advent of the Bradfield Scheme was then topped off by the southwards military push by Japan after Pearl Harbour which promoted the 'populate or perish' imperative to develop rapidly the unoccupied central and northern areas of the continent or risk losing them to Asiatic invaders.

It would appear that all of these influences were important in firing the enthusiasm of the two Jacks — Bradfield and Idriess — and their like-minded contemporaries for inland hydraulic engineering activities. However, there was another, somewhat darker strand to their thinking that appears to have been neglected by other historians, but which is tied crucially to the limbic tendencies of our national perceptions of the inland described in Part I.

Part 3 — 'First parch, then panic!'

It is no accident that the periods of most intense political interest in the Bradfield Scheme — the late 1930s and early 1940s, the early 1980s and, most recently, the 2000s — all coincide with periods of major drought across Australia. Most rural Australians have been aware for many decades that periodic droughts, sometimes lasting five years or more, are an endemic occurrence in most parts of inland Australia. One would think that the prospect of drought would be too familiar to provoke undue panic or despair. However, over the past century or so, a number of politicians, journalists and other opinion leaders have shown a recurring tendency during major droughts to become the harbingers of a future nightmare scenario in which a state of permanent drought will be imposed on inland Australia as a form of divine punishment for the heedless and selfish ways in which we have used resources such as water, soil, forests and native grasslands.

This type of thinking first came to the fore during the Federation Drought of 1895 to 1902, which triggered the collapse of a high proportion of the pastoral enterprises in far western NSW and many other inland areas. The most immediate causes of the catastrophe were the absence of rain for several years, the impact of plagues of rabbits and dingos, and the accentuation of land degradation due to the overstocking of many properties. However, it is likely that an equally important cause of the collapse of many pastoral enterprises was the inevitable bursting of an investment bubble, fuelled by a flood of funds from around the world, which had promoted the over-capitalisation of the sector.

We might, therefore, with some justification, choose to interpret the economic and social catastrophe in the inland during the Federation Drought as being largely the result of a combination of natural causes, undue optimism and inexperience. However, some contemporary observers preferred to adopt a harsher and more judgemental position, tinged with a vision of apocalyptic doom that could only be averted through grand gestures of redemption. One of the foremost of these observers was the journalist C.E.W. Bean, who covered the aftermath of the Federation Drought in the inland for the *Sydney Morning Herald* and who later achieved greater fame as a war correspondent and official historian of World War I.

In an article about the region around the Darling River, which was given the lurid title 'The Rape of the West', Bean wrote of how:

> ... by 1895 the rabbits and the sheep had got to their work, and the drought was over the land. A series of terrible, lean years saw the West turn into nothing else than a desert. The sheep were held on the runs, in the hope of rain, till they were too weak to travel. There was not a blade of grass on the surface; but the stock walked over it until it was worked into a hard crust. Over parts there swept a loose sand which covered up even the fences, and actually turned patches of grass land into sandy wilderness. When the rain came, it beat off the hard ridges as it sweeps a galvanised roof. Such scrub as the sheep had left, the rabbits ringbarked. Every station was reduced to a tithe of its stock.[21]

Bean, whose appreciation of environmental issues was advanced for the time, argued that the solution to these problems was for Australians to develop a better understanding of the physical characteristics of the inland, and to adopt farming practices more sympathetic to its cycles of change. However, many of his contemporaries preferred to seek salvation in grand gestures: for instance, the South Australian Parliament, as we have already seen, briefly revived the earlier proposal to flood Lake Eyre with water from the Spencer Gulf. The Burrinjuck Dam and the Murrumbidgee Irrigation Area were also products of the prevailing mentality of this era.

The pastoral industry of the eastern interior had largely recovered from the ravages of the Federation Drought by the time Bradfield was dreaming up his Scheme in 1937, but another major drought began in that year and persisted across much of the country until the mid-1940s. Once again, a strong flavour of much contemporary public debate was that the drought was to a significant extent the result of unsympathetic and unsustainable human uses of the inland. The spectre of the 'dust bowl' that engulfed many North American crop-growing areas from 1933 to 1939 was frequently raised, as was the fact that Lake Eyre and the major rivers feeding it (Coopers Creek, the Georgina and the Diamantina) had been largely dry for many decades.

This was a period in which the first glimmerings of what were to become the Australian environmental movement could be detected in the pages of magazines such as *Walkabout* and *Wild Life*. Intellectuals and scientists began to express concern about the role played by deforestation in promoting salinity and soil erosion, and Bradfield himself began to refer to these issues in his public speeches, as well as becoming increasingly preoccupied with a rather fanciful notion that, because the palaeontologic record of the eastern interior showed that much of it was once covered by a vast inland sea this, rather than desert, was its natural state and that his Scheme therefore represented nothing less than a means of restoring the inland environment to its authentic state.[22]

Bradfield always presented his views in measured prose, but his supporters and fellow travellers — particularly Idriess — could at times work themselves up into a state of hysteria. *The Great Boomerang* contains many instances of such purple prose, but my personal favourite is the following evocation of an Old Testament prophet in the form of a shepherd who allegedly spoke to Idriess during the dark night of the western plains of NSW:

> … the shepherd says 'Listen!' There was no sound. 'It is too small for an ordinary man to hear….A few of us hear it. It is what is going to move a thousand leagues of sandhills. To make a sea of sand and dust to smother a generation to come … Teeth … millions and millions of teeth. And the years go on. And millions and millions more teeth are born eating, eating, eating. Eating down into the scanty grass-roots, killing the binding that binds the sandhills together. And every year the winds keep on blowing.'[23]

Bradfield, Idriess and some of their contemporaries had convinced themselves that the impact of grazing in the interior had turned marginal land into permanent desert that could only be redeemed by vast irrigation works. This pessimistic perception was dispelled by the impact of several years of heavy rain in the late 1940s and early 1950s, which filled Lake Eyre several times and submerged large areas of western Queensland and New South Wales for periods of six months or more, following which the formerly arid lands bloomed with grass, wildflowers and other flora. This was the prelude to three decades of above average rainfall and high fertility in the eastern interior during which the Australian wool industry reached its economic apogee.

This golden post-war era for the inland began to draw to an end in the late 1970s and was largely extinguished in the short, but severe drought of the early 1980s, at which time the Queensland Government and others chose once again to promote the Bradfield Scheme. Then, during the more prolonged drought which commenced in 2001, Alan Jones, Richard Pratt, Peter Beattie and others once again raised the idea of 'turning the coastal rivers inland' to 'drought proof this great brown land'.

Conclusion

It would appear that the level of fear of an ecological apocalypse in the Australian inland — and the level of faith in the possible panacea of a vast irrigation scheme of the type proposed by Jack Bradfield — waxes and wanes in a labile fashion that parallels the tendency for inland Australia to shift in and out of periods of major drought over the medium to longer term. In the first decade of the twenty-first century, we are once again in a period in which political, media and public interest in the state of our inland waterways has intensified during a prolonged drought. Have we simply descended once again into a state of panic, which will be dispelled as soon as the drought breaks, or have we managed this time to instigate a national policy process, which will lead us to an objective and emotionally balanced approach to managing the land and water of inland Australia? It is too early to say for certain, but we can perhaps be encouraged by how rapidly the proposition was removed from the table after being raised by Premier Beattie in February 2007.

It is impossible not to be impressed, and perhaps even inspired, by the grandeur and daring of Bradfield's Scheme as a nation-building vision for the future of Australia, and by the energy and enthusiasm with which he and others promoted it. But, as is the case with many other problems facing inland Australia, the issue of how to manage — and possibly augment — its limited supply of water is far too intricate and complex to be fixed simply by reaching out for a grand solution: no matter how tempting this might be to us in our urgent need to quell a rising state of panic.

The dilemmas currently facing inland Australia arise from aspects of the physical environment which date back many millennia (and, in some cases, millions of years), combined with problems of our own making which have arisen over the past two hundred years. Having taken a long time to develop, these problems are not capable of being solved through a single engineering blueprint. They will only be overcome through the slow growth of insight and a sustained and concerted effort on behalf of governments and the inland's inhabitants.

ENDNOTES

[1] The Hon John Howard, Prime Minister of Australia, 'Address to the National Press Club', Parliament House, Canberra, 25 January, 2007; Australian Government, *A National Plan for Water Security 25 January 2007*, Canberra 2007; Peter Beattie, Premier of Queensland, 'Open letter to Australians', February 2007; Australian Broadcasting Commission, 'Beattie suggests redirecting Queensland river water' (Reporter: Tony Eastley), *AM*, 19 February 2007; Australian Broadcasting Commission, 'Beattie denies water proposal far-fetched' (Reporter: Kerry O'Brien), *7.30 Report*, 19 February 2007; 'Inland lake aired again', *Courier Mail*, February 20, 2007.

[2] Australian Broadcasting Commission, 'River plan divides farmers, scientists', (Reporter: Louise Willis) *The World Today*, 19 February 2007; Australian Broadcasting Commission, 'Environmentalists react to Beattie's water proposal' (Reporter: Kathryn Roberts), *PM*, 19 February 2007; Rosemary Odgers and Stephen Wardill, 'Experts baulk at scheme, *Sunday Mail*, February 20, 2007.

[3] For example, G.W. Leeper, 'Restoring Australia's parched lands, a comment', *Australian Quarterly*, June 1942, 50-2; Ann Marshall, 'Climactic Aspects of the Bradfield Scheme', *Journal of the Australian Institute of Agricultural Science*, 10, 4, 1944, pp. 165-8; Commonwealth Meteorological Bureau, 'Bradfield Scheme for watering the inland, meteorological aspects', *Commonwealth Meteorological Bureau Bulletin*, 34, Commonwealth of Australia, Melbourne, 1945; Rural Reconstruction Commission, *Irrigation, Water Conservation and Land Drainage*, Eighth Report to the Honourable J.J. Dedman MP, Minister for Post-war Reconstruction, Commonwealth of Australia, Canberra 1945; Queensland Government, Bureau of Investigation under the Land and Water Resources Development Act of 1943, 'Third Annual Report' (1946) in *Queensland Parliamentary Papers 1947-48, Volume II*, Government Printer, Brisbane 1947, pp. 639-59; Bruce Davidson, *Australia Wet or Dry? The physical and economic limits to the expansion of irrigation*, Melbourne University Press, Carlton 1969; J.M. Powell, *Plains of Promise, Rivers of Destiny, water management and the development of Queensland 1824-1990*, Boolarong Publications, Brisbane 1991; Fereidoun Ghassemi and Ian White, *Inter-Basin Water Transfer, case studies from Australia, United States, Canada, China and India*, Cambridge University Press, New York 2007.

[4] Tom Griffiths and Tim Sherratt, 'What if the northern rivers had been turned inland?' in Stuart Macintyre and Sean Scalmer, eds., *What if? Australian history as it might have been*, Melbourne University Press, Carlton, 2006, pp. 234-54.

[5] A one-in-1000 year drought', *The Age*, 8 November 2006.

[6] A.W. Noakes, *Water for the Inland*, Railings and Railings, South Brisbane 1947; JW Gregory, The Dead Heart of Australia, a journey around Lake Eyre in the summer of 1901-1902, with some account of the Lake Eyre basin and the flowing wells of central Australia, John Murray, London 1906, pp. 342-52; F Ghassemi and I White 2007, *op cit*, pp. 144-47 and 379-83.

[7] Richard Raxworthy, *The Unreasonable Man, the life and works of JJC Bradfield*, Hale and Iremonger, Sydney 1989, pp. 46-8; Legislative Assembly New South Wales, Parliamentary Standing Committee on Public Works, 'Report relating to the Proposed Construction of Locks and Weirs on the River Darling' in New South Wales, *Votes and Proceedings of the Legislative Assembly during the Session of 1896, Volume 5*, Government Printer, Sydney 1896, pp. 559-61; Legislative Assembly New South Wales, Parliamentary Standing Committee on Public Works, 'Report relating to the Proposed Locks and Weirs on the River Darling between Bourke and Menindee' in New South Wales, *Votes and Proceedings of the Legislative Assembly during the Third Session of 1899, Volume 5*, Government Printer, Sydney 1900, pp. 32-3; JJC Bradfield, 'Address to the Millions Club Luncheon', undated, *Bradfield Manuscripts, National Library of Australia (BMNLA)*.

[8] R. Raxworthy, *op cit*, pp. 132-4, B Davidson, *op cit*, p. 62-3.

[9] R. Raxworthy, *op cit*, p. 136.

[10] *Ibid*, pp. 136-7.

[11] Bradfield to Lyons, 21 November 1938, 29 November 1938, *BMNLA*; RG Casey to Bradfield, 29 November 1938, *BMNLA*; Bradfield to Menzies, 23 May 1939; Menzies to Bradfield, 30 May 1939, *BMLNA*; Bradfield to ET Quayle, 29 July 1941, *BMNLA*; JJC Bradfield, 'Rejuvenating inland Australia',

Walkabout July 1941, pp. 7-15 (JJC Bradfield, 1941a); JJC Bradfield, 'Watering inland Australia', *Rydges*, October 1941, pp. 586-606; JJC Bradfield, 'Restoring Australia's parched lands', *Australian Quarterly*, March 1942, pp. 27-39.

[12] Ion L. Idriess, *The Great Boomerang*, Angus and Robertson, Sydney, 1941; Ion L. Idriess, *Onward Australia, Developing a Continent*, Angus and Robertson, Sydney 1945; F.R.V. Timbury, *The Battle for the Inland, the case for the Bradfield and Idriess plans*, with Foreword by Ion L. Idriess, Angus and Robertson, Sydney 1944; A W Noakes, *Water for the Inland*, Railings and Railings, South Brisbane 1947; F. Ghassemi and I. White, *op cit*, pp. 135-7.

[13] C.H. Hay New South Wales Government Offices, London to J.J.C. Bradfield, 19 January 1939, *BMLNA*.

[14] Rural Reconstruction Commission, *op cit*; Commonwealth Meteorological Bureau, 'op cit'.

[15] Queensland Government, Bureau of Investigation, 'op cit'.

[16] F. Ghassemi and .I White, *op cit*, pp. 131-4; Parliament of Australia, *Hansard*, House of Representatives, Wednesday 13 February 2008, p. 62.

[17] G.W. Watson to J.J.C. Bradfield, 1 March 1939, *BMNLA*; F. Ghassemi and I. White, *op cit*, p. 134, T. Griffith and T. Sherratt, 'op cit', p. 253, 'Pratt willing to aid Bradfield Scheme' *National Nine* News, February 23 2007.

[18] E.T. Quayle, 'Possibilities of modifying climate by human agency, with special application to south-eastern Australia', Proceedings of the Royal Society of Victoria, XXXIII, 1921, pp. 115-32; E.T. Quayle, 'Local rain producing influences under human agency in Central Australia', Proceedings of the Royal Society of Victoria XXXIV, 1922, pp. 89-104; Legislative Assembly New South Wales, Parliamentary Standing Committee on Public Works New South Wales (1896), p. 607; Commonwealth Meteorological Bureau, 'op cit'; A. Marshall, 'op cit'; Pandora K. Hope, Neville Nichols and John L. McGregor, 'The rainfall response to permanent inland water in Australia', Australian Meteorological Magazine, 53, 2004, pp. 251-62.

[19] B. Davidson, *op cit*, p 68.

[20] For further details about this school of thought, see J.M. Powell, *An Historical Geography of Modern Australia, the restive fringe*, Cambridge University Press, Cambridge 1988 and J.M. Powell, 'Griffith Taylor and `Australia Unlimited'' *John Murtagh Macrossan Memorial Lecture 13 May 1992*, University of Queensland Press, St Lucia 1993.

[21] C.E.W. Bean, *On the Wool Track*, Angus and Robertson, Sydney, 1963 (originally published 1910), p. 48.

[22] 'Developing Australia by J.J.C. Bradfield CMG' undated, *BMNLA*; J.J.C. Bradfield (1941a); J.J.C. Bradfield (1942).

[23] I.L. Idriess (1941), p. 14.

7. Australia's fiscal straitjacket

Fred Argy

Abstract

State governments are finally waking up to the need to get more actively involved in financing of public infrastructure. But at the Federal level, with the current commitment of Coalition and Labor to zero net borrowing over the economic cycle, the public debt straitjacket is becoming even more entrenched. The notion that, over the medium/long term, all general government investment should be financed out of current revenue or through the private sector is plain silly. It is impeding the Government's capacity to meet the nation's infrastructure needs and forcing it to adopt financing options that are economically less efficient than borrowing. It is also contributing to the run down of social capital and denying Australians a genuine, well informed choice on the appropriate balance between public and private goods. The policy needs a rethink.

Introduction

As John Butcher reminds us in Chapter 2, nation-building is about: (a) taming (or should we say working constructively with) nature; (b) building economic infrastructure (such as roads and railways) to remove physical bottlenecks to economic growth; and (c) investing in human capital such as public health, education, housing, employment programs, among others, in order to minimise the risk of skills bottlenecks and, more importantly, to ensure a fair society with genuine equality of opportunity).

If a government is interested in nation-building, the last thing it should be doing is tying itself up in a fiscal straitjacket. Yet this is exactly what the new Rudd Labor Government has done.

The medium term fiscal straitjacket

Like its predecessor, the Rudd Labor Government has promised that over the business (and electoral) cycle:

* tax receipts will not increase relative to gross national product; and
* there shall be no net government borrowing (no increase in public debt).

Effectively, Prime Minister Rudd and his Treasurer, Wayne Swan, have set a ceiling on tax rates and promised that, over the medium term,[1] all federal government spending — recurrent or capital —will be fully paid for out of tax revenue.[2] This extreme form of 'fiscal conservatism' may have helped Rudd win the election but it will make it very difficult for him to deliver a strong report card on his education, health and infrastructure goals.

The structural fiscal goals are not as rigid at the state level[3] but, under our lopsided federal system, it is the Federal Government that has the largest and fastest growing revenue base and the greatest capacity to borrow. So it is the federal fiscal stance that will be crucial for nation-building.

Yet, in my view, (and I am far from alone on this), the federal fiscal stance makes no economic sense. It is based on eight myths or, at best, eight half-truths, which I will explore below.

First myth — that 'higher taxes are bad for economic growth'

Few economists would accept this proposition as a generalisation. Tax increases can have significant incentive costs (although even here there is controversy[4]), with the so-called 'deadweight' (choice distorting, welfare-reducing) costs of higher taxes as high as 20 cents in the dollar. But the net economic cost of tax increases depends on:

- the initial tax levels (as the efficiency costs increase approximately with the square of the tax rate);
- how the revenue is raised (how much it impacts on work incentives and capital movements and how much it distorts choice); and
- how productively the money is spent[5] (how great are the offsetting benefits on the spending side) — for example, the offsets are nil if spending takes the form of 'middle-class welfare' transfers but they are much higher with productive investment in human capital.

With a careful choice of tax instruments and well designed spending programs, the economic benefits of public spending often outweigh the costs, especially in a low tax country like Australia. That is why it is hard to find a significant statistical correlation between size of government (levels of government spending and taxation) and a nation's economic performance.

People who want governments to spend less can mount a general argument based on 'government failure' and the need for a 'disciplined and restrained approach' to public spending. Equally, those who want governments to spend more on infrastructure, education, health care or early childhood intervention can make a general argument for additional spending based on increased wellbeing and social capital gains. But, at this generalised level, the arguments are based on ideology — not economics. Each proposal requiring higher taxation needs to be assessed on its individual merit without any prior presumption for or against.

Second myth — that a 'public debt freeze is the key to sound public finance'

This claim is plainly ludicrous. Net public debt — the difference between the government's stock of financial (mainly debt) liabilities and its financial assets — is not an appropriate measure of a government's balance sheet strength. The focus should be on net public worth — all financial and non-financial assets minus all liabilities. If governments borrow money to invest in real 'productive' assets with a comparable life to the debt, this adds to net public debt but it does not detract at all from net worth and, depending on the investment, could even increase net worth in the long term.

The only prudential requirement on governments should be ensure that, over the medium term, they run a net operating surplus (an excess of current revenue over *current* expenses) and borrow only to invest in physical or human capital projects that have met the standard cost-benefit criteria and have the potential to increase the revenue base in the long term. This should ensure net government worth is stable or rising and that public debt levels are kept at a sustainable level in terms of capacity to service. This is the stance now adopted by state governments and by most other OECD governments.[6] It is only the Commonwealth government that is out of line.

The irony is that Australia's public debt levels are among the very lowest in the developed world (less than five percent of the OECD average, relative to GDP). All Australian governments have very strong balance sheets[7] and our credit rating agencies are generally relaxed about some increase in government borrowing for investment purposes.[8] This should give Australia more — not less — freedom to borrow than other OECD countries.

Third myth — that 'the private sector is always a more efficient owner-manager of infrastructure than government'

As a generalisation, this proposition is simply untrue. While there is little doubt that the private sector is generally better than the public sector in design, construction and operation of infrastructure, capturing these benefits does not require private ownership. Governments can and do out-source most operational matters to private companies and consultants.

The efficiency case for *private ownership* of infrastructure is based on a number of premises which may or may not be correct.

Firstly, it assumes that the equity risks of the infrastructure project are largely commercial in character. But the equity risks are often more regulatory and political in character and in such cases the private sector is likely to demand a very high risk premium.

Secondly, the government is not always able to effectively transfer to the private sector the ultimate risk of default. Whatever the formal contracts might say, if a privatised hospital, school, road or railway network fails to perform, the government is held responsible.

Thirdly, private ownership is able to deliver benefits to users only if there is sufficient contestability in financial and service markets. The market for infrastructure finance has now matured and the up-front transaction costs such as fees to financial intermediaries, while still high, are now more reasonable than they were. But it remains hard to avoid quasi-monopoly market power in many infrastructure service markets. In such circumstances, privatisation would require close regulation and monitoring to ensure prices are reasonable and there is adequate accountability and transparency. This could nullify many of the efficiency advantages of private participation.

A fourth assumption is that private ownership will lead to improved managerial incentives. But will it? Government agencies are often derided for their lack of modern management expertise but in recent years they have developed ways to auction out community service obligations to avoid opportunistic political interference while also giving managers clear goals and well-structured performance incentives. There are many successful state-owned enterprises across the world, one example being Singapore Airlines. Private ownership of infrastructure, especially in listed companies, comes with its own problems such as the overriding desire to satisfy the short term demands of financial markets.

Finally, assigning infrastructure ownership risks predominantly to the private sector can lead to a misallocation of capital resources. For example, it tends to create a bias in favour of infrastructure investments with good commercial potential and against social infrastructure with high social returns (an issue I return to later). As well, in the case of new roads, privatisation can distort patterns of usage (forcing motorists to take less time-saving alternatives).

A recent OECD study of country experiences finds there are only 'limited' efficiency gains from extensive involvement by the private sector in the ownership and provision of non-self-funding social infrastructure and in social protection.[9]

In short, while private equity ownership of infrastructure will often be able to save taxpayers money and offer a service that is cheaper and more responsive to consumer preferences, governments should not start with a universal presumption that it is always superior to public ownership (which is what the embargo on net public borrowing implies). Each case needs to be assessed on its merit.

Fourth myth — that 'government borrowing for infrastructure investment puts upward pressure on inflation and interest rates'.

This view about the implications for interest rates and inflation is widely held, even by people who should know better, including the former Treasurer, Peter Costello.[10] Yet it has very little validity. Here it is important to distinguish between interest rate pressures stemming from capacity constraints ('real crowding out') and those stemming from financial market reactions ('financial crowding out').

If Australia's productive capacity is fully stretched, any new government infrastructure investment financed out of borrowings will, if other policies remain unchanged, add to inflationary and interest rate pressures — at least in the short term until the investment starts to pay off. However, against this, I would make the following observations:

1. on past experience, there is likely to be some longer term offsetting shift in private saving (e.g. through the so-called Ricardian equivalence' effects on anticipated future taxes) which will dampen the initial impact on demand of additional borrowing by about a third to a half (Comley et al 2002);
2. transferring financing responsibilities to the private sector will not help much to ease interest rate pressures since the short term effect on aggregate demand will be broadly the same; and
3. the fiscal authorities can avoid short term inflationary and interest rate effects by taking action to discourage or defer other types of national spending and by timing well the infrastructure investment program over the business cycle.

What of 'financial crowding out' — the risk that global financial markets will require an extra interest rate 'loading' for country and sovereign risk? This can happen in two ways. The first is by impacting on global capital markets, although this can be ruled out as Australia is a price-taker in these markets. The second is through effects on inflationary expectations. This has been a problem in the past because credit rating agencies tended to get skittish when a major new program of infrastructure investments was financed by public sector borrowing (rather than by private interests) because of unease about the lack of commercial and market disciplines in decision-making and the fear it might create useless 'white elephants' and make the additional debt hard to service. However, with public debt now at historically very low levels, and assuming new infrastructure decisions are made on the basis of sound cost-benefit evaluations, rating agencies and financial markets can be expected to take a more sensible and relaxed view of both public sector and external deficits.[11]

Fifth myth — that 'if a particular infrastructure project cannot be sensibly financed by the private sector, revenue can fill the gap'

Relying on current revenue to pay for the full cost of new social investment is not a sensible or viable alternative to government borrowing.

Firstly, we cannot count on a continuation of the extraordinary revenue windfall from the mining boom. When that boom ends, a federal government will have limited capacity to fund the up-front capital costs of infrastructure out of current revenue because of its self-imposed tax ceiling.

Secondly, there would be an economic cost if governments chose to crowd out economically desirable recurrent outlays (such as on education) or if workers were forced into higher than desirable effective marginal tax rates (Argy 2007 p. 149).

Thirdly, and most fundamentally, it is unfair to ask present Australians to pay upfront for new capital spending that will yield returns over a period of several years or even decades. Revenue should be used to pay for annual accrual expenses only (interest, depreciation, operational and maintenance costs).

Sixth myth — that 'there is no evidence that the fiscal straitjacket has impeded infrastructure investment'

This is an important issue because one of the key concerns of critics of the present fiscal straitjacket is that it has led to neglect of Australia's public infrastructure — and especially social infrastructure. To explore this issue further, I would ask two questions:

1. Is there hard evidence of neglect?

It is true that the evidence of infrastructure neglect is inconclusive, however, there is plenty of prima facie evidence — especially social and environmental — if one looks at:

- the steep relative decline in public investment over the last 15 years;
- the wide range of studies identifying specific infrastructure bottlenecks (such as coal ports in Newcastle and Dalrymple and electricity supply);
- cost-benefit studies pointing to high social returns from new investment; and
- opinion polling and anecdotal evidence of community dissatisfaction with the state of our infrastructure.

Public investment is lower today as a proportion of GDP than it was 15 years ago (in the late 1960s it was equal to one-half of private investment and today it is barely one fifth). This alone does not prove fiscal neglect. It may, for example, reflect such factors as more cost-based pricing (affecting demand), past over-investment in some areas and a shift from public to private financing. But the most marked decline has been in areas of social investment that do not lend themselves easily to private equity funding. It is also significant that the decline in public investment has been more rapid in Australia than in many other comparable countries.[12]

Sector-specific studies and anecdotal evidence reveal deficiencies in:

- economic infrastructure such as in power generation capacity, telecommunications, seaports and coal terminals;[13]
- social infrastructure such as pre and public schools, hospitals, urban roads, public transport, child care, training, lifelong learning institutions, community and preventative health care, domestic electricity supply, age and disability care and public housing; and
- environmental infrastructure such as water supply.[14]

In addition, there are many credible cost-benefit studies showing that social investments (especially in early childhood development and targeted labour market programs) yield high marginal social returns.

Finally, opinion polling shows a widely held and growing disenchantment with the standard of public services, especially in big cities and in regional areas, and a strong willingness to pay more taxes to improve the quality of services.[15]

All this is inconclusive but it is strongly suggestive of infrastructure neglect over the last decade.

2. Is the fiscal stance to blame for the apparent deficiencies?

Accepting that there are some infrastructure deficiencies, is fiscal policy to blame?

In my view, the deficiencies in economic infrastructure are more likely to be due to bad planning, poor management or tax disincentives than lack of finance. This is because such infrastructure can be readily financed by government trading enterprises (which have relative freedom to borrow and whose spending has held up fairly well) or by the commercial sector.

But there is little doubt that the fiscal stance is largely to blame for the neglect of social and environmental infrastructure (education, health, housing, transport, water and community amenities) because:

- such infrastructure does not lend itself easily to private financing as, typically, such projects are relatively complex, long lived and capital intensive, have long pay-back periods and seldom generate a steady cash stream sufficient to make them even approximately self-funding (paying for interest and depreciation);

- such infrastructure relies heavily on 'General Government' fixed capital non-defence spending, which has been declining relative to other investment (ABS 5204.0); and
- there is evidence of a trend decline in the share of non-cash government benefits going to the poor.[16]

As I will argue later, the fiscal straitjacket is creating an artificial bias against investments or recurrent government outlays of a social or environmental kind.

True, some of the gaps in social infrastructure supply are capable of being corrected by means other than new investment. For example, there may be a problem of misallocation of public capital (for example, relatively too much spending on roads and not enough on public transport) and there is certainly a need for pricing reforms to reduce demand in some areas (such as through congestion or carbon taxes). As the above discussion strongly suggests, the fiscal straitjacket has compounded infrastructure deficiencies.

Seventh myth — that 'running structural fiscal surpluses is good for national productivity'.

Unless one starts with the simplistic premise that 'governments always stuff everything up' (as some exponents of *Public Choice Theory* argue), the argument that fiscal surpluses boost productivity can be turned on its head.

As already discussed, the embargo on government borrowing tends to have efficiency costs because it overloads the tax burden in the early years and encourages governments to use private financing when it is not the optimal choice.

A more fundamental productivity cost of the present fiscal stance is that it artificially constrains the ability of governments to choose between social and economic infrastructure and between private goods and collective services, even when the latter offers relatively high marginal social returns. In particular, as noted earlier, it creates a bias in the allocation of capital against many types of social investment such as public schools, hospitals, urban roads and transport, child care development, training, lifelong learning institutions and community and preventative health care facilities.

Capital markets work very imperfectly. They have a tendency to ignore wider economic benefits for 'third parties' (benefits not directly captured by market transactions), such as effects on the environment, travel time, accidents, and the productivity of the unpaid household sector. And they tend to under-invest in merit goods such as health, education, job search, specific training and certain kinds of infrastructure (that crowd in private investment).

While government failure is also rife and needs to be allowed for, it is ideological bigotry to assume that governments are always incapable of correcting for market failures. A number of credible studies have found national economic returns (in terms of real incomes per head) of between \$2 and \$10 per dollar of government outlays on early childhood disadvantage and broader access to health, education, housing, public transport and improved urban freeways,[17] with gains coming in the form of a better educated and skilled workforce and citizenry; greater geographic and occupational mobility of labour; less waste of potentially successful entrepreneurs; higher employment participation rates; diminished health costs; lower imprisonment rates; less spending on welfare and juvenile delinquency; savings in commuting time; lower accidents and reduced pollution.

Cross-country studies show that governments (notably the Nordic countries, Ireland, the Netherlands and Austria) who choose to give relatively high priority to social investment have been very successful in reconciling high levels of social redistribution with good — or even superior — economic outcomes.[18]

There is another, more subtle, productivity bonus to be earned from increased social investment. It arises because of the signal it gives that governments are serious about achieving genuine equality of opportunity — where everyone can achieve their full potential irrespective of the circumstances of their birth. This positive perception helps to reduce the risk of a community backlash against further efficiency-driven economic reform.

Eighth myth — that 'the community prefers lower taxes and does not like the idea of governments borrowing'.

This proposition (although not a complete myth) is debatable. When Australians are simply asked if they want lower taxes, there will always be a majority saying 'yes'. But when they are asked to express a preference for lower taxes relative to additional spending on such things as health, education and the environment, the responses are much more positive for spending.[19]

On government borrowing, it is true that there is probably some public hostility. But this is because politicians misleadingly call it a budget deficit and equate it with bad management and higher interest rates. Australians would respond much more positively if:

- government borrowing were linked specifically to particular investment projects;
- the benefits (shorter commuting times, fewer accident risks, improved power availability and water quality, etc.) were clearly spelt out; and
- they were told that government borrowing for investment purposes is prudentially sound and that, if fiscal policy was well managed, it would have no adverse effects on interest rates.

The present fiscal stance poses a basic democratic problem: by setting arbitrary fiscal targets, governments are restricting their own ability to respond to the preferences and expectations of the community. Society is being prevented from exercising the full range of choices available to it.

Why the present fiscal stance needs a rethink

In summary, Australia has got itself into a fiscal straitjacket, which is open to six objections:

- it has no prudential rationale;
- it starts with an arbitrary presumption in favour of private financing and spending instead of looking at each case on its merit;
- it impedes the government's capacity to meet the nation's infrastructure needs;
- it creates a bias in the capital market against high-yielding investment in human capital (because social investment has relatively less access to finance from commercially oriented financial institutions and enterprises);
- it forces governments to adopt financing options that are economically less efficient;
- it denies Australians a genuine, well informed choice on the appropriate balance between public and private goods.

A policy stance that militates against public investment in infrastructure thus gets low marks for both social and economic efficiency as well as on grounds of democratic legitimacy. With Australia's public debt and tax levels at very low levels (historically and compared with the rest of the world) and with our social and environmental infrastructure perceived by most Australians to be in a state of neglect, it seems to be clearly in the national interest to relax the present fiscal straitjacket.

A proposed new fiscal stance

Instead of damning the States for their current modest borrowing programs, the Federal Government should be taking a lead role in developing, with the States, a set of national infrastructure investment priorities. Labor's idea of a national infrastructure audit is a good starting point.

As to financing, governments should continue to support viable private-public partnerships but, where the benefits of private involvement do not stack up, they should not rule out the alternative option of government net borrowing (or, what is effectively the same thing, drawing on the Future Fund) over the economic cycle — subject to a commitment to maintain or increase public sector 'net worth' in the medium term on an accruals accounting basis.

The Commonwealth should then use its increased borrowing capacity, as well as some of its windfall revenue from the commodity price boom, to make capital grants to the States earmarked for specifically agreed projects which meet the standard cost-benefit criteria. In the longer term, one hopes the imbalance in the federal system will be rectified and the states given more financial autonomy but there is no immediate prospect of that.

The government infrastructure spending program should be sensibly timed over the business cycle. If there is an expectation that the economy will continue to operate at full capacity for many years to come, fiscal action will be needed to defer other low priority spending (such as on middle-class welfare) and to discourage some forms of private consumerism.

References

Abelson, P., G. Withers and M. Powall. 2003. *Financing Public Infrastructure for urban development,* Conference paper, September.

Argy, F. 2006. *Equality of opportunity in Australia*, Discussion Paper no. 85, The Australia Institute, April.

—— 2006-2. 'Employment Policy and Values'. *Public Policy*, volume 1, no. 2.

—— 2007. 'Distribution effects of labour market deregulation', *AGENDA*, volume 14, no. 2.

—— 2007-2. 'Economic freedom: The good and the ugly', *Australian Quarterly*, July/August.

Comley, B., S. Anthony and B. Ferguson. 2001. 'The effectiveness of fiscal policy in Australia', *Commonwealth Treasury Economic Round Up*, Winter.

FitzGerald, Vince. 2003. 'Public investment in road and other infrastructure: the economic case', *CEDA Chief Executive*, July.

Gruen, D. and A. Sayegh. 2005. *The evolution of fiscal policy in Australia,* Treasury Working Paper 2005 -04, November.

Kamps, Christophe. 2006. *New estimates of Government net capital stocks for 22 OECD countries*, IMF Staff Papers vol 53, no. 1.

Keating, M. 2004. *Who rules?* Federation Press, Sydney.

ENDNOTES

[1] No one denies the need for governments to set their budget strategy in a sustainable medium term framework (i.e. over the business cycle as a whole) because it is good for policy predictability, financial market stability and public accountability. The debate is about the precise medium term (structural) fiscal goals that governments should set for themselves.

[2] Paul Kelly, *The Australian* 2/6/07.

[3] State *public trading enterprises* are allowed to carry debt in the same way as private corporations and even *at the general government level,* some state governments are tentatively moving towards a fiscal stance that aims for a surplus *in the operational account* but which leaves some room for net borrowing for new capital expenditure. But total state debt levels are not expected to exceed four or five percent of state GDP over the next five years, compared with 25% in the early 1990s.

[4] Keating (2004) points to literature which finds that 'there is not much empirical evidence of taxation affecting the supply of labour or saving' (p. 29)

[5] Argy 2006, pp. 57-60 and 2007-2.

[6] The UK, for example, seeks only to keep the operational account in the black and borrows if it needs to invest in excess of its annual savings. The EU countries are bound not to exceed a cash deficit of 3% of GDP over the cycle.

[7] NSW, like most other states, has a high and rising net public worth.

[8] See for example, the comment by Standard and Poor that the AAA rating of NSW is not under threat 'because of its strong balance sheet' (Alan Wood, *The Australian* 24/2/06). Hugh Emy, in *Australian Fabian News* June 2005, observes that 'it is clear from comments by Standard and Poor that investment aimed at expanding long-run economic capacity is more likely to support than diminish credit ratings in the long run'.

[9] 'Should we extend the role of private social expenditure?' *OECD Social, Employment and Migration Working Paper* no. 23.

[10] Mr. Costello blasted the states for 'running deficits' (borrowing) because it would put upward pressure on interest rates. But in the same interview he said that he had 'no problem with bank financed private debt' (Marc Moncrief, *The Age* 8 June 2006).

[11] Two papers by Treasury officers (Gruen and Sayegh 2005 and Comley et al 2001) lend strong credence to the view that financial markets are more relaxed about an increase in government and external debt when public debt levels are low.

[12] Kamps (2006) shows that the government net capital stock as a percentage of GDP at 1995 prices was 19th lowest out of 22 countries in 2000 compared with a ranking of 11 in 1980. See also Hugh Emy in *Australian Fabian News* June 2005. If one assumes a stable relationship between the desired stock of capital and level of GDP, then in a period of accelerating economic growth, like the present, the ratio of infrastructure investment to GDP should be rising in Australia. It is only in the most recent year that public investment has taken off, driven by state government infrastructure spending.

[13] For example, in transport, much has been said of the problems of the Pacific Highway and the lack of an inland north-south rail freight link or corridor. Also there are concerns about coal supply bottlenecks such as the Dalrymple Bay terminal in Queensland (report by Adele Ferguson in *The Australian* 18/7/07).

[14] Argy 2006, chapter 4.

[15] Twenty-five percent of Australians don't have faith they would receive adequate hospital treatment if they had an accident, according to a recent Roy Morgan Research survey. See also Argy 2006, pp. 47 and 55.

[16] Sources: ABS *Household Expenditure Survey* (ABS 6537.0); Commissioned study by Victorian Government, *Shared Future* (2004) and analysis by Ann Harding in *The Australian* 25/2/02.

[17] See Argy 2006-2. pp.64-65. See also Abelson et al (2003) and Fitzgerald 2003. The Business Council of Australia commissioned a study in 2005 which estimated a $16 billion permanent increase in GDP from $90 billion spent on infrastructure — mostly economic rather than social. Research modelling by The Brotherhood of St Laurence indicates that every dollar of investment in community enterprises that tackle local, long term unemployment could yield societal benefits of $14 (Tony Nicholson in *Australian Policy Online* 12/09/2007).

[18] See Argy 2006-2. pp. 66-7 and 75ff.

[19] See sources in Argy 2006 p 58.

8. The 'Building Better Cities' program 1991-96: a nation-building initiative of the Commonwealth Government

Lyndsay Neilson

Abstract

The Building Better Cities Program (BBC), initiated during the term of the Hawke Labor Government and administered by the then Department of Housing and Regional Development (DHRD), can be credited with leading the revival of Australian inner cities, the most significant change in urban Australia since the introduction of consumer credit post World War II.

The genesis of the Building Better Cities Program was a Special Premier's Conference held in July 1991 at which the Commonwealth, State and Territory Governments agreed to co-operate in a program focused on improving urban development processes and the quality of urban life. Its aims were to demonstrate better urban planning and service delivery as well as co-ordination within and between the various levels of government.

The Program was first funded in the 1991-92 Commonwealth Budget. The overall purpose of the Program was 'to promote improvements in the efficiency, equity and sustainability of Australian cities and to increase their capacity to meet the following objectives: economic growth and micro-economic reform; improved social justice; institutional reform; ecologically sustainable development; and improved urban environments and more liveable cities'.

The Commonwealth Government agreed provide up to $816.4 million over the period December 1991 to June 1996 in order to meet these objectives. The Program operated through formal agreements with individual State and Territory governments and targeted 26 distinct areas throughout Australia.

Initially as Chief Executive of the National Capital Planning Authority and then as Deputy Secretary of the Department of Housing and Regional Development (responsible to the Deputy Prime Minister and Minister for Housing and Regional Development — the Hon. Brian Howe) Lyndsay Neilson oversaw the creation, development and implementation of the program, and observed the aftermath following the 1996 Federal election.

The chapter reflects on the successes and shortcomings of the Building Better Cities program and addresses those aspects of the program that offer lessons for Commonwealth-State engagement in the contemporary environment.

I gratefully acknowledge the assistance of Pem Gerner, Geoff Campbell, Brian Howe and Bruce Wright in preparing this chapter. The views expressed are mine and I am also responsible for any historical inaccuracies or misstatement of facts.

Introduction

The 'Building Better Cities' program (BBC) was a major initiative of the Hawke Labor Government. It was initiated by the Honourable Brian Howe MP, first in his role as Minister for Health, Housing and Community Services then later as Deputy Prime Minister and Minister for Housing and Regional Development.

It was the first Commonwealth engagement in urban Australia since the Whitlam Government in the 1970s, with Minister for Urban and Regional Development, Tom Uren, led a major shake-up of thinking about managing Australia's cities and towns.

The shock of the 1970s initiatives and the acrimony they created with the States meant that the 1990s program needed to be built in a collaborative way, bringing State and Territory Governments into a new partnership with the Commonwealth, sharing responsibility and working together to achieve agreed outcomes.

This meant that BBC not only broke new ground with the style of intervention undertaken (focussed on capital works initiatives) but it also created new forms of intergovernmental agreements built around *outcomes* — an approach that was, at the time, at the leading edge of intergovernmental financial arrangements.

This chapter focuses on the development of the initiative, the building of collaboration with the States and Territories, and the impact of the program both over the period it was funded and, more importantly, in the years after. It was in the latter period that the urban initiatives began to have real impact on the pace, nature and character of development across Australian cities, most importantly in the inner cities and in strategic areas of urban renewal.

The issues at stake

During the 1980s, with the election of the Hawke Government there developed an atmosphere of exciting reform created by the decisions of Hawke and Treasurer Paul Keating to pursue the opening up of Australia to global economic competition.

Macroeconomic reform involved addressing efficiency within the economy as well as removing barriers to trade and international investment and currency exchange. The debates about efficiency turned, inevitably in an economy and society as urban as Australia's, to the place of cities in economic growth.

Traffic congestion, needed infrastructure investment, inner urban decline in population and employment, rising car dependency, restructuring of labour markets leading to rising structural unemployment in the old industrial suburbs, concerns with consequent rising inequality across society, all became issues of debate.

The economics profession, unashamedly non-spatial in its outlook, remained recalcitrant in acknowledging any role for spatial policies — interventions directed at particular places rather that the economy as a whole — arguing that markets should sort out spatial issues through structural adjustment over time and that government intervention would only impede market progress.

The Commonwealth Treasury, having a sufficiently long memory to recall the bitter battles of the 1970s with Tom Uren's Department of Urban and Regional Development (DURD) over economic policies, remained totally opposed to any revival of interest at Commonwealth level in dealing with cities. Policies and programs with spatial effect were to be avoided because these matters were State responsibilities and the Commonwealth should stay out of them.

The counter view was that there were common trends across the nation that resulted from Commonwealth economic and social policies (such as the effect of structural unemployment, the lack of investment in infrastructure due to strictures on borrowing) and that the economy as a whole would substantially benefit from interventions that addressed impediments to change in urban Australia and so speed adjustment to new realities.

In other words, there were market failures in the urban system, often spatially based (such as lack of players and confidence in the inner city property market) that needed focused spatial policies to correct them.

Further, trends such as declining population and employment in inner cities threatened the increasing underutilisation of capital already invested in infrastructure and services — an inefficient outcome — and placed more pressure on the need for new investment in outer suburbs to accommodate new growth.

Urban consolidation was seen as an economically efficient way of catering for population growth, offsetting the car-based sprawl that characterised Australian urban expansion.

At the same time, urban expansion was seen as necessary to accommodate most growth, given the high propensity among Australians to seek to own their own home on a spacious suburban lot and issues of affordability for first home buyers in particular — the ability to buy a block of land and build later when savings allowed, was still a significant factor.

But outer urban development could be more efficient and more equitable if it was planned and delivered better — more focus on public transport infrastructure and networks, more attention to employment opportunities in outer suburbs, more timely provision of services for arriving residents — all matters addressed in the past and reflected in the work of Australia's government Development

Corporations in several States and in the work of some of the larger estate developers.

Organisations like the Albury-Wodonga Development Corporation, the Macarthur Development Board in Sydney, and the most significant, the National Capital Development Commission in Canberra had extensive experience in organising and managing 'whole community' developments on an integrated basis, on government owned land.

Private companies like Lend Lease and Delfin were experimenting with similar approaches on their own estates, with some success. But more needed to be done to demonstrate how to make suburban development better — more efficient, more equitable, more liveable.

A further imperative was the development of non-metropolitan Australia. Regional development (decentralisation) was a long-running mantra of all governments across Australia, and the pressures were being raised by structural adjustment in the economy that removed protection progressively from many region-based industries.

The resulting unemployment, coupled with the impacts of technological change, led to rural and small town population decline that was a major political issue for rural-based political parties, including the Labor Party, which was trying to shore up a rural and regional city base.

Brian Howe MP was the leader of the Left of the Labor Party in Canberra and a reformer by instinct. As Minister for Health, Housing and Community Services he was a senior player in the Hawke Government and a senior Cabinet Minister. Howe worked hard to get the Prime Minister and his Department interested in 'spatial disadvantage' arising from economic changes, and the social problems associated with existing settlement patterns emerging in Australian cities.

In response, to address the issue, the Department of the Prime Minister and Cabinet funded a series of economic and social studies on spatial disadvantage, and later a major piece of work by The Institute of Family Studies on living standards and communities.

The Australian Living Standards Study looked at living conditions and experiences in around a dozen differing communities around Australia, including several in remote areas.

This work was never released, but was followed by discussion within the Council of Australian Governments in 1990 on urban settlement patterns and the implications of the dispersed city model for broader economic and social policy. This latter work was coordinated by Meredith Edwards in the Department of the Prime Minister and Cabinet.

At the same time the Prime Minister was advancing his 'New Federalism' agenda, forming more cooperative relationships with the State and Territory governments to advance projects and initiatives he saw as being firmly in the national interest.

All these factors, and more, combined to create a moment that was 'ripe' for an initiative in urban and regional development.

The Commonwealth's interest stirred

Howe had an interest in urban issues from his past, and was undoubtedly being lobbied frequently by members of the left and people previously associated with the Whitlam Government (notably Pat Troy, former Deputy-Secretary of DURD, and possibly Tom Uren himself) who urged him to take up urban issues again within the Commonwealth.

Howe and his Chief of Staff, Tom Brennan, attended a conference organised by the Regional Science Association of Australia where, among other things there was considerable discussion of urban and regional development and its relationship to Australian economic reform — particularly discussion of what a cogent policy agenda for the Commonwealth might be.

I attended the same conference, then in my role as Chief Executive of the National Capital Planning Authority in Canberra, and had a number of informal conversations with Howe and Brennan touching on the need for urban initiatives, who was influential in the field of urban planning and development and related matters.

Some weeks after the event I received a call from Brennan inviting me to a meeting with Howe to discuss a possible Commonwealth urban initiative. Brennan relayed that Howe felt I 'might be interested in helping build an urban agenda' and asked that I give the matter some thought prior to meeting Howe.

In the spirit of 'New Federalism' it was clear that the Government wanted an alternative approach to the more centralist DURD model taken by the Whitlam Government.

Having been a party to the Whitlam-Uren urban and regional programs of the 1970s I had some experience to draw on in thinking about what might be a successful approach for the Commonwealth to take in the 1990s, especially in the face of continuing suspicion among the States about a Commonwealth 'takeover'.

When I met with Howe I set out to make a number of points.

Firstly, the 'DURD era' was still regarded with suspicion by the States and within the Commonwealth and anything that suggested a 'return of DURD' would be unacceptable. Howe was aware of this sentiment and agreed with it.

That meant a new approach that drew the States and Territories into collaboration with the Commonwealth was needed, rather than subjecting them to an initiative 'imposed from Canberra'.

Secondly, the possible scale of any Commonwealth urban initiative could not encompass all the potential urban and regional issues that, politically, the government might like to address. I used a simple calculus that divided $1 billion among six States and two Territories (everyone had to benefit, irrespective of obvious difference in need) and pointed out that $120 million per State didn't deliver a lot when dealing with urban development.

That meant that any Commonwealth initiative, to be effective, needed to be selective. Politically that would create problems because funds would not flow across all electorates but to only a selected few — a difficult call for any Minister whose job, in part, is to assist the back bench retain seats, as well as the Party to win new ones. Howe reserved his judgement on this, while fully understanding the issue.

My proposal was that there needed to be a program of investment that had a strong demonstration effect — rather like the Whitlam-era 'Green Street' program that demonstrated how good design could achieve very acceptable and environmentally friendly forms of higher density housing in existing suburbs. 'Green Street' was very influential in impacting expectations and practice in the market place in small scale urban renewal.

To address urban renewal alone though, was not sufficient — there needed to be 'demonstrations' of how to manage better the development of outer suburban estates and also investments that worked in 'the bush' — some initiatives for Australian regional cities that would change expectations and outcomes.

Howe also wanted a social agenda in the program, and we discussed a range of ideas, including my proposal that we look at the deinstitutionalisation programs of some States that were freeing up large properties formerly the home of mental health or intellectual disability institutions and of jails. (I had previously prepared, as a consultant to the Victorian Government, a review of the Victorian Corrections system that led to jail closures and also the 10-Year Plan for the Office of Intellectual Disability Services in Victoria that was, in part, targeted at closure of a number of major institutions).

Howe was interested but sceptical, wanting to understand examples of what might be worthwhile projects, so he asked that Brennan and I work together to contact people around the States, confidentially, and produce some examples of locations and projects that might be worthy of support and that might constitute elements of a program that met solid reform principles from a Commonwealth perspective.

Over the following week Brennan and I spoke with contacts in the States — his political, mine professional, for the most part — and sought their suggestions as to what the States might welcome by way of 'a Commonwealth urban initiative' and, if there were projects to be supported with capital, what kinds of projects might be 'investment-ready' and significant in influencing urban growth and change.

Varied suggestions came back: some for pieces of infrastructure, usually transport; others for particular redevelopments on underused land, others for regional infrastructure such as port improvements. One or two were for comprehensive urban projects (redevelopment of Melbourne's Flinders Street rail yards, for example); none were for outer urban locations (other than suggestions for new roads).

Nevertheless there were plenty of suggestions, more than enough for Brennan and I to go back to Howe and state a number of things.

Firstly, there was no shortage of projects in which the Commonwealth might invest and where investment would be welcomed — with the emphasis on capital investment.

Secondly, in order to create a significant urban demonstration effect talking up individual investments in items of infrastructure was not enough; we needed to be more specific about wanting to take an 'area-based' approach, where multiple outcomes could be gained from Commonwealth involvement — physical renewal, affordable housing, employment, public transport access, environmental initiatives, social gains and so on. We wanted comprehensive and linked effects wherever possible.

Third, there was a potentially very receptive atmosphere among the States and Territories if we were dealing with a capital program that could breathe new life into key aspects of urban and regional growth and change.

It was enough for Howe to feel he could have a discussion with his senior Cabinet colleagues, most importantly the Prime Minister and the Treasurer. He had undoubtedly also been canvassing his own contacts for their views and expectations.

Howe's overtures and explanations were well received and he was given authority to commence informal consultations with the State Premiers, on a confidential basis.

Consulting the States

I first learned of this when I received a telephone call from Mike Codd, Secretary of the Department of the Prime Minister and Cabinet, inviting me to meet with him. I went to the meeting with some trepidation, to discover that Howe had suggested to Hawke, and Hawke had agreed, that I be asked to call on each of the State Premiers and open up informal discussions with them about their likely response to a Commonwealth urban initiative and their suggestions about what form it might take.

Codd would clear the proposal with the other two relevant Departmental Secretaries — Tony Blunn, Secretary of the Department of Territories (within which the National Capital Planning Authority was located) and Stuart Hamilton, Secretary of Howe's Department of Health, Housing and Community Development.

I accepted the proposal with enthusiasm, and proceeded to plan the process, which would be opened up by a letter from Prime Minister Hawke to each Premier requesting their assistance and cooperation. Howe and I agreed that I would be accompanied to these meetings with a member of his advisory staff, Onella Staggoll.

So, during the latter months of 1990 we set out to win the cooperation of State Premiers in preparing an urban and regional initiative for Australia in which they would participate as a partner with the Commonwealth.

We provided State Premiers with some outline indications of the types on investments that might attract Commonwealth attention and the broad purpose of the Commonwealth's interest, but otherwise not a great deal of detail was given for obvious political reasons — notably there was as yet no Commonwealth commitment to a program and the Government didn't want speculative leaks to the media about the potential initiatives.

Our reception was mixed.

Premier Greiner of New South Wales was perfectly happy to receive funds from the Commonwealth provided he got to spend them on his project priorities with no strings attached. He wasn't particularly interested in a partnership.

Premier Kirner of Victoria was similarly inclined in relation to receiving money, but with a potentially more sympathetic view of partnering with her Labor Party colleagues from Canberra. She had several 'pet projects' to advance, none of which met the general criteria we advanced (closing Swanston Street in Melbourne's CBD was a key priority for Premier Kirner).

Premier Lawrence of Western Australia did not meet us but sent her senior staff to do so. They expressed political suspicion about the Commonwealth's motives but saw a number of initiatives of value in Perth — especially redevelopment in and around Fremantle,

In Queensland we met with the effervescent Deputy-Premier Tom Burns on behalf of Premier Goss, and the powerful Mayor of Brisbane, Jim Soorley. Both had suggestions and ideas, a number of them (notably the redevelopment of some of inner Brisbane's run-down neighbourhoods) very consistent with the objectives we were then forming and testing.

Premier Bannon in South Australia also had his office and government officials meet with us and expressed an interest in addressing the social problems of Elizabeth in Adelaide, a rapidly declining area of former car-industry-worker housing that had become a welfare-housing nightmare for his Government.

This initial round of meetings also enabled us to invite each of the States (and later the Territories) to submit a list of proposals to the Commonwealth, in writing, as a guide to what they might be interested in undertaking in a partnership, given the general criteria we spelled out — area-based, multiple outcomes, capital investment, demonstration effect, with inner urban, outer urban and regional projects all to be considered. A couple of weeks were provided for these initial responses.

The 'Yellow Book'

With some prompting, initial ideas for Commonwealth support flowed in from States and Territories — still on a highly confidential basis (confidentiality *was* respected — no material was leaked). With the help of NCPA staff and consultant David Hain, Tom Brennan and I categorised, assessed and assembled the proposals into the so-called 'Yellow Book' — an A4 landscape document on yellow paper for discussion with Brian Howe.

Over a series of meetings with Howe we rejected, sought more information and details about, or regarded as serious propositions about 50 proposals from State governments, most of them still single-purpose infrastructure investment proposals. We refined the contents of the Yellow Book to produce a list of possibilities across the country and in inner urban, outer urban and regional locations. Interestingly, we did not locate them within electorates.

When Howe was satisfied that there were enough proposals that could be potentially developed to fit our broad criteria (area-based, multiple outcomes for the area, with economic, social and environmental features and benefits, capital in nature, demonstrating new ways of approaching urban renewal or new development) he decided he would take the proposals to Cabinet to support the allocation of funds in the 1991-92 Budget.

He now involved the Secretary of his Department, Stuart Hamilton, in the discussions. Stuart, in a memorable exchange in a lift in Parliament House asked me how much money the initiative would need.

'About a billion dollars' was my reply, and I explained to him the same logic that I had presented to Brian Howe.

The funding decision

Howe held private discussions with the Prime Minister and the Treasurer and with other influential Cabinet Ministers (such as Hon. John Button MP) to gain support for his proposals.

Howe personally persuaded the Prime Minister that the Government needed to invest in the nation's development through capital programs, in the major cities for example, and that a program could be devised that addressed major issues emerging in Australian cities. This program should be an important aspect of Hawke's New Federalism agenda.

Because of the sensitivity of the proposals and the desire to move quickly, Tom Brennan and I prepared a Cabinet Submission, but one not intended for circulation among other agencies of government. Howe had the agreement of his colleagues that the submission would not be circulated prior to Cabinet, but, rather, tabled at the Cabinet meeting.

The submission was supported in Cabinet, with final financial allocations to be decided in the Budget 'round-up', but an 'in principle' allocation to the initiative of $800 million in capital (which later became officially $816.4 million when the Department of Finance properly constructed the $800 million number).

The allocation of the funds as capital raised an interesting challenge. Practice was that capital was normally provided to States (where there was capital involved in Commonwealth-State funding) as general purpose funds, with no conditions attached. In order to be able to have States use the funds in ways that met the Commonwealth's objectives, we would need to utilise a different approach.

Tom Brennan took on this task with the Treasurer's Office and it was agreed that the Loan Council arrangements for General Purpose Capital Grants would provide a suitable vehicle, provided we could reach agreement with the States that, while the funds were untied capital, the States would use them for proposals agreed with the Commonwealth. This was to prove to be a major challenge, but one that was, in due course, fully met.

The final financial arrangements are explained in more detail in documentation cited from the Australian National Audit Office

The 1991-92 Commonwealth Budget Papers therefore showed an allocation of $816.4 million to the Building Better Cities program, allocated across States and Territories in accordance with population — an outcome of Department of Finance instructions about how to allocate General Purpose Capital Grants.

State/Territory	BCP Allocation ($ million)
New South Wales	278.1
Victoria	209.0
Queensland	139.4
Western Australia	78.3
South Australia	68.7
Tasmania	21.7
Northern Territory	7.5
Australian Capital Territory	13.7
Total	816.4

Source: Australian National Audit Office, Audit Report No. 9 1996-97

Getting the program started

It was decided that to initiate the program and drive collaboration with the States, leadership would rest with the Department of the Prime Minister and Cabinet (PM&C). The Secretary, Mike Codd, arranged a meeting between Stuart Hamilton and Tony Blunn, at my NCPA offices, to ensure they were clear about the role of PM&C but also to ensure they accepted that the National Capital Planning Authority (in Blunn's portfolio) would act as a consultant to PM&C, while reporting to Hamilton's Minister. There was a certain tension to these unusual arrangements.

Codd established a Better Cities Task Force, an interdepartmental group to get the program under way and, just as importantly, to provide informed advice to Cabinet on the proposals to be put forward by the States and Territories. I chaired the Task Force, and the major relevant Departments participated — PM&C, Treasury, Transport, being the most significant among them.

Funding was provided to NCPA to recruit a team to work on establishing program guidelines, assessment criteria for proposals, and procedures for decision-making by Cabinet, where all the allocations of funding were finally to be approved — a concession in the light of the scale of the program and its unusual passage through Cabinet in the first place.

This process was to be objective and rigorous.

The approach to funding meant that, in effect, the capital had been already allocated to the States and Territories. But funds were not to flow without several requirements first being met.

First, each State and Territory had to sign up to an 'umbrella' Intergovernmental Agreement that set out the objectives of the Program and the nature of the collaboration it required. The funding was not provided in a set ratio — dollar-for-dollar, for example — but instead would be paid into a pool of funds provided by the State, the Commonwealth, local government and the private sector in some cases, to go towards implementation of an agreed development plan (an Area Strategy) for each area to be funded.

Each Area Strategy proposed by a State or Territory would need to demonstrate how outcomes would be achieved, consistent with the objectives of the program. Each strategy would have to estimate the cost of delivering those outcomes and the contribution sought from the Commonwealth to make the Strategy effective.

Once the Commonwealth and the State both signed up to an Area Strategy, funds could flow. The Commonwealth would monitor progress against Strategy milestones, and if progress was inadequate, the Commonwealth could turn off the funding tap until the State or Territory government made up for lost effort.

In this way it was intended that the States could not simply show an allocation of funds to a Strategy and then not actually spend their share, using only the monies provided by the Commonwealth.

The Task Force was assisted by NCPA staff and a team of consultants (initially David Hain and Dianne Berryman, later joined by Geoff Campbell, formerly Chief Planner of the National Capital Development Commission). It needed first to clarify and adopt program objectives and guidelines to be provided to States and Territories as a basis for preparing their formal bids for funding.

The overall purpose of the Program was described as being to promote improvements in the efficiency, equity and sustainability of Australian cities and to increase their capacity to meet a range of social, economic and environmental objectives.

The objectives were determined to be as follows:

- economic growth and micro-economic reform — including the location and level of development needed to encourage economic activity and promote increased productivity;
- social justice — including better access to employment, training, appropriate health care, family support and education;
- institutional reform — including rationalisation of, and improved access to, key community and health services and reduced dependence on expensive outmoded types of institutional services;
- improved urban environments and more liveable cities; and
- ecological sustainability — improved sustainability of cities through urban consolidation.

This ambitious span of objectives was made more complex in terms of project definition by a number of additional factors:

- each area strategy proposed had to try to satisfy elements of each objective; and

- each state (but not the territories) had to provide proposed area strategies in inner urban, outer urban and regional settings.

The relationship between the objectives, project selection criteria and intended project outcomes was complex and set high performance standards, forcing examination of linkages between activities and investments in an area, and those investments and actual urban outcomes.

Figure 1, adapted from one used in a report by the Victorian Auditor-General, *Objectives, Selection Criteria and Intended Outcomes Established for Program*, illustrates the hierarchy:

Figure 1

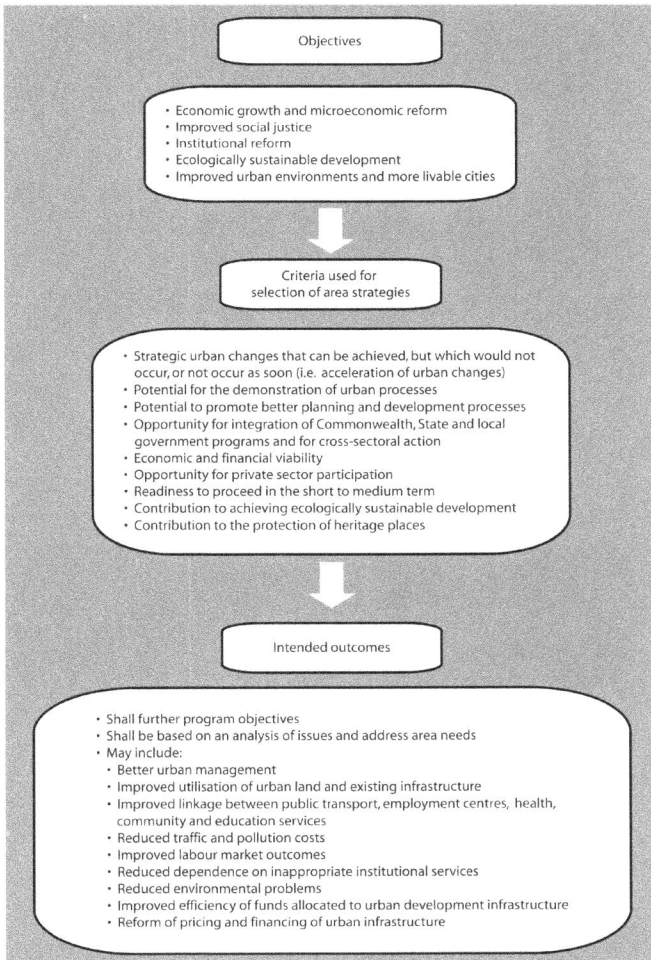

Objectives

- Economic growth and microeconomic reform
- Improved social justice
- Institutional reform
- Ecologically sustainable development
- Improved urban environments and more livable cities

Criteria used for
selection of area strategies

- Strategic urban changes that can be achieved, but which would not occur, or not occur as soon (i.e. acceleration of urban changes)
- Potential for the demonstration of urban processes
- Potential to promote better planning and development processes
- Opportunity for integration of Commonwealth, State and local government programs and for cross-sectoral action
- Economic and financial viability
- Opportunity for private sector participation
- Readiness to proceed in the short to medium term
- Contribution to achieving ecologically sustainable development
- Contribution to the protection of heritage places

Intended outcomes

- Shall further program objectives
- Shall be based on an analysis of issues and address area needs
- May include:
  - Better urban management
  - Improved utilisation of urban land and existing infrastructure
  - Improved linkage between public transport, employment centres, health, community and education services
  - Reduced traffic and pollution costs
  - Improved labour market outcomes
  - Reduced dependence on inappropriate institutional services
  - Reduced environmental problems
  - Improved efficiency of funds allocated to urban development infrastructure
  - Reform of pricing and financing of urban infrastructure

Source: Adapted from Victorian Auditor-General's Office, 14 November 1996, accessed 3 April 2008 at http://archive.audit.vic.gov.au/old/sr45/ags4502.htm

The Guidelines and Criteria were all agreed by the Better Cities Task Force and endorsed by Cabinet, and the urgent process of seeking formal bids from the States and Territories commenced late in 1991 — with a view to having bids received and assessed before the end of that year. Geoff Campbell stressed the need to engage quickly with State and Territory governments and their agencies, following up our previous exploratory contacts. A round of visits started.

The urgency was simple — to gear up capital expenditure in the urban environment is normally an extensive and time-consuming process. If Better Cities funds were to be spent usefully and with good effect during the five years of the program, spending needed to start as soon as practical. That was why one key criterion for proposals to be accepted was that they were 'investment-ready'.

States were now provided with draft material covering all aspects of the program — the umbrella Intergovernmental Agreement, the requirements for Area Strategies, the Selection Criteria — and were invited formally to submit proposals for funding agreement.

Seeking State and Territory bids

Given the prior consultation process, most States and Territory governments and their agencies were by now well prepared with proposals for Commonwealth consideration.

New South Wales remained reluctant to conform to the program's requirements, seeking the straightforward allocation of the Commonwealth's capital to State-determined priorities.

Victoria was struggling to agree proposals within the Victorian Government, as the selective nature of the program caused evident political difficulties in that State.

Queensland and Western Australia were the most advanced with preparation of proposals and both had worthwhile Area Strategies ready for consideration.

The NCPA's team of staff and consultants began travelling to all States and Territories and working with teams of officials in each to try to ensure proposals came forward that would satisfy the program criteria when tested by the Better Cities Task Force and, eventually, by Cabinet.

At the same time the negotiation of the Intergovernmental agreement was under way to ensure that there was commitment by all parties to collaboration and to an outcomes-based approach to delivery.

Slow but steady progress was made through late 1991 and into early 1992, with State and Territory officials visiting Canberra, and vice-versa, to carry on negotiations. There was little political intervention, but Brian Howe, impatient to see agreements signed and spending started, urged his State counterparts to get on with the tasks needed.

There was tangible excitement as worthwhile proposals emerged: the revitalisation run-down suburbs of inner Brisbane; the redevelopment of contaminated and disused industrial land in East Perth; the redevelopment of the Launceston rail yards in Tasmania; the redevelopment of the Honeysuckle area of industrial Newcastle; the transformation of institutional land at Janefield in Melbourne into a new suburb; the major transformation of old industrial land at Ultimo-Pyrmont in Sydney; relocation of fuel storage tanks away from valuable seaside real estate in Darwin; and others.

The program had been understood and accepted and visionary new things were about to happen.

Two other aspects of the program that came to the fore at this time warrant mention. Firstly, one of the significant impediments of markets for urban renewal emerging in Australian cities was the lack of surplus capacity in old, inner city infrastructure systems — especially sewerage systems. Another was the predominance of often highly contaminated old industrial sites in the inner city areas, land that was too costly to rehabilitate and sat idle, occupied by redundant gasometers and fuel and metal-impregnated rail yards.

A key strength and selling point of BBC was that it would provide the funding to *remove these barriers to change* — something players in the market place could not afford individually to do. This turned out to be a major factor in the success of BBC in sparking urban renewal.

The second was that the Program sought specific management arrangements for each Area Strategy that would bring strength and commitment to delivery of the spending and the outcomes. Our view was that normal departmental working arrangements would fail because the needed integration of activity and cooperation would not occur. We were encouraging experimentation in urban governance as well.

This too turned out to be a key factor — those Area Strategies where the arrangements for management were the most focused and where management teams were 'on site' (East Perth, Inner Brisbane, Ultimo-Pyrmont, Honeysuckle in Newcastle) all turned out to be the most quickly and most efficiently delivered.

Selection of Area Strategies

Over a number of months the Better Cities Task Force met, and debated and argued the strengths and weaknesses of State and Territory bids, and sought improvements and refinements. Progressively these were made.

At the same time more of the Intergovernmental Agreements were signed and working arrangements set in place for the necessary ongoing intergovernmental collaboration in the delivery, monitoring and assessment of programs.

A particular feature of the Agreement was that States and Territories had to agree to report annually to their Parliaments on the progress made under the Building Better Cities program. The Commonwealth would also report as a matter of course under the Annual Reports from the relevant Departments.

Finally, a number of submissions to Cabinet led the Commonwealth to endorse 26 Area Strategies across the nation to be funded under the program. The Area Strategies were as follows:

State	Area Strategies
New South Wales	Ultimo/Pyrmont High density affordable housing, planned light rail, sewerage and water systems, and a new neighbourhood park.
	Transit West (West Sydney) Development of Parramatta and Blacktown as key regional centres; construction of Blacktown bus and rail interchange and the Merrylands-Harris Park 'Y' rail link.
	Honeysuckle and Environs (Newcastle) Rejuvenating inner Newcastle; improving employment opportunities, public transport and housing choices.
	Eveleigh Medium density housing and open spaces; development of an Advanced Technology Park to encourage employment in knowledge-based industries and scientific research.
Victoria	Plenty Road Transport improvements — tram line extension to Mill Park; improved public housing; development of former institutional land; R&D commercialisation facility at La Trobe University.
	Inner Melbourne and Rivers Higher density public and private housing; city circle tram service; flood mitigation works.
	South West Development of Bio-Technology precinct at Werribee including the Australian Food Research Institute; upgrade Geelong-Werribee-Melbourne rail line; redevelopment of the Norlane Public Housing Estate (Geelong).
	South East Rail infrastructure improvement, including redevelopment of Dandenong Railway Station; joint venture development of residential housing; promoting Dandenong as a regional employment and service centre.
Queensland	Brisbane-Gold Coast Corridor Extension of railway from Beenleigh to Robina; higher density housing, including public housing, with access to improved transport interchanges.
	Brisbane — Inner North Eastern Suburbs Conversion of former industrial sites for residential housing; higher density housing, including low cost housing and public housing; improvements to public transport; cycle path network and public footpaths.
	Inala — Ipswich Institutional reform, including closure of Wacol Rehabilitation Centre and the Challinor Centre for persons with intellectual disabilities and rehousing residents; infrastructure improvements including flood mitigation works; construction and upgrade of public housing.
	Mackay Urban Consolidation Project Provision of low cost housing and student accommodation; increased urban densities.
	South Townsville Inner City Village High density housing adjacent to Townsville CBD; better traffic management; improvements to community services.

State	Area Strategies
Western Australia	East Perth Infrastructure upgrades including water, sewerage, drainage, power and road works; affordable housing and promotion of an urban village concept. Experiment with environmentally responsible buses for public transport.
	Stirling Infrastructure upgrades — sewerage system, road and rail links, Stirling bus-rail interchange.
	Bunbury New public housing, tourist and recreational facilities; environmental and infrastructure works, including removal of oil storage facilities, waste water treatment system, and waterfront public open space areas.
	Fremantle Infrastructure upgrades — sewerage, stormwater drainage and water recycling systems; higher density housing including affordable housing and housing for the elderly.
	Perth Urban Innovative housing close to employment and transport.
South Australia	Elizabeth — Munno Para Infrastructure improvements - stormwater drainage, water storage and landscaping; affordable housing initiatives, innovative housing loans.
	North West Sector Development of Northwest Crescent of Adelaide; road links and environmental improvements, Virginia pipeline to reuse treated sewage.
	Southern Areas Improved infrastructure — sewerage disposal, roads and cycle paths; employment opportunities at Noarlunga.
	Western Area Higher housing densities; improved community facilities; better traffic management, clean up of Patawalonga.
Tasmania	Launceston Inner City Increased housing densities; development of cultural, community and conservation sites, redevelopment of railyards and sheds.
	Hobart Western Shore Improved urban environment and land use including decontamination of sites; institutional reform and conservation of historical sites.
Northern Territory	Darwin New deep water port for Darwin at East Arm Peninsula; environmental improvements.
ACT	North Canberra Waste water recycling plant scheme; an energy efficient rating system for new residences; higher density housing and institutional reform.

Source: ANAO 1996

NSW and Victoria provided only limited regional initiatives (Geelong and Newcastle were the focus), unlike Queensland and Western Australia, where regional projects were very important. Otherwise the spread of Area Strategies was impressive, and the scope for innovation and demonstration very sound.

The above summaries give no illustration of the complexity of individual area strategies. Appendix 1, showing the expenditure for Victorian Area Strategies illustrates better the nature of their content. The Victorian strategies were rather weak in that their component parts were scattered and management arrangements were too informal for our liking, but they were accepted for funding.

The Victorian Area Strategies also illustrate the contributions made by the State as well as the Commonwealth — a little over 50 cents for each Commonwealth dollar. This level of State/local contribution varied widely across the Area Strategies.

Appendix 2 provides a descriptive summary of one Victorian Area Strategy — the Plenty Corridor. The actual Strategy documentation was, in each case, between 10 and 15 pages long.

Getting implementation going

Once the Area Strategies were signed off and Intergovernmental Agreements signed, longer-term arrangements needed to be set in place for management of the Program. The initial role of the NCPA in acting as the agent to get the initiative established was no longer appropriate and program administration needed to pass to the Department of Health, Housing and Community Services.

This was done, with the NCPA being retained as consultant to the Department for technical services, and indeed, the Authority did commission and produce a large number of BBC Technical Papers over the ensuing years, and these provide an ongoing and valuable reference source for urban initiatives today.

The Australian National Audit Office described the changing administrative arrangements for implementation thus:

> BCP [Better Cities Program] was initially administered by the Department of Health, Housing and Community Services. With changes in Commonwealth administrative arrangements, it was managed by successor Departments in the Health Portfolio and transferred to the Department of Housing and Regional Development (DH&RD) in 1994. At the time of the audit, BCP was managed by DH&RD's Urban Programs Branch. The National Capital Planning Authority (NCPA) provided the managing Department with consulting services in connection with BCP. In March 1996 following the change of government, the program was transferred to the Department of Transport and Regional Development.

> The Department notes that the original formulation of BCP was under the Department of the Prime Minister and Cabinet with the assistance of the National Capital Planning Authority. This included the Better Cities Task Force, an interdepartmental committee which endorsed the Area Strategies and advised the Government on the content of State/Territory agreements. Source ANAO 1996

Working with the States was a constant struggle to keep activities aligned with objectives, agreements and milestones, and did lead to both later modifications of agreements and area strategies to reflect the realities of implementation and also to the Commonwealth ceasing funding on at least two occasions until, States/Territories achieved pre-agreed milestones.

Geoff Campbell moved from the NCPA's team of consultants to the office of Deputy Prime Minister and Minister for Housing and Regional Development, Brian Howe, as a ministerial consultant with a special remit to oversee the implementation of the program.

Howe had his own challenges with the program as it started implementation. First, the selective nature of the initiative, with only 26 areas covered, disturbed some among the back bench. They did not accept that a national initiative needed to be selective to have any effect, and argued for extension of the program on a more generous geographic (electoral?) basis. To their credit Howe and his fellow leaders resisted these calls, with their focus firmly on the national benefits of the program's demonstration potential.

The challenge with Better Cities strategies was, nonetheless, the time taken simply to organise to spend capital. In the inner areas of Australia's cities the major barriers to change were, as discussed, lack of capacity in key infrastructure services and contamination of large areas of former industrial land in good locations for urban development.

Overcoming these barriers meant a lot of preliminary work and spending needed to be done. Before new urban development and uses could rise on old railway yards or old industrial sites, land had to be cleaned up, sewers and pumping stations had to be built and acceptable economic development projects planned and designed.

A very large proportion of the Commonwealth's investment through BBC went 'underground' in this way, and Ministers became impatient to see the above-ground results.

When new developments did start to appear, (early examples being the redevelopment of Dandenong Railway Station in Melbourne and Blacktown Railway Station in Sydney as part of Area Strategies designed to revitalisate areas in decline) there was much celebration, especially among those who benefited from these new facilities. When Paul Keating, by then Prime Minister, arrived by train to open the new Blacktown Station, he was greeted with rapturous and sustained applause.

At the other end of the scale simple steps also produced great results. Victorian Premier Jeff Kennett and Brian Howe agreed that as part of Melbourne's inner urban Area Strategy a small tramline extension along Spring Street would be made to enable a complete City Circle tram route to be set up, taking visitors and others on a loop around Melbourne's CBD tourist attractions. Howe provided the capital, Kennett the running costs, and a lasting and highly valued contribution to inner Melbourne's liveability and economic performance was delivered in short order.

Nothing was more dramatic and long-lasting in effects, both direct, and indirect through demonstration, than the revitalisation of the inner city areas of Sydney, Perth and Brisbane. The work of the Inner Brisbane Urban Renewal Authority, led by the late Trevor Reddacliffe, and the East Perth Redevelopment Authority, was transformative. Both Authorities pulled both government and private sector funding into complex and lasting renewal projects.

In contaminated, industrial East Perth the task was more complex. But before too long new inner-urban town houses in well designed environments were rising, selling and becoming occupied. The success over the subsequent years led to the Authority being mandated to continue its work in other areas of Perth.

In Sydney, the transformation of old industrial sites in Ultimo-Pyrmont and the introduction of the light rail link to central Sydney were catalytic events, along with the reuse of the Eveleigh rail yards.

Appendix C, prepared by Pem Gerner from his Doctoral Thesis on the Better Cities program, narrates and evaluates a selection of area strategies from today's perspective.

Creating momentum, giving the freedom to State and Territory agencies to experiment and innovate, while ensuring the fundamental parameters of the program were being addressed and milestones met, was a juggling act of significant complexity, well beyond the demands of usual government programs which handed out money for one-off projects with usually single-purpose objectives. BBC broke new ground even at this most basic of levels.

What was fundamental to success, however, was the fact that the private sector backed the program in all States. Better Cities both created and freed up investment opportunities, and developers, guided by the agencies managing the program and each Area Strategy, found these opportunities increasingly attractive.

As confidence built in the reality of government's commitment to these areas, with funding being spent on real infrastructure and other assets, private companies took the projects seriously.

Trevor Reddacliffe in Inner Brisbane, with his private development background, was especially adept in convincing private investors of the merits of investing in 'his' area, and they did. Millions of dollars poured into his projects, and inner Brisbane rapidly became a national exemplar in urban renewal.

But East Perth, Ultimo-Pyrmont and Eveleigh in Sydney and Lynch's Bridge and Kensington Banks in inner Melbourne also rapidly drew in private investment and the Area Strategies began to take real shape. Today, investment still is flowing, an important understanding in terms of how best to assess the overall impact of the Better Cities initiative.

The Phase 2 initiative

As the first five years of the Building Better Cities program came close to an end, the Government, led by Prime Minister Keating, had to debate and decide upon an extension of the Program. While Keating had little to do with Better Cities after its establishment (he was on the back bench for a significant period) when he became Prime Minister he began to take considerable interest — especially after he attended the opening of Blacktown Railway Station and saw the enthusiasm of the impressive crowd.

The Minister for Finance, Kim Beazley, was firmly opposed to any extension of the program, arguing that it had achieved its objectives and was, in any event, too tightly focused.

Brian Howe argued strongly for a new round of the initiative, focused on new objectives but keeping the emphasis on integrated, multiple-outcome Area Strategies as the means of delivering Commonwealth funds.

The new emphasis was to be on the nation's economic 'gateways' — the major linkages between our physical economy and the rest of the world, where opportunities for port and airport expansion combined with urban renewal initiatives were both very evident and very necessary. The privatisation of airports had left large areas of land available for new economic initiatives and the Government wanted to take full advantage of this, as well as create better access to and from airports and seaports as an efficiency measure.

Urban renewal and urban growth management remained key components.

Phase 2 of Better Cities was put forward also as part of Keating's 'One Nation' initiative, and he supported it in this context.

In the event, Howe won the debate, but only with the personal support and intervention of Keating, who directed that a further $200 million of Commonwealth funds be included in the 1995 Budget.

The *Sydney Morning Herald* around that time reflected the uncertainty of the likely outcome with a headline that read 'Keating to scrap the Better Cities Program'.

The Australian National Audit Office records the subsequent history:

> A second phase of the program (BCP Mk.II) was announced in the 1995 Budget with estimated Commonwealth funding of $200 million over four years. This was to deal with national economic gateways such as air and sea ports, urban growth management and urban renewal. The Commonwealth entered into BCP Mk.II agreements with four States (New South Wales, Queensland, South Australia and Tasmania) before the March 1996 election.
>
> Following the election, the Government announced that the program would not be continued. The 1996 Budget provided funding to meet existing contractual commitments. Appropriations and expenditure for BCP Mk.II are set out in Table 4.

Table 4: Building Better Cities Mark II
Commonwealth Appropriations and Expenditures

Financial Year	Appropriation ($m)	Expenditure ($m)	Appropriation spent
1995-96	20.0	20.0	100%
1996-97	2.6	--	--

Source ANAO 1996

The Howard Government wanted nothing to do with urban Australia, and signalled its intentions in its first Budget by scrapping the BBC program, apart from final funding commitments under BBC Phase 1. It had also abolished the Department of Housing and Regional Development in which it was located, transferring the residual program management to the Department of Transport and Regional Development under National Party Minister, The Hon. John Anderson MP.

Continuing activity and impacts

Of course the nature of the program was such that the activity it generated continued on. The States now had no supporting Commonwealth funds, but also, largely, the area strategies no longer *needed* Commonwealth funds — private investment was now sufficient, along with some State contributions, to maintain development momentum.

By 1996 in most BBC areas, the market had well and truly picked up on the development opportunities BBC had created and facilitated, and with active agencies such as the Inner Brisbane Urban Renewal Authority, the East Perth Redevelopment Authority, Honeysuckle Creek Board, and elsewhere committed State agencies, investment continued to flow.

Appendix 3 provides examples of the later stages of development as the areas matured.

Post 1996 there emerged even stronger private sector support for the Better Cities initiative as more developers took advantage of the policy certainty, development opportunities and supportive environment of the Better Cities Area Strategies. Various evaluations of the initiative from an economic perspective (see Appendix 4) point to significant multiplier benefits (ranging from 1:5 to as high as 1:12 for each government dollar invested in BBC) along with employment and population growth outcomes that continue to rise, most evidently in the inner urban Area Strategies where the urban renewal processes sparked new market demands for inner urban lifestyles.

In fact the turn-around in inner urban populations in Australia that commenced after 1991 was sparked by the new opportunities created as BBC removed obvious impediments to markets investing in these locations, and gave new confidence to both producers and consumers of urban property alike. This was the most obvious large-scale effect of the program across the nation as a whole.

A corollary effect, less welcome, was the accompanying increase in property values and 'gentrification' process in the inner city, that BBC sought to counter with affordable housing initiatives (with some success in Brisbane, Sydney and Melbourne, and less in Perth).

But the initiatives in regional locations in all States also had marked impacts in terms of the confidence with which cities like Geelong, Newcastle, Townsville, Launceston, and Bunbury set about further renewing old port and railway lands and inner urban property that was decaying and run-down, setting examples and lessons from which others have since learned.

There is less evidence that the outer urban projects had significant demonstration effects, although individual projects that revolved around infrastructure upgrades progressively have led urban development in potentially new directions — the Gold Coast railway; the Patawalonga rehabilitation in Adelaide along with the Virginia pipeline for recycling treated sewage; the transport interchanges at Stirling in Perth, Dandenong in Melbourne and Blacktown in Sydney; the flood mitigation along the Maribyrnong in Melbourne; the alternative fuel bus system in Perth. These were all valuable experiments in addressing urban issues that did not immediately result in the achievement of associated urban development changes but led in new directions because of their innovation and scale.

A careful examination of the elements of each Area Strategy on which funds were spent, and an assessment today such as that undertaken in 2006 by Pem Gerner for his PhD Thesis, would show two things, in my view:

- firstly, that many of the elements of the Area Strategies as well as the Strategies themselves, were highly innovative and led to new levels of expectation and confidence about how urban infrastructure investments could be managed and delivered in ways that satisfy multiple objectives (efficiency, sustainability, design quality) without sacrificing any of the functionality of the system being provided; and

- secondly, that these innovations have formed the basis for work elsewhere and improved the overall quality and capacity of both government and the private sector in managing urban growth and changes and the elements within it.

In 1996 the Australian National Audit Office prepared its report on BBC, and concluded that it was difficult to evaluate the effectiveness of the initiative because baseline measurements had not been taken against the objectives to be achieved. There were baseline measures, but only where statistics were available that matched the geographic coverage of each of the Area Strategies — often difficult because some were spread over a wide area, with complementary investments but no common statistical 'area'.

A longer passage of time is needed to evaluate BBC fully, and it would be of value to have further work undertaken to examine and assess effects more than a decade after funding for the initiative ceased. Certainly many in the private sector and State and local governments have urged the Commonwealth, at various times, to commence a similar initiative.

One important set of findings from the ANAO report was to do with the innovations of BBC in terms of public administration.

The ANAO concluded that:

> The BCP was an important addition to Commonwealth-State financial assistance models. While it was a general purpose capital assistance program, BCP payments to States and Territories were predicated on the achievement and reporting of outcomes and progress in implementation. Adopting a similar outcomes oriented approach is under consideration for other Commonwealth-State programs as a means of reducing duplication of administration with improved accountability. ANAO 1996

While commenting on the lack of adequate measures to fully assess performance against outcomes, the ANAO was very supportive of the outcomes-based approach to programs in the intergovernmental context.

> In conducting a performance audit of BCP, the ANAO had the opportunity to consider the practical features of managing a program in which outputs and outcomes were important and delivery was by another level of government than that providing the funds. Some of these features are sufficiently important to merit consideration in the design of future Commonwealth programs. ANAO 1996

Further, the ANAO acknowledged that it might take some years beyond the funding period of the program to observe outcomes as real results.

Conclusions

BBC was a major Australia-wide urban initiative, and it had significant impacts in each State and at least one Territory — the Northern Territory. While not widely known among the general population, in the urban development industry and in government it became well known, was widely respected and is still a point of reference in the industry today.

It contributed to the transformation of inner urban Australia, to the development of new approaches to the future of regional cities, and to innovations in infrastructure and the management of resources such as urban water.

Because BBC did result in significant innovations, both in terms of approaches to urban design and the built environment, and because it produced outcomes in each State and Territory, it qualifies as a nation-building initiative, in my view. Yet it was a selective program geographically, intended to demonstrate new approaches, which it did. If it had not been selective it would not have been effective. This remains a dilemma for national programs.

BBC also demonstrated a new, collaborative approach between the Commonwealth and the States and Territories, where cooperation was essential to achieving shared objectives, and where the States and Territories delivered the program on behalf of the Commonwealth, while also contributing their own funds.

The outcomes basis of the program was unique at the time and the Agreements that enabled the program were new in approach and format.

The use of Area Strategies was particularly effective in most cases but especially so where managing organisations with real powers were established for an Area Strategy.

Because it was ahead of its time on issues like sustainability and the decentralisation of services, BBC also facilitated significant innovation in the development of both physical and social infrastructure.

Experiments with water reclamation and reuse in a number of areas broke new ground, public transport initiatives spurred renewed interest in the place and role of public transport, and the experience gained in cleaning up contaminated sites was invaluable for the future.

In terms of intergovernmental relations a many lessons were also evident.

The umbrella Intergovernmental Agreements served well as a means of having all governments agree to shared and common goals and objectives while allowing for variations in emphasis to reflect experience and conditions in each State or Territory.

Having an Area Strategy agreement below the 'umbrella' setting out what as to be achieved in each area receiving funding, and determining the various funding contributions (again with flexibility to reflect case-by-case variations) maximised the opportunity to 'design' program inputs and outcomes enabling experimentation and demonstration in each area — potentially driving a lot of learning. (Indeed, bringing together managers from each area for frequent sharing of information and experiences was a feature of the program).

And having dedicated management teams capable of working across government departments in each State to bring together and integrate the contributions of different agencies (and professions) was important. As stated earlier, this worked best when the managers also had some statutory powers or equivalent standing and authority (as in Inner Brisbane).

Ultimately the major investment in the areas where Commonwealth funding was provided came from the private sector, and the capacity to support and facilitate market activities, create confidence in new market directions and lead the market into new development products, were all fundamental to the success of BBC. Where this was best managed, the end results were the most impressive.

Finally, as a collaborative initiative, BBC showed how clear government policies, backed by committed investment in removing barriers to and creating opportunities for market activity, while mobilising the capacity of governments to deal with complex challenges, can lead to major changes in outcomes for society, in real development on the ground, and in social and economic opportunity.

Appendix 1

Funding Allocation, Victorian Area Strategies

Area strategy	Project title	Australian Government funding	State Government funding	Total funding
Inner Melbourne and rivers	North Melbourne public housing redevelopment	17.3		
	Lynch's Bridge housing development:flood mitigation and site works	8.2		
	Lynch's Bridge stage 2 land release	2.5		
	City Circle Tram Loop	6.4		
	South Melbourne release of surplus land for housing development	0.5		
Total area strategy funding		34.9	47.0	81.9
Plenty Road	Redevelopment and devolution of institutional services	52.0		
	Housing development (public and private)at East Preston	16.7		
	Light rail extension - Bundoora	12.6		
	Institutional land release for medium density housing	12.0		
	La Trobe Technology Precinct	4.0		
Total area strategy funding		97.3	52.3	149.6
South-East	Public transport improvements: Cranbourne line	27.1		
	Public transport improvements: Dandenong-Pakenham line	7.7		
	Land release and development at Lyndhurst	-		
Total area strategy funding		34.8	34.0	68.8

Area strategy	Project title	Australian Government funding	State Government funding	Total funding
South-West	Australian Food Industry Science Centre	18.0		
	Public transport improvements(heavy rail)	11.0		
	Housing development (public and private)at Norlane, Geelong	5.3		
	Geelong woolstores redevelopment: education facilities	4.5		
	Geelong transport interchange	2.0		
	Infrastructure works at Werribee Bio-Technology Precinct	1.2		
Total area strategy funding		42.0	6.4	48.4
Total Program funding		209.0	139.7	348.7

Appendix 2: A Better Cities Area Strategy

Area Strategy — Plenty Road — Victoria

The strategy

1. The target area was in the suburbs of Melbourne. Its predominant feature was under-utilised State and Commonwealth land. It included large residential medical institutions and large public housing estates characterised by obsolete and inappropriate housing. The uses to which this government land was put were considered inappropriate and lacking integration with surrounding areas. Employment opportunities in some parts of the area were limited and there was a need to improve public transport.

The budget

2. The total budget for the Area Strategy was $149.7 million over the five-year implementation period to 1995-96, made up by:

- Commonwealth (BCP) contribution $97.4 million

- State contribution $52.3 million

This estimate did not include any value attributable to Commonwealth or State land and facilities made available to the strategy, nor the cost to the State of capital expenditure on other facilities in the area.

Objectives

3. The objectives of the Area Strategy were:

- to achieve reforms in institutional services for people with psychiatric and other disabilities;

- to promote labour mobility and services accessibility by improvements in public transport;

- to improve the utilisation of available social infrastructure in the corridor;

- to promote urban consolidation with mixed use development and higher density housing in under-utilised land in established areas and thereby to reduce the demand at the urban fringe; and

- to encourage development of employment opportunities close to residential areas.

4. The Area Strategy was implemented through a number of developmental projects and activities.

111

Redevelopment and devolution of institutional services

5. The task called for the amalgamation and consolidation of the services provided at a number of the residential institutions in the area. It included the development of methods of delivering alternative services in the community, at other locations throughout Melbourne.

Institutional land release for medium density housing

6. Land freed by institutional redevelopment and adjacent Commonwealth land no longer required was incorporated into a master plan for the area. Land is to be released for private sale and public housing construction.

Housing development

7. The strategy included redeveloping public housing units in the area and making land available for the development of private housing.

Light rail extension

8. Tram services were extended into the area ahead of residential development. This was aimed at providing better access and establishing a public transport habit among current residents. The service is also intended to support the increased area population that will follow housing development.

Technical precinct

9. The strategy also provided for the building of a technical business facility located within La Trobe University to encourage more employment in the area.

Area coordination

10. The area was the responsibility of four Local Government authorities. The strategy called for significant coordination between Commonwealth and State agencies and local government to introduce new planning approaches and methods in developing the area.

Source: ANAO 1996

Appendix 3: An example of a Better Cities Area Strategy from each State.
Prepared by Pem Gerner

NEW SOUTH WALES

Ultimo Pyrmont. (pp 107–117)

This still rolls on and so continues to mature as continuing works in progress. It has some excellent built and circulation outcomes, but some of the built elements are less than satisfactory, particularly the apartment blocks at the water's edge. Very USA in design and out of scale. But for its few faults, it is a huge leap forward from what it was. It also tackled the issue of affordable housing and a massive site clean-up.

Ultimo-Pyrmont's rebirth under BCP cannot not be underestimated as its 300 ha site constituted Sydney's most significant urban renewal project. It is projected that over a 20 to 30 year period it will receive somewhere in the range of 15,000–17,000 residents and that a possible work force of between 40,000–50,000 will eventually be accommodated there.

Historically, Ultimo-Pyrmont's wheat handling, wool storage and sugar processing industries were embedded in Sydney's history, but the area was too close to the heart of Sydney's CBD, and the land far too valuable, for these industries to perpetuate. They have, in any case, chartered new ways of doing business.

- The area was identified in the 1988 Central Sydney Planning Strategy as suitable for mixed residential and commercial uses. The study by DEM and COX Richardson, required an examination of Sydney's regional context to establish the potential for Pyrmont's future and its role beside Sydney's CBD. The study produced a framework to allow the above mix to proceed. The recommendations were of assistance to the Property Services Group and the Department of Planning in the formulation of the gazetted *Regional Environmental Plan No. 26* for the areas rejuvenation, but it was the Federal BCP funding that brought this project alive and provided the impetus for its realisation.

- It is a massive rebirth of a worn-out part of the City of Sydney and on the whole a great credit to all those involved.

VICTORIA

Inner Melbourne and Rivers — Lynch's Bridge and Kensington Banks (pp 154–160)

This is essentially a massive medium-density housing redevelopment and handled very well. It contains provision for public housing and elderly people and so met the requirements of the BCP criteria in this regard.

The development is essentially complete and its landscaping is brilliant, integrating as it does with the heritage base of the much earlier use of the site as stockyards. Pedestrian and vehicular traffic separation is superb.

It is claimed to be the largest housing project of its kind in Australia with some 360 residential units at Lynch's bridge with a further 1200 units at Kensington Banks.

QUEENSLAND

Inner North Eastern Suburbs (pp 176–182)

This Area Strategy was centred on the advancement of inner city living by revitalising the Brisbane suburbs of Fortitude Valley, Teneriffe, New Farm, Newstead and Bowen Hills. All the suburbs are adjacent, bounded by the Brisbane River and Breakfast Creek and close to the CBD. Included in the strategy were improvements in the choice of housing, together with some affordable housing and upgraded traffic management.

The Area Strategy contained a number of components including low cost medium-density housing on the Church Street site; consolidating the Bowen Hills residential area; redevelopment of Newstead as an urban village; the construction of a limited number of public housing units; Fortitude Valley advanced as a mixed-use centre; Teneriffe became an urban centre with residential, retail and institutional facilities; New Farm was consolidated through public consultation and a pedestrian/cycleway between Newstead Park and the city Botanic Gardens.

This Area Strategy was important as the catalyst for the successful resuscitation of this inner city area, and although the individual intrusions were inherently infill, and isolated from each other, they were of sufficient number and design quality to bring a large measure of revitalised coherence to this area.

WESTERN AUSTRALIA

East Perth (pp 203–212)

The East Perth Area Strategy is an area of 120 ha, approximately two kilometres from the Perth CBD, and centred on the Claisebrook Inlet where its waters merge with those of the Swan River. The site was one of the BCP's waterfront rebirth

Area Strategies, and by any standard it would take its place with any similar project in the world, as an example of best design practice.

Historically, the site was heavily industrialised, containing a gas works, sewage pumping station and electrical pumping station amongst its cluster of polluting industrial activities. These activities meant that much of the land was in government ownership and was also under-utilised. The site required a complete reappraisal in terms of its remediation and establishment of new infrastructure. The core of the strategy was to create an innovative urban village containing a diversity of activities including residential, commercial and recreational.

By any measure whether it be: site decontamination, landscape design, heritage and adaptive re-use, new built form, circulation, public art or any other criteria this project was an absolute winner, and its lessons successfully integrated into the neighbouring Area Strategy of Subiaco (Perth Urban)

SOUTH AUSTRALIA

ELIZABETH — Munno Para — Rosewood Village (pp 239–243)

Twenty-five kilometres to the north of Adelaide lies the City of Elizabeth originally conceived during the Playford Government era of the 1950s as a satellite city. Given the passage of time, the extensive single storey public housing (SA Trust homes) were aged, appearing decidedly jaded, and demanding serious maintenance.

Rather than demolish the housing stock whose redeeming feature was its solid construction — if little else — the houses were given, what is in contemporary TV language termed as a 'make-over' with new carports, internal plumbing and fencing, as well as the street planting being greatly strengthened.

The outcome of these operations was a transformation, but the most important objective of this Area Strategy was to accomplish a reduction in rental housing and an increase in home ownership achieved through the refurbishment of the public housing stock and its sale to tenants in the open market.

The instrument to achieve this was the concept of the 'HomeStart' and was accessible to those on incomes as low as $300 per week. A deposit of $1,000 under the bonus HomeStart provided a subsidised loan to $15,000 inflation adjusted, to be repaid when the house was sold or earlier if possible. The loan was later modified to become the Rosewood 'Advantage Loan'.

The social and economic advantages of this Area Strategy are clearly demonstrable. The one-time tenants could now enjoy both the greatly enhanced physical environment in their home and surrounding public domain and also the dignity of achieving home ownership.

TASMANIA

Launceston Inner City (pp 271–277)

The objectives of this Area Strategy included those of consolidated the CBD's role; the maintaining of industrial activity to designated areas and diminishing effects of industrial pollution along the Tamar River. Urban consolidation opportunities existed on the site of the Inveresk railway workshops, adjacent to the CBD and although contaminated from previous industrial usage contained a large number of buildings, some 70 in total, being almost a surfeit of buildings, available for adaptive re-use.

It is the ingenuity of finding community uses for this staggering stock of buildings that makes this project, within the Launceston Inner City Area Strategy, one of merit.

Appendix 4: Reviews of the Better Cities Program (list provided by Pem Gerner)

1. National Capital Authority — December 1997. *A Report on the Commonwealth Better Cities Program 1991-1997*. Volume 1, pp 162.
2. National Capital Authority — December 1997. *A Report on the Commonwealth Better Cities Program 1991-1997*. Volume 2, pp 222.
3. Australian National Audit Office. 1996. *Building Better Cities: Department of Transport and Regional Development*. Audit Report No 9, 1996-97.
4. National Institute of Economic and Industry Research (NIEIR) Better Cities Economic Evaluation prepared for National Capital Planning Authority — NIEIR Clifton Hill, Vic.
5. Gerner, Robert. 2002. 'Urban Design and the Better Cities Program — The Influence of Urban Design on the Outcomes of the Program'. PhD Thesis.

9. Stumbling towards nation-building: impediments to progress

Anthony F. Shepherd

Abstract

On the fiftieth anniversary of the Snowy in 1999, I called for unwavering political support for major infrastructure projects. Support such as was enjoyed by the Snowy project and was essential for its success. Some eight years on we see signs of cautious political support for big projects. Our economic infrastructure still suffers from major gaps particularly in transport (public and private), water, power and ports. We are suffering also from a technical skills shortage. Political support is emerging but is cautious because of the plethora of noisy single-issue groups encouraged by a media greedy for the 20 second grab. Furthermore, defects in our Constitution are exacerbating the problem as Federal and State Governments grapple with problems best dealt with on a national basis.

Introduction

On the fiftieth anniversary of the Snowy in 1999, at a forum not too far from here, I called for unwavering political support for desperately needed major infrastructure projects. I said at that time:

> In the last 50 years, it is difficult to think of a major development which has successfully harnessed not just the support of the Australian people but an overwhelming sense of their pride and goodwill … Development has become an unpopular word; a necessary, if somewhat unfortunate incident of everyday life. A bit boring, a bit inconvenient and definitely bad if it happens anywhere near where somebody lives. (Shepherd 1999)

I went on to observe:

> I do not accept that the fact that the tightening of the public purse with respect to major infrastructure projects is the only reason for stalled developments. The private sector is now sufficiently mature to accept responsibility for funding also. With a range of boo [Build, Own and Operate] and boot [Build, Own, Operate and Transfer] projects it has demonstrated its capacity to facilitate and promote the timely provision of high quality public infrastructure.

> The Snowy was conceived in the heady excitement for Australia's prospects following WWII. Today, the gung-ho enthusiasm that saw the planning wrapped up in 3 years, public goodwill extend to all the

workers, and record breaking feats of engineering daring and excellence has largely gone. Today's community is highly informed, highly urbane and generally, anti development.

Political leaders are reluctant to risk popularity through championing projects which may not have overwhelming public enthusiasm. I suggest that such leadership is now critical to pursuing the development of major infrastructure projects. (Shepherd 1999)

What have we done in the eight or so years since then? Have we indeed lost the pioneering nation-building spirit? I am afraid that the score sheet is not all that impressive, especially given the unprecedented prosperity we have enjoyed in this period. We have made some progress but, as a nation, we still face considerable challenges.

Of course, we have the technical capability to undertake major infrastructure projects, as evidenced by projects such as the Lane Cove Tunnel, the Alice to Darwin Railway, Sydney's Cross City Tunnel, Melbourne City Link and the Sydney Airport Railway Link. Some of these projects have been a great success and will continue to make a significant economic contribution for the foreseeable future.

However, if we do a stock take we find that we rank twentieth out of 25 OECD countries for investment in public infrastructure as a percentage of GDP. In a practical sense we find:

1. The queues of ships waiting to load at Newcastle and most of our other coal loading ports are unacceptably long and demurrage cost exporters some $400m in Newcastle alone last year;
2. Public transport is not keeping pace with development as our major cities continue to sprawl and under investment also makes public transport even less attractive when one can buy a brand new air conditioned car for $15,000;
3. We still do not have a divided highway linking Melbourne, Sydney and Brisbane, and if we take a lane out on the Sydney Harbour Crossing or the Monash Freeway at peak then Sydney and Melbourne are gridlocked for hours;
4. The rail freight system between Melbourne, Sydney and Brisbane has not improved in 50 years and is still too slow, expensive and unreliable to compete with road transport. Rail has 11–19% of market share in land freight north and south, whereas investment on the East-West rail link has taken rail freight to over 80% of market share and shows what can be achieved;

5. Water supply to major cities and regions in most States is so stressed by the drought that severe water restrictions are now a fact of life and we have no national plan for urban or rural water security;

6. Most of our sewerage still goes into the seas and rivers with limited treatment and there is very limited recycling of sewerage;

7. Broadband access and speeds are amongst the slowest in the OECD where we rank seventeenth out of 30 in terms of broadband penetration;

8. Our public hospitals are reportedly in bad shape and waiting lists continue to grow;

9. Our public education system — once our pride and joy — continues to slip in world terms. As a result, parents are making huge sacrifices to put their children in the private education system;

10. The country, which was once a pioneer in skills training and apprenticeships, now cannot attract enough people with appropriate skills to service the resources boom. We can attract bright students into medicine and law but not many into engineering and the sciences; and

11. We do not have an integrated national plan for power, water or transport nor do we have a truly national market in any of them.

Why is it so? My view, based on 17 early years in the federal public service and followed by 28 years in the private sector, is that it is due to a combination of circumstances.

When I came to Canberra in the late 1960s, the Snowy Project was going strong and the Government and the top federal public servants were focussed almost entirely on national development. Whether that be by direct investment, or by immigration, export policies, education, health or by facilitation. It was an accepted non-debatable truth. We were a young, resourceful country, brash at times, but we were going places. Development was a way of life. The Department I worked for was building and operating NASA tracking stations for the Apollo and other space programs and launching rockets at Woomera. We were also building Mirage fighters. It was all 'go, go, go'!

The same focus applied in each of the States irrespective of their political colour. National development was essential and it was accepted that we could not leave ourselves as vulnerable and defenceless as we were when the Second World War hit Australia like a tsunami.

If we were fortunate enough to travel overseas in the 1950s and 1960s we saw a UK and Europe still struggling to recover from the War and an Asia, both north and south, with a far lower standard of living. Only the United States was booming and investing heavily in its national and industrial infrastructure. The United States was the country we emulated.

The momentum continued in the 1970s but started to slow coming into the eighties. Other parts of the world not only caught up, but began to surpass us. Western Europe made a remarkable recovery from the War. Asia — particularly countries like Japan —started to really fire. Perhaps we had not so much 'slowed', but rather the competition has lifted.

But the momentum did slow and the current gaps in our economic and social infrastructure and our skills shortages in engineering and science are undeniable. The fact that we are not close to being the number one country in the world on most social and economic indicators is a further sign of our relative decline.

There was no single factor influencing this decline so I will deal with them in no particular order and highlight those I see as interrelated.

The growth of single issue groups with their inevitable opposition to any proposed major development has weakened the political will. The growth and acceptance of these groups is due to a combination of: increasing cynicism about the political process; vastly improved and simplified methods of communication; more sophisticated activism; significant increases in personal wealth; a new libertarian spirit; genuine concern about the environment; and, of course, NIMBYism (Not-In-My-Back-Yard). Furthermore, these groups have been encouraged and fed by a media which can often be disappointingly superficial and sensationalist.

Every major project I have worked on whether it be the Sydney Harbour Tunnel, Melbourne City Link, Eastlink in Eastern Melbourne, the redevelopment of Walsh Bay or even the construction of the ANZAC warships has been criticised by one element of the media at some stage of its development. Negative lobby groups seem to be given better than a 'fair run' by an Australian media that feeds on confrontation. The quality of analysis by the bulk of the print or electronic media is superficial or non-existent.

Could you imagine Sydney today without its Tunnel? Well, Ted Mack, the venerated former Mayor of North Sydney and local Federal MP could. As did that venerable journal of record, the *Sydney Morning Herald*, when the project was first launched. If you waded through the media at the time Melbourne City Link was getting off the ground you would think it was the end of civilisation as we knew it.

I do listen to the ABC from time to time to find out what the 'Dark Side' is thinking. Recently, the new Premier of NSW announced the Government's intention to construct a desalination plant. Now, putting aside whether this is a good solution, how did the ABC deal with this issue? The ABC's main concern was the potential for disruption in a few streets where a new pipeline would be buried: disruption, which, at worst, would last four weeks. There was no analysis of whether this is a good way to drought proof Sydney or any assessment of the Government's published motives and logic.

Under this skewed perspective, the automatic assumption is that the Government is a bunch of fools or knaves. Look at the treatment given to so-called 'development' politicians such as Jeff Kennett, Laurie Brereton, Carl Scully and Nick Greiner. No wonder politicians are nervous about big projects.

A second and related factor leading to a downturn in investment in infrastructure is a combination of political correctness and a planning process in most jurisdictions that appear designed to exhaust any Minister, government department, council or developer.

We still have one of the world's great democracies but we also have a lot of government: three levels all wanting to be involved and to justify their existence. I say, 'For heaven's sake, we elect a Government, let them govern. If you don't like their decisions throw them out at the next election'. Now, even minor decisions must have a major public enquiry going on for months at great taxpayer expense so that every special interest group can have their say. Why bother? They are still going to complain vociferously if the project goes ahead in whatever form.

Don't get me wrong, I'm in favour of community consultation, but it is a matter of degree. If the Government based on all the evidence makes a decision that is in the best interests of the whole community, then let's get on with it.

The third factor has been the anti-debt philosophy developed — quite correctly, in my view — by the Commonwealth and the States in the late 1980s. Although frequently derided as a symptom of 'economic rationalism', this was, at that time, a rational response to some States effectively borrowing to meet recurrent operating expenditure — borrowing to buy your groceries as they say. Fortunately, the Commonwealth and the States, aided by the rating agencies, shut down this binge and governments thereafter went for budget surpluses.

However, the States and the Commonwealth are now pillars of financial rectitude and it is time again to look at Government borrowing to invest in our infrastructure, particularly in those areas which are not attractive to the private sector. These are generally where the private sector does not or cannot take a long enough view. The Sydney Harbour Bridge was vastly overbuilt for the foreseeable requirement at the time. Thank heavens we had visionaries such as Bradfield then. Who is the new Bradfield?

This brings me to another factor. Although I am a fervent supporter and promoter of outsourcing and privatisation, we have taken out of our public service a lot of its talent and we have reduced the breeding grounds necessary to grow and develop the public service. If we are to have leadership and vision from the public sector then we must have a talented and motivated Public Service which can initiate, plan, prioritise and supervise the provision of our national infrastructure.

The final factor is an outmoded Constitution. Although the Constitution served us reasonably well for the first 50 or so years of Federation (with a bit of manipulation, and astonishingly progressive interpretation by various High Courts) its drafters did not recognise the need for an integrated national approach to economic and social infrastructure. For example, the Commonwealth is awash with cash from income and company tax. Some of the States are battling financially, particularly with a downturn in revenue from stamp duty. Unfortunately, gambling revenue has been seen as an offset but that is another story.

The Federal AusLink initiative, while far from perfect, has been one of the few exceptions where the Commonwealth and the States have endeavoured to work co-operatively to develop and fund some national priorities in transport. It is not perfect but it is a good start and an example of where the future should lie.

The infrastructure sector is very pleased that the new Rudd Labor Government is onto this issue. The Commonwealth intends to conduct a 'national infrastructure audit' to identify the gaps and establish priorities. It has established a statutory body —Infrastructure Australia — to develop and implement plans for national infrastructure and a special fund — Building Australia — to back it. For the first time, Australia has a dedicated national Infrastructure Minister. These are welcome breakthroughs and should help to depoliticise decision-making. The challenge is not to replicate existing federal and state bureaucracy and not to slow down the process.

Roads, rail, power, water, ports, airports, communications, health and education are all national issues. We are a single nation. We must have an organised and integrated approach. The Commonwealth cannot do it alone as it does not have the bureaucratic infrastructure nor the skills. Subject to my earlier comments about strengthening the public service, the States have a lot more of the skills and experience required to deliver infrastructure. Therefore the Commonwealth and the States must work together. It sounds simple, but it has taken 107 years to get there.

Governments should concentrate on what they do well: that is initiate, plan, prioritise and regulate. The private sector should do what it does best, which is deliver and operate. I could go on forever about the relative efficiencies of government and the private sector, but a simple quotation from that great American philosopher, Will Rogers says it all:

> If you want to eliminate traffic congestion then get the private sector to build all the roads and the Government to build all the cars.

The private sector has the capital, expertise and the will to make an increasingly significant contribution to our nation's economic and social infrastructure. What we need is the market and the political will and, importantly, leadership.

Of course, the development spirit is not totally dead. It lives on in our resources companies that quietly get on with the job in remote parts of the country where they have become virtual governments, effectively and efficiently providing most of the economic and social infrastructure; it lives on in the PPP market where the private sector takes on massive risks and invests huge sums of capital; and it lives on in various premiers, ministers, mayors and public servants who, despite the risks and the counter pressures, assiduously move major projects forward.

References

Shepherd, A.F. 1999. 'The Spirit of the Snowy — Fifty Years On', Australian Academy of Technological Sciences and Engineering, AATSE Symposium, November 1999, accessed 26 February 2008 at http://www.atse.org.au/index.php?sectionid=296

10. Broadbanding the nation: lessons from Canada or shortcomings in Australian federalism?

Michael de Percy

Abstract

At federation, the former Australian colonies readily agreed to the Commonwealth's ownership and control of the national telecommunications network, enshrined principally in section 51 of the Australian Constitution. Conversely, Canada's telecommunications industry developed in diverse, regionally based markets consisting of a variety of private sector businesses and provincial and municipal government-owned enterprises. As telecommunications technologies converged with media and Internet-based technologies, the changing industry structures in both countries have led to quite different outcomes in high-speed broadband. Canada embraced the plurality of its industry structure with federal policy focused on educating the diverse policy communities, aggregating demand in local and regional markets, and 'forbearance' from regulatory interference in an effort to promote cross-platform competition. Canada's policy choices resulted in Canada ranking fourth in the Organisation for Economic Cooperation and Development (OECD) in 2007 in terms of broadband infrastructure access and speed of the services. On the other hand, Australia's device-based industry structure, combined with its centrally-controlled communications policies, struggled to keep pace with the converging technologies and effectively prevented local and regional interests from being heard in a debate dominated by the federal government, the Australian Competition and Consumer Commission (ACCC), Telstra, and professional lobbyists. Local and regional interests were effectively ignored while Telstra blamed the federal government and ACCC for the state of Australia's broadband infrastructure and speeds which rank well below the OECD average. During the 2008 federal election, Kevin Rudd announced the Labor Party's intention — if elected — to massively extend the reach of broadband technology as an essential element in nation-building. This chapter reflects on the implications for nation-building of Australia's centrally-controlled federal communications policy, and its long history of government-controlled, one-size-fits-all infrastructure solutions.

Introduction

This chapter reflects on the implications for nation-building of Australia's centrally-controlled federal broadband policy, and its long history of government-controlled, one-size-fits-all infrastructure solutions. Drawing on early qualitative findings from a series of interviews with telecommunications industry elites conducted in Canada and Australia during 2006 and 2007, this chapter posits that Australia's nation-building future rests on a reinvigoration of federalism to enable local and regional communications solutions to address local and regional communications problems. The reasons for this are twofold. First, research on the social uses of broadband technologies indicates that improving the infrastructure is not, as some would believe, about providing entertainment or solving a digital divide issue which may not justify significant public expenditure — it is 'a social network and productivity issue ... [and] an investment in social capital' (CEDA 2006: 22) which is necessary if Australia is to maintain its current standard of living. Traditional social networks exist physically at the local and regional levels, while broadband technologies enable digital social networks which extend beyond geographical bounds, providing numerous social and economic benefits. In this social environment, broadband technologies require physical infrastructure which is necessarily situated amidst the local as established by geography and the needs of the citizen. Thus local issues are important if the broader 'digital' needs of citizens are to be met. After all, it will be difficult for governments to justify public expenditure on a broadband network which does not meet the needs of its citizens as users (this concept is explored by Coleman & Skogstad 1990; Coleman 2007).

Second, where social capital is defined as the 'social norms, networks and trust that facilitate cooperation within or between groups... [which] can generate benefits to society by reducing transaction costs, promoting cooperative behaviour, diffusing knowledge and innovations, and through enhancements to personal well-being and associated spill-overs' (Productivity Commission 2003: viii), a single national solution may be regarded as paternalistic in circumstances where citizens as users are not involved in the decision-making process.[1] Given the specific knowledge requirements for citizens as users to be gainfully involved in communications policy processes, paternalistic solutions tend to detract from social capital rather than create it. Where the citizen as user is excluded from decision-making processes due to a lack of policy experience, they are subsequently excluded from gaining skills to participate effectively in future policy processes. The nation-building project may be largely finished in terms of large-scale infrastructure projects (Butcher 2007), but the future of nation-building in the global information economy is one of increasing social capital by establishing communications networks which are accessible and deliver the services which citizens as users need and can afford. Increasing social capital in this environment requires citizen engagement — a requirement that is likely to become more important as technology provides citizens with greater access to information and interactive media.

The key argument developed in this paper is that contemporary nation-building requires citizen participation and strategically-focused policies which facilitate citizen engagement and federal systems are well-placed to enable such approaches. Various commentators have indicated that if Australia is to maintain its current standard of living, high speed broadband is a necessity (Smarr cited in Hartcher 2007). However, evidence of the advantages of public investment in broadband infrastructure remains incomplete (Crowe 2007a) or lacks empirical rigour (see for example Bell Canada Enterprises 2006; Business Council of Australia (BCA) 2008a; Crandall et al. 2007; Douglas 2007; Foreshaw 2006). Moreover, academic challenges to the status quo (the single national solution) in Australia continue to be regarded as 'left-field' (Sainsbury 2006). To shine some light on the 'left-field' debate, two approaches to broadband infrastructure deployment in two most-similar federal jurisdictions are compared from a nation-building perspective in Canada and Australia. The following sections focus on the Australian way of 'doing' communications policy, the influence of history on nation-building, and the persistence of the single national policy solution in the broadband era.

The Australian way of 'doing' communications policy

Historically, telegraphy was a major component of the nation-building projects in both Canada and Australia. The technology is significant today in that it ushered in the information age (Copp & Zanella 1993: 14; Livingston 1996: 6-7; Williams 2001: 15) and established a conceptual framework for policy-makers responding to modern communication challenges. While broadband technologies have surpassed the capabilities of the broadcasting and telecommunications technologies of the twentieth century, conceptual remnants from the initial stages of the information age tend to circumscribe policy choices for deploying contemporary broadband infrastructure in Australia (Gans 2006). At federation, the former Australian colonies readily agreed to the Commonwealth's ownership and control of the national telecommunications network, enshrined principally in section 51 of the Australian Constitution. Conversely, Canada's telecommunications industry developed in diverse, regionally-based markets consisting of a variety of private sector businesses and provincial and municipal government-owned enterprises. As telecommunications technologies converged with media and Internet-based technologies, the changing industry structures in both countries have led to quite different outcomes in high-speed broadband.

Canada embraced the plurality of its industry structure with federal policy focused on educating the diverse policy communities, aggregating demand in local and regional markets, and 'forbearing'[2] from regulatory interference in an effort to promote competition. Such policy choices resulted in Canada ranking fourth in the Organisation for Economic Cooperation and Development (OECD) in 2007 in terms of broadband infrastructure access and speed of the services. On the other hand, Australia's device-based industry structure,[3] combined with its centrally-controlled communications policies, struggled to keep pace with converging technologies and effectively prevented local and regional interests from being heard in a debate dominated by the federal government, the Australian Competition and Consumer Commission (ACCC), Telstra, and professional lobbyists (Crowe 2007c; Lee 2007; Warne-Smith 2007). Local and regional interests were sidelined (Marris 2007; Sainsbury 2005) while a passionate debate over responsibility for the state of Australia's broadband infrastructure and speeds, which rank well below the OECD average, raged publicly between Telstra, the Howard government and the ACCC (Crowe & Boyd 2005; Lee & Bajkowski 2007; The Australian 2007). During the 2008 federal election, Kevin Rudd announced the Labor Party's intention — if elected — to massively extend the reach of broadband technology as an essential element in nation-building. Following Rudd's election victory, 'broadband' has been elevated in status to a ministry[4] however a single national solution continues to dominate the broadband policy discourse in Australia.

Research suggests that single, national broadband solutions do not 'create a program delivery system that is cost-effective, easy to use and highly responsive to the needs of citizens' (Information Technology Office 2005: 14). The increasing trend toward centralisation appears to be reinforcing 'state paternalism' which is at odds with the need to create 'social capital'. To Kelly (Kelly 1992: 98), 'state paternalism' was an historical approach to policy-making in Australia which was 'familiar and comfortable' to organised interests. While many have critiqued Kelly's concept of the Australian Settlement (see for example DeAngelis 2004; Smyth 2004; Stokes 2004), 'state-paternalism' provides a useful conceptual framework for understanding the Australian way of 'doing' communications policy (see Castles cited in DeAngelis 2004; also Stokes 2004). However, the paternalistic approach appears to have had its day. As Rhodes (Rhodes 1996) suggests, active policy communities operating independently of centralised systems of control tend to be 'a challenge to governability because they become autonomous and resist central guidance'.

A new way of 'doing' communications policy in Australia is likely to improve access and equity in relation to policy programs which to date have been unsatisfactory. For example, in its performance audit of the federal government's program 'Networking the Nation —The Regional Telecommunications Infrastructure Fund', the Australian National Audit Office (Australian National Audit Office 1999: 13) found that significantly more funding through the program went to Coalition-held electorates. Although the audit report found that 'decision-making was equitable, with no obvious weighting in the allocation of funds to particular political parties', 72% of the funds allocated went to Coalition seats with only 23% of the funding allocated to Labor seats. Centralised power in this regard clearly benefited the Coalition for electoral purposes. Further, the allocation of funds to the states was based on proportion of population with 'no other needs assessment undertaken to implement the Government's decision on the allocation of funds' (Australian National Audit Office 1999: 15). It is not unreasonable to assume that local needs in electorates held by other parties received fewer benefits from the program. Moreover, the central administration's ability to deliver program funding to citizens has also been called into question, especially in administrative efficiency and effectiveness in terms of actually delivering programs. The 1999 audit report suggested that 'given the Department now has some experience in administering the program', administrative costs could be reduced. Yet seven years later, the Metropolitan Broadband Connect program announced in March 2006 to provide $50 million to improve suburban broadband services indicated that the central administration was still struggling to deliver broadband programs (Crowe 2007b). Indeed, by February 2007 most of the funding remained unspent except for $1.3 million in 'administrative costs' and Australia was still well behind Canada in the OECD broadband rankings.

Canada's results in deploying broadband infrastructure and the key themes emerging from interviews with industry elites suggest that sound policy outcomes result from: encouraging bottom-up engagement with diverse policy communities through provision of municipal (local), provincial (state), and federal representation of local and regional interests; educating policy actors through formal involvement in policy processes; enabling local and regional solutions to broadband infrastructure through partnerships between various combinations of public, private and third sector organisations; reorganising the formal boundaries of the converging communications industries; and 'forbearing' from competition where different service providers are competing for customers who require similar services which can be provided by a variety of different media. The latter concept is referred to here as 'technological neutrality' where functionality, rather than a particular technology, is regulated (Computer Laboratory 1997). Most of these approaches are absent in Australian broadband policy programs, suggesting that an old way of 'doing' communications policy persists. To this end, attention is now focused on early approaches to nation-building in an effort to determine history's influence on the 'Australian way'.

The influence of history on nation-building concepts

Historically, the term 'nation-building' in Australia and Canada meant 'building infrastructure' (see Vance cited in Infrastructure Canada 2006; Putnis 2002).[5] However, these two countries adopted very different approaches to the nation-building project — differences reflected in their distinct approaches to the practice of federalism today. Watts (cited in Mathews 1982: 13; see also

Brown & Bellamy 2006: 12) states that Australia began as a decentralised federation which has since moved toward a 'centralised coordinative federalism'; in effect a unitary system of government in-waiting. Canada, on the other hand, began highly centralised but has since become 'largely coordinate and even conflictual in character'. More to the point, Watts (cited in Mathews 1982: 14) suggests that Canada has both strong national communities *and* provincial communities as a result of competing 'nation-building' and 'province-building' processes which have occurred concurrently since Confederation in 1867.

The existence of a 'vibrant French-Canadian component' in Canada helped establish a 'heterogeneous federal society' and competition between national and provincial institutions resulted in political legitimacy 'oscillating between periods of centralisation and decentralisation' over time (Watts cited in Mathews 1982: 17). This is in stark contrast to Australia's trend toward centralisation which has gathered momentum in recent times. The extent of the federal government's attempts to take control of traditionally state-run policy areas include, for example, public housing (ABC News 2007b), hospitals (ABC News 2007a), industrial relations (Shaw 2006), courts (Attorney-General of Victoria 2007), education (Ferrari 2006), and social policy (AAP Australian Associated Press (AAP) 2007), indicating that Watts' (cited in Mathews 1982) observations some three decades ago remain extant.

Geography also played a part in the different practices of federalism in Australia and Canada. Australia's remoteness required a greater focus on communications technologies to overcome the tyranny of distance and cooperation between the dispersed colonies (settled mostly in coastal regions) commenced well before[6] the Overland Telegraph Line was connected with the submarine cable from Java in 1872. At federation, section 51 (v.) of the Australian Constitution gave the federal government legislative responsibility for 'telegraphic, telephonic, and other like services'. This level of cooperation was peculiar to communications. For example, while the states retained responsibility for railways at federation, the communications network was considered 'properly a national enterprise' by all jurisdictions (Putnis 2002: 2). Australia had a national telegraph network connecting it to the rest of the world but it did not have a national, uniform-gauge rail network as a result of railways being deployed independently by colonial governments (Department of Infrastructure 2008). Conversely, Canadian federalism was concerned with connecting communities which formed predominantly along the overland northern border of the United States and focused on 'railway-building and the expansion of Canadian territory' (Burgess 1990: 43). Telegraphy, although preceding the construction of the Canadian Pacific Railway, did not acquire the same level of importance as the railway (Boyce 2000). Indeed, the impetus for confederation was the condition that 'the Dominion government build a railroad' to connect the provinces (Velaz 1997: 54). Consequently, Canada's rail network was transcontinental while provincial governments tended to facilitate local telegraph infrastructure to the north of the transcontinental railway line through local combinations of public, private and community ventures.

The Australian and Canadian experiences of deploying railways and telegraph technologies suggest there are advantages in single solutions for building 'national' infrastructure where none exists. Indeed, railways and communications networks were often regarded as conceptually similar because of their concurrent historical deployment. Yet the institutions responsible for communications policy are still grounded in the principles of their early federal predecessors in that Canada's communications network tends to be developed at the local and regional level while Australia persists with a single national solution.[7] As the convergence of communications technologies is making the railway/telegraph concept less relevant — one might think of modern communications technologies such as broadband as more of an entire transport system rather than simply one element of the system — it is timely that Australia's nation-building model is reconsidered.

The conceptual separation of transport and communications is a recent phenomenon. The telegraph was largely responsible for the information age and Livingston (Livingston 1996: 6) suggests that telegraphy enabled the separation of transport and communication in a practical sense. Nevertheless, 'distinguishing communication from transportation' conceptually in scholarly works mostly occurred in the late 1980s. Indeed, some industry elites still adopt the 'railway' concept in discussing broadband deployment, but this concept relates to the 'carriage' of data via a 'line' rather than the approach to deploying the infrastructure. However, single national solutions were only referred to by Canadian industry elites in their historical context. Diverse policy actors and market players tended to focus on how they serve citizens or customers respectively rather than debating the merits of federal communications policy. Most industry elites spoke of communications policy in terms of simply 'forbearance' and it was apparent that greater cooperation exists among policy actors in Canada. In sharp relief to Australian industry elites, most Canadian policy actors were focused on providing solutions to local problems while business people generally discussed market competition issues rather than focusing on problems with the regulatory system.

Australia's nation-building approach to deploying communications infrastructure was enabled by a collaborative culture resulting from some 50 years of cooperation between the various colonial governments before federation (Putnis 2002). During that time, government distaste for privately owned networks was obvious. For instance, the first privately-owned telegraph network was established in South Australia by James McGeorge, a business owner who ignored the Colonial government's opposition to privately owned infrastructure (Moyal

1984: 20). Once his network was established, the Colonial government promptly purchased the competing network and simply dismantled it. Government control of telegraphic infrastructure also thwarted Samuel McGowan's[8] desire to create a business out of the new technology and despite some success as a telegraph construction contractor, he was eventually coerced into becoming 'general-superintendent of the new electric telegraph in Victoria' (Moyal 1984: 18). Following federation, the Australian government retained responsibility for the communications network and invariably controlled the broadcasting and telecommunications industries (see Australian Heritage Commission 2003 for details). Seven decades later, deregulation of the telecommunications industry commenced with the corporatisation of Telecom Australia in 1975 and market-based solutions have proven popular for many years since. However, federal intervention in media and communications remains a popular policy tool for Australian governments, despite the private nature of most communications providers.

Australian industry elites focused on very different themes to their Canadian counterparts. Government intervention, various obstacles to infrastructure deployment, *ex-ante* regulation[9] (ITU International Telecommunications Union (ITU) 2008) and an unpredictable industry environment coupled with suspicion of other policy actors were recurring themes. These themes suggest that contemporary market-based approaches to communications services provision in Australia are yet to achieve the level of acceptance which has accompanied the relative 'market maturity' experienced in Canada (Spool 1997; Total Telecom Magazine 2007).[10] The overview of Australian communications history above provides some insight into these phenomena. Nonetheless, a single national solution designed by the federal government persists as the dominant paradigm for fixing Australia's broadband problems. Much like the telegraph solution, the focus on a single part of the communications infrastructure suggests that the out-dated transportation concept of communications deployment continues to inform Australian policy choices. Regrettably, the 'Australian way' is of little value in appropriately connecting citizens as users in a time of rapid technological change.

The persistence of the single national solution in the broadband era

Nation-building in Australia has generally been neglected since major government-led infrastructure projects such as the Sydney Harbour Bridge and the Snowy Hydro Scheme were completed. The rise of 'economic rationalism' in Australian policy (see Pusey 1991), which has seen a shift from government-led to business-led infrastructure development, is often blamed for contemporary infrastructure problems. Aside from government neglect of infrastructure, the shift from public to private funding has created its own problems, particularly in the way that governments have attempted to keep the details of public-private partnerships shrouded in secrecy (see for example Scott & Allen 2005). Consequently, the public's support for major, government-led engineering feats has not been forthcoming for private sector infrastructure projects, despite the obvious engineering significance of major private-sector projects (Shepherd 1999). In some instances, businesses have agreed to commercial documents being released for public scrutiny but it has been governments who have resisted. For example, public-private partnership projects such as Sydney's Cross City Tunnel have been the subject of significant public opposition (Smith 2005)[11] toward both the public and private proponents of the project with many citizens regarding themselves as 'collateral damage' in the negotiation process (Fullerton 2006). Changing the provider of funding for infrastructure projects has not changed the single policy solution. In the foreseeable future, it is unlikely that Australia will reduce the use of public-private partnerships to fund large infrastructure projects. Nevertheless, consumer groups are concerned that governments will 'sell out consumers' long term interests by caving into industry pressure' in their 'haste to appear to have the instant answer on broadband' (Choice 2007).

The major differences between Australia and Canada are reflected in the two approaches to deploying broadband networks. Lehr et al (2005: 3) provide a simplified explanation of these two approaches, in that the differences 'may be caricaturised as a battle between the traditional service provider business model for providing network services versus one based on end-user equipment', with Australia adopting the former, and Canada more closely resembling the latter. History has influenced the current structure of Australia's telecommunications industry and the impact of technological convergence on policy-making has been neglected for many years. This has led to false industry boundaries between the telecommunications and various media industries in Australia, where regulation is designed predominantly for communications industries which remain traditionally structured on devices rather than functionality.

The phenomenon where industry changes remain elusive is often referred to as 'excess inertia' in game theory where 'no one benefits from the new [way of doing things] alone, [so] each participant may rationally stick to the old, inefficient [way of doing things]' (Boyer et al. 2001: 406). For example, competitors in the Australian telecommunications industry are often restricted to second-mover strategies (for an overview of the concept, see Hanson et al. 2002: 168-9) because of Telstra's market dominance. This forces competitors to 'imitate' the market leader rather than venture new approaches (Boyer et al. 2001: 406-7; see also Dosi cited in Carter 1981: 182-202). Moreover, successive federal governments have encouraged Telstra's competitors to imitate the market leader by persisting with outdated industry structures. Telstra Chief Executive Officer Solomon Trujillo (Trujillo 2006) refers to these converging sectors as the 'media communications' industry and the term is adopted here to differentiate the new industry from the traditional telecommunications and media broadcasting industries.

Local interests persist despite the Australian preference for national communications solutions and federalism is an important element in addressing these competing local and national interests. Indeed, federal systems have traditionally provided political solutions to overcome political issues associated with uniting regional jurisdictions and interests into a single nation-state. However, the secrecy and push to further centralise power under the Howard regime impacted upon communications policy and has effectively limited the involvement of local and regional interests in the policy process (Sainsbury 2006). Centralisation of power is important from a social capital perspective, in that the institutions of government 'set the rules: 'routines, procedures, conventions, roles, strategies, organisational forms and technologies around which political activity is constructed' (March & Olsen 1989: 22). The centralisation of power can, over time, become the 'new way of doing things' which decreases opportunities for local and regional institution-building. Crick (Crick 2006) suggests that social capital is reduced where political activity is restricted to certain 'non-revolving' elites by providing little opportunity for others to add to the debate. In Australia, this occurs at two levels which are absent in Canada. First, the centralisation of power in the federal government reduces the ability of sub-national governments to deal with regional and local issues. Second, traditional industry boundaries mean that businesses compete in the market on functionality, but are regulated by the devices used to provide the function. Each level of restriction contributes to the latent protection of entrenched interests, thus reducing access to citizens both as policy participants and users of technology.

Canada's 'oscillating legitimacy' between federal and provincial custodianship is noticeable in the media communications industry and improves citizen and user access to policy debates through greater policy transparency. For example: 'It is decidedly wrong to say that only the appropriate provincial legislature can regulate what its provincially incorporated companies do in any respect. It is likewise wrong to say that only the federal parliament can regulate what federally incorporated companies can do in any respect' (English 1973: 344). This institutional arrangement is largely responsible for Canada being a world leader in broadband infrastructure and services. According to the OECD (Organisation for Economic Cooperation and Development (OECD) 2002: 6):

> Low prices, good quality service and relatively rapid diffusion of new technologies characterise the Canadian telecommunication landscape. The regulatory framework is transparent and allows for full participation

of all interested parties. Consensus building has been a key factor in the development and implementation of regulations.

Canada has focused on 'technological neutrality'[12] in determining the structure of the industry for cross-platform competition purposes. The integrated regulatory system supports competitive practices through the CRTC's 'mandate of making the telecom market as competitive as possible' (Surtees cited in Martin 2003). This approach does not only focus on large competitors such as Bell Canada, Telus and Rogers Communications. Indeed, decisions by the CRTC demonstrate that federal policy can be actualised for smaller entrepreneurial firms. For example, Xit Telecom, a Quebec-based private fibre network developer, tested the policy by complaining to the CRTC that the large providers were selling dark fibre[13] to 'end customers at rates less than the cost of new construction, while charging more to potential competitors' (see Martin 2003). The CRTC ruled that Bell Canada and Telus Communications (Quebec) were to 'file proposed tariffs for inter-exchange dark fibre access' to promote competition in the private network market to lower costs to potential customers. The complaint was lodged in April 2003 and the CRTC's *Telecom Decision CRTC 2003-59* was issued on 22 August 2003. The CRTC often resorts to its 'expedited procedure for resolving competitive issues', enabling rulings on competitive issues to be delivered relatively swiftly. Obviously similar examples of competition regulation exist in Australia, but this case relates directly to competition policy enabling private networks to be built on a competitive basis, not simply the wholesale pricing issues often associated with the battles between Telstra and the ACCC.

In Australia, the Business Council of Australia (BCA) (see Maiden 2007) has recently called for 'greater investment on the 'supply side' of the economy', particularly in the areas of infrastructure, skills and workforce participation. In its report entitled *Infrastructure: Roadmap for Reform*, the BCA (Business Council of Australia (BCA) 2008b: ii) suggests that insufficient infrastructure development in ports, roads, rail, power, and water require a 'cross-jurisdictional framework for appropriate, timely, and coordinated investment in infrastructure to meet future growth needs' along with the 'development of fully operational national markets' as essential reforms (see also Williams 2008). The report also states that broadband services are problematic in terms of low penetration and speed of broadband services. However, while broadband networks are regarded as important, and it is recognised that Australia's broadband services are falling behind the rest of the developed world, very little attention is given to the details. For instance, the BCA's focus on the 'development of a quality broadband system with comprehensive access for businesses and households' (Business Council of Australia (BCA) 2008b: 8) is, unlike all the other types of infrastructure mentioned in the report, given no indication of the anticipated improvement to

Gross Domestic Product (GDP) (Business Council of Australia (BCA) 2008b: 6). Further, communications infrastructure occupies just a few lines of the report, leaving government to provide a 'policy framework that can stimulate the investment required to match a clear view of the productivity and innovation advantages available from higher broadband speeds, a view of the competitive framework for access, and a statement on implementation timing' (Business Council of Australia (BCA) 2008b: 14).

There are two reasons for the BCA to expect the government to provide direction on the communications network. First, the federal government has constitutional responsibility. Second, and more importantly, the federal government has always dealt with communications policy.

Lessons from Canada

As early as 1994, Canada not only had a clear federal policy advocating community involvement in establishing communications networks, but the federal government's leadership, particularly from the Communications Minister, had encouraged the diverse policy communities to 'buy-in to the Minister's vision'.[14] The federal government's leadership in communications policy encouraged the involvement and subsequent education of a diverse group of policy actors, representing a plurality of interests, who helped to shape communications policy at various levels of government and civil society. This particular group of policy actors remains influential today, with many of the community leaders involved in Canada's Information Superhighway conferences of the early 1990s occupying leadership roles including First Nation communications network developers, industry and public advocates, communications infrastructure entrepreneurs, and academics. Indeed, many of the original conference attendees were active participants in the recent Canadian Radio-television and Telecommunications Commission (CRTC) review of telecommunications regulation. Others conducted an alternative telecommunications review panel to enable citizen voices to be heard through media coverage. This alternative review panel was particularly important, ensuring community issues were included alongside the lengthy and expensive submissions put forward by the large telecommunications carriers, particularly Bell Canada.

Particularly in areas of market failure, Canadian communities have been able to work with businesses and governments at various levels to facilitate broadband infrastructure deployment. The extraordinary extent of government cooperation, at federal, provincial and municipal levels, and civil society and business involvement in the deployment of broadband infrastructure, facilitates accessibility and take-up of broadband services. For example, governments, businesses and civil society groups in Laurentian Hills, Renfrew County, Ontario, were engaged by Xit Telecom in an innovative approach to bring high-speed broadband services to communities where most other providers are unable to make a profit. Xit Telecom uses a combination of dark fibre and microwave infrastructure and requires (generally) 30 customers in a given area to justify their infrastructure deployment. The technology is cheaper than that provided by the larger telecommunications carriers because the intelligence is in the applications (the boxes at each end), not the network itself.

Xit Telecom claims that consumers will pay CAD$39.95 per month for their broadband connection, a price which is comparable to many Australian broadband plans. Yet the firm's innovative approach to network deployment was not a result of any particular technological development, but more a case of establishing strong working relationships with governments and communities. In Laurentian Hills, community frustration at the lack of broadband services prompted federal Member of Parliament Cheryl Gallant to initiate the Broadband Renfrew Access Valley Ontario (BRAVO) project (Walker 2007a). Robert Proulx, owner of Xit Telecom, addressed a community meeting, sponsored by the BRAVO project, to put forward his proposal to establish a private network for the community, using Xit Telecom's business model. The community agreed to a small test to trial the technology's capabilities. While tests are still in progress at the time of writing, with topographical problems interfering with the line-of-sight microwave infrastructure, it appears that some more investment in infrastructure may be required to bring broadband to the community.

Despite some problems with the early trials, the integrated nature of Canadian broadband policy is likely to enable Xit Telecom to bring broadband services to the Laurentian Hills community as the approach enables local problems to be dealt with by the policy and deployment process. For instance, the local Member of Parliament has negotiated some CAD$30 million funding from the federal, provincial and municipal governments which is available for community infrastructure projects in partnership with private sector investors and infrastructure providers. Further, issues of access to property for locating microwave, satellite and wireless infrastructure and providing access to cable ducts is coordinated by the project leaders; often volunteers from the BRAVO project. Such small scale operations occur throughout Canada regularly, enabling the deployment of private networks using various business models.

An earlier federal policy initiative, run by the Internet Highway Applications Branch (IHAB) at Industry Canada, used market aggregation to improve broadband penetration in communities. Communities were encouraged to submit a Request for Proposal (RFP) for broadband infrastructure deployment. This involved various partnerships between governments, businesses and community groups in the policy process and has helped citizens as users to receive the type of infrastructure they need. For instance, Kuhkenah Network (K-Net) is a community group which has established a private network to service indigenous communities in the remote northern regions. The fibre network enables the provision of e-health services (called tele-health in Canada) to these communities. Medical and education services can be provided remotely via an advanced video conferencing system. The growth of some of the remote northern communities may well be due to the advanced connectivity provided by K-Net.

In comparison to Gungahlin in Canberra, a relatively new suburb to the north of the national capital, Canadian communities do not face the same barriers brought about by the federal system. Telstra is the major provider in Gungahlin, although there are other providers using Telstra's network or their own wireless networks to service the area. Telstra denies there are problems with broadband in the area but residents have experienced unsatisfactory broadband services which some believe to be a result of insufficient infrastructure development (Frost 2007). Further, alternative providers available elsewhere in the Australian Capital Territory (ACT), such as the ACT government-sponsored TransACT fibre network provider, are not available in the Gungahlin area. TransACT has been able to lay fibre cable throughout the ACT on the infrastructure owned by ACTEW, the ACT's major electricity provider. Gungahlin, however, was built by developers and government joint-ventures which meant that access to the underground conduits for the electricity network did not facilitate access for TransACT's network. Here local problems favoured Telstra and, in effect, hindered local competition. In the meantime, the Gungahlin Community Council, a community group designed to represent the interests of community members, is limited to media coverage as its major influence on the policy process and the deployment of local infrastructure.

Reinvigorating federalism

Attempts to reinvigorate federalism in Australia are not new (Brown & Bellamy 2006). Indeed, the Rudd Labor government is currently in the process of delivering 'new federalism' (Franklin 2008) through harnessing 'the goodwill of wall-to-wall State and Territory Labor governments'. In effect, the Coalition of Australian Governments (COAG) is more cooperative under Labor than it was under the previous Howard government. Nevertheless, COAG is still a centralised institution and while it does take into account state and territory issues, it is still focused on the single national policy solution. Canada's broadband outcomes from a nation-building perspective have enabled nation-building to commence from within the citizenry, rather than from an externally imposed central body. Canada's approach provides the social capital that enables communications networks to function beyond the technical capabilities and into the realm of the tacit where most social benefits can be derived.

Reinvigorating federalism in an Australian context is unlikely to move beyond the 'Australian way' if recent infrastructure initiatives offer any insight to the future. The old way of thinking about communications policy is unlikely to develop the human element of the national network where 'the edge-nodes are both end-users and relay points that may be interconnected into a mesh to provide wide-area connectivity … [where] there is no centralized network coordination … [and] the 'network' grows 'virally' as end-users add equipment to the network' (Lehr et al 2005: 3). The establishment of Infrastructure Australia (see Walker 2007) will no doubt improve some aspects of Australia's infrastructure crisis, but treating broadband infrastructure in the same way policy–makers treat other types of infrastructure is conceptually narrow and unlikely to meet the needs of citizens as users. Canada provides a number of lessons for Australia in reinvigorating federalism — considered here an enabling quality of modern nation-building. Regrettably, the 'Australian way' persists and is likely to do so into the foreseeable future unless 'left-field' ideas which challenge the status quo are considered seriously in policy debates.

References

ABC News. (2007a) 'Howard in hospital power grab'. *ABC News Online*. 1 August 2007.

ABC News. (2007b) 'States fight public housing 'power grab". *ABC News Online*. 24 August 2007.

Attorney-General of Victoria. (2007) *Ruddock makes a power grab over court appeal*. Media Release. <http://www.dpc.vic.gov.au/domino/Web_Notes/ newmedia.nsf/b0222c68d27626e2ca256c8c001a3d2d/398b9b3d0c39439bca257323007 feb74!OpenDocument>.

Australian Associated Press (AAP). (2007) 'PM denies federal power grab'. *news.com.au*. 1 August 2007.

Australian Heritage Commission, (ed) (2003). *Linking a Nation: Australia's Transport and Communications 1788–1970*. Australia: Our national stories.

Australian National Audit Office. (1999) *Networking the Nation — The Regional Telecommunications Infrastructure Fund*. Australian National Audit Office.

Bell Canada Enterprises. (2006) *Successful broadband program completed ahead of schedule — New Brunswick one of the most connected provinces in Canada*. Bell Canada Enterprises. <http://www.bce.ca/en/ news/releases/aliant/2006/06/29/73706.html>.

Boyce, R.W.D. (2000) 'Imperial Dreams and National Realities: Britain, Canada and the Struggle for a Pacific Telegraph Cable, 1879-1902.' *English Historical Review*. 115.460.

Boyer, M., J. Robert and H. Santerre. (2001). 'Industrial Restructuring in the Knowledge-Based Economy'. In *Doing Business in the Knowledge-Based Economy: Facts and Policy Challenges*, eds L.A. Lefebvre, E. Lefebvre and P. Mohnen. Boston: Kluwer Academic Publishers and Infrastructure Canada.

Brown, A.J. and J. Bellamy, (eds) (2006). *Federalism and Regionalism in Australia: New approaches, new institutions?* Canberra: Australian National University Press.

Burgess, M. (1990) *Canadian Federalism: Past, Present and Future.* London: Leicester University Press.

Business Council of Australia (BCA). (2008a) *Infrastructure: Roadmap for Reform.* Melbourne: Business Council of Australia. <http://www.bca.com.au/ Content.aspx?ContentID=101167>.

Business Council of Australia (BCA). (2008b) *Infrastructure: Roadmap for Reform.* Melbourne: Business Council of Australia.

Butcher, J. (2007). 'Nation-building renaissance? The job's not finished yet'. In *The Canberra Times.* Canberra: 5 June 2007.

Carter, C., (ed) (1981). *Industrial Policy and Innovation.* London: Heinemann.

Choice. (2007). 'The future of broadband.' *Choice Magazine.*

Coleman, S. (2007) 'Just hit the red button'. *The Times Higher Education Supplement.* 4 May 2007.

Coleman, W.D. and G. Skogstad. (1990) *Policy Communities and Public Policy in Canada.* Mississauga, Ontario: Copp Clark Pitman.

Computer Laboratory. (1997) 'Technological Neutrality.' Cambridge University. <http://www.cl.cam.ac.uk/~rja14/dtiresponse/node11.html>.

Copp, N. and A. Zanella. (1993) *Discovery, Innovation and Risk: Case Studies in Science and Technology.* Cambridge: MIT Press.

Crandall, R., W. Lehr and R. Litan. (2007) 'The Effects of Broadband Deployment on Output and Employment: A Cross-sectional Analysis of U.S. Data.' *Issues in Economic Policy.*

Crick, B. (2006) 'Keynote Address.' Paper presented to CitizED International Conference, University of Sydney.

Crowe, D. (2007a) 'Study undermines broadband claims'. *The Australian Financial Review.* 15 May 2007.

Crowe, D. (2007b) 'Bulk of $50m broadband funding still not spent'. *The Australian Financial Review.* 13 February 2007.

Crowe, D. (2007c) 'Coonan plan to shake up broadband'. *The Australian Financial Review.* 5 June 2007.

Crowe, D. and T. Boyd. (2005) 'It's War: And the Telstra share price could be the victim'. *The Weekend Australian Financial Review.*

DeAngelis, R. (2004) 'Debate: A Comment on the 'Australian Settlement' Symposium.' *Australian Journal of Political Science*. Vol. 39:pp. 657-9.

Department of Infrastructure, T., Regional Development and Local Government. (2008) 'History of Rail in Australia.' Canberra: Department of Infrastructure, Transport, Regional Development and Local Government. <http://www.infrastructure.gov.au/rail/trains/history.aspx>.

Douglas, J.-V. (2007) 'Internet spreading work opportunities far and wide'. *The Australian Financial Review*. 29 May 2007.

English, H.E., (ed) (1973). *Telecommunications for Canada: An Interface of Business and Government*. Toronto: Methuen.

Ferrari, J. (2006) 'National syllabus 'a power grab''. *The Australian*. 7 October 2006

Foreshaw, J. (2006) 'Video prescribed fo rchildren's health'. *The Australian*. 31 January 2006.

Franklin, M. (2008) 'Rudd delivers new federalism'. *The Australian*. 27 March 2008.

Frost, C. (2007) 'Internet Battle: Broadband blues in Gungahlin'. *The Northside Chronicle*.

Fullerton, T. (2006). 'Whealing and Dealing'. In *Four Corners*. 20 February 2006: Australian Broadcasting Corporation.

Gans, J. (2006) *The Local Broadband Imperative: Appropriate high-speed Internet access for Australia*. <http://ceda.com.au/public/publications/info_paper/docs/ip86.pdf>.

Hanson, D. et al. (2002) *Strategic Management*. Southbank, Victoria: Nelson - Thomson Learning.

Hartcher, P. (2007) 'Australia lags, says net guru'. *The Sydney Morning Herald*.

Information Technology Office. (2005) *2005-6 Provincial Budget Performance Plan*. <http://www.ito.gov.sk.ca/documents/2005-06%20Performance%20Plan.pdf>.

Infrastructure Canada. (2006) 'Infrastructure and Identity: 'Building Canada: People and projects that shaped the nation'.' Ottawa: Infrastructure Canada. <http://www.infrastructure.gc.ca/research-recherche/result/alt_formats/pdf/rp15_e.pdf>. Consulted 16 March 2008.

International Telecommunications Union (ITU). (2008). 'Ex Ante and Ex Post Regulation'. In *ICT Regulation Toolkit*: International Telecommunications Union.

Kelly, P. (1992) *The End of Certainty: The Story of the 1980s*. St Leonards: Allen & Unwin.

Lee, T. (2007) 'ACCC won't hang up on Telstra'. *The Australian Financial Review*. 6 June 2007.

Lee, T. and J. Bajkowski. (2007) 'Doubt over Telstra campaign'. *The Australian Financial Review*. 3 May 2007.

Livingston, K.T. (1996) *The Wired Nation Continent: The Communication Revolution and Federating Australia*. Melbourne: Oxford University Press.

Maiden, S. (2007) 'Opposition attack Rudd double standard'. *The Australian*. 25 February 2008.

March, J.G. and J.P. Olsen. (1989) *Rediscovering Institutions: The Organisational Basis of Politics*. New York: Free Press.

Marris, S. (2007) 'Coonan's wireless push angers Nats'. *The Australian*. 13 June 2007.

Martin, M. (2003). 'CRTC shines light on dark fibre.' *Network World Canada*.

Mathews, R.L., (ed) (1982). *Public Policies in Two Federal Countries: Canada and Australia*. Canberra: ANU Press.

Moyal, A. (1984) *Clear Across Australia: A history of telecommunications*. Melbourne: Neslon.

Organisation for Economic Cooperation and Development (OECD). (2002) *Regulatory reform in Canada: From Transition to New Regulation Challenges*. Paris: OECD.

Productivity Commission. (2003) *Social Capital: Reviewing the Concept and its Policy Implications*.

Pusey, M. (1991) *Economic rationalism in Canberra: a nation-building state changes its mind*. Melbourne: Cambridge University Press.

Putnis, P. (2002) 'The concept of the 'national' in the history of news discourse in Australia.' Paper presented to International Association for Media and Communication Research Conference, Barcelona, July 2002.

Rhodes, R.A.W. (1996) 'The New Governance: Governing without Government.' *Political Studies*. Vol. 44:652-67.

Sainsbury, M. (2005) 'Just a phone call away'. *The Australian*. 10 August 2005.

Sainsbury, M. (2006) 'Red faces on the cards once documents made public'. *The Australian*. 7 December 2006.

Scott, S. and L. Allen. (2005) 'Documents reveal secret tunnel deals'. *The Australian Financial Review*. 21 October 2005.

Shaw, M. (2006) 'Federal IR power grab 'suspicious'. *The Age*. 11 May 2006.

Shepherd, A.F. (1999) 'Selling Projects to the Community.' Paper presented to Academy Symposium: The Spirit of the Snowy - Fifty Years On, Melbourne.

Smith, A. (2005). 'Now there's proof: drivers dodge tunnel'. In *The Sydney Morning Herald*. Sydney: 26 September 2005.

Smyth, P. (2004) 'Comment: Australian Settlement or Australian Way?' *Australian Journal of Poltiical Science*. Vol. 39:pp. 39–41.

Spool, J.M. (1997) 'Market Maturity.' North Andover, MA: User Interface Engineering.   <http://www.uie.com/articles/market_maturity/>. Consulted 25 March 2008 2008.

Stokes, G. (2004) 'The 'Australian Settlement' and Australian Political Thought.' *Australian Journal of Political Science*. Vol. 39:pp. 5–22.

The Australian. (2007) 'Sol's sour grapes'. *The Weekend Australian*. 15-16 September 2007.

Total Telecom Magazine. (2007). 'Editorial: Reaching Maturity.' *Total Telecom Magazine* (June 2007): 21.

Trujillo, S. (2006) 'The New Telstra: A Transformation Story.' Paper presented to Address to the National Press Club of Australia, Canberra, 29 June 2006.

Velaz, F. (1997) 'Build it and they will come.' *IIE Solutions*. December 1997:54-5.

Walker, J. (2007) 'Priority list to come first'. *The Australian*.

Warne-Smith, D. (2007) 'The Telstra Mouth'. *The Weekend Australian Magazine*.

Williams, C. (2001) *Canadian Social Trends*.

Williams, F. (2008) 'Playing catch-up'. *Herald-Sun*. 1 March 2008.

ENDNOTES

[1] Coleman (2007) also suggest that while the 'public, whose power as consumers has been enhanced by opportunities to talk back to companies and form networks around common interests, is still largely locked out of the political system'.

[2] In accordance with Canada's *Telecommunications Act 1993*, the Canadian Radio-television and Telecommunications Commission (CRTC) may refrain (that is, 'forbear') 'in whole or in part and conditionally or unconditionally, from the exercise of any power ... in relation to a telecommunications service or class of services provided by a Canadian carrier, where the Commission finds as a question of fact that to refrain would be consistent with the Canadian telecommunications policy objectives'.

[3] Canada's CRTC is a specialist regulator and is responsible for regulatory functions regarding technical, content and competition issues of both broadcasting and telecommunications services as a result of the *Canadian Radio-television and Telecommunications Commission Act 1976*. Australia, on the other hand, did not merge its broadcasting and communications authorities until 1 July 2005 when the Australian Communications Authority (ACA) and Australian Broadcasting Authority (ABA) merged to form the Australian Communications and Media Authority (ACMA). Nevertheless, the Australian Competition and Consumer Commission remains the main regulator of competition issues under its telecommunications

authority outlined in Part XIB of the *Trade Practices Act 1974*. The industries, however, remain for the most part separated on the basis of 'device' — that is, radio, television, computer, telephone, mobile telephone — rather than by function (that is, communication).

[4] Stephen Conroy is the Minister for Broadband, Communications and the Digital Economy.

[5] Note that while Putnis (2002) claims that the news media was responsible for 'creating' the nation, he acknowledges that telegraph infrastructure enabled the news media to do so.

[6] The first inter-colonial telegraph line connected Melbourne and Mt Gambier in 1858, and soon after Sydney and Albury (Department for Environment and Heritage 2007: 4). Various inter-colonial conferences were held in the 50 years preceding federation.

[7] During the 2007 election campaign, broadband became a major issue. However, Australian voters were effectively given a choice between a national solution with mostly private sector solutions by the Coalition, or a national solution focusing on public-private partnerships by Labor.

[8] McGowan was a young Canadian entrepreneur responsible for the 'first transfer of modern telecommunications technology to Australia' (Moyal 1984: 16).

[9] Interviewees were familiar with the two approaches to regulation know as *ex ante* and *ex post*. According to the ITU (2008), '*Ex ante* regulation is mainly concerned with market structure, that is the number of firms and level of market concentration, entry conditions, and the degree of product differentiation, [whereas e]x post regulation is mainly concerned with market conduct — the behaviour of a firm with respect to both its competitors and its customers'. *Ex ante* regulation was commonly deemed 'undesirable' by industry elites in both Canada and Australia.

[10] 'Market maturity' usually refers to the various stages of 'product life'. However, in the telecommunications industry, it also suggests the state of play between market competitors. Given that Canadians tend to focus on competing in the market, whereas Australians tend to focus on the regulatory system, Canada's industry appears to be at a greater level of 'maturity'.

[11] A traffic count conducted by the *Sydney Morning Herald* (see Smith 2005a) demonstrated that motorists were not using the Cross City Tunnel. The NRMA had also published a 'rat run' map to show motorists how to avoid using the tunnel (and paying the toll fee).

[12] For example, Canadian telecommunications companies compete on an equal footing with cable television companies on the basis of the type of service provided, not the infrastructure 'platform' the service is delivered on. Technological neutrality is an essentially contested concept but in principle, various CRTC and International Telecommunications Union papers refer to the concept as 'natural selection' of particular technologies to perform particular functions, that is, the function and not the technology is regulated. Nevertheless, voice-over-Internet-Protocol (VoIP) services have challenged these principles in both Canada and Australia and the issues of 'neutrality' remain largely unresolved.

[13] Dark fibre refers to cable which has been deployed but is not in use. The cable does not have any electronic signalling equipment which enables businesses to 'light up' the cable using various technologies. Dark fibre is often used to build private networks for customers such as municipalities, school boards and large enterprises (see Martin 2003).

[14] Numerous industry elites from various policy actor groups acknowledge the Minister's leadership and sponsorship in the deployment of communications infrastructure.

11. Re-imagining the Australian state: political structures and policy strategies

Ian Marsh

Abstract

Can the State reasonably pursue the task of nation-building if governments are not prepared to adapt the machinery of State in step with the evolving nature of society and emerging challenges? Australia's present political system was conceived in, and designed for, the very different social conditions that existed in the early nineteenth century. At that time, the two major parties broadly articulated a real social divide and developed organisational machinery that effectively mobilised the surrounding society: that provided opportunities for debate of emerging issues, engaging activists and providing cues to their followers about how to judge issues. Now the social base of the political system has been transfigured. Domestically, the community is pluralised and differentiated, class identity has decomposed and variety of new issues has undermined both the older collectivist identities and the autonomy of domestic politics. Consequently, the public agenda has expanded, differentiated and become more complex. Over this same period, the party organisational machinery that formerly mediated citizen and activist mobilisation and engagement has been jettisoned. No compensating machinery has been developed. As a result, the public conversation about major emerging issues languishes. How, then, can governments hope to chart a path for nation-building? What institutions will we require to support a truly 'national' dialogue about the meaning of 'nation' and the kind of society we're trying to create? I argue that a reconfigured Parliament might engage citizens and interest groups in 'government by discussion'. For that to occur public disaffection will doubtless need to attain new heights, and new political entrepreneurs will be needed to champion the message that there is another way.

Introduction

Building a nation requires the establishment of civil and legal institutions as well as a political culture within which some sort of collective vision of national destiny might be forged. These are the essential prerequisites for nation-building as they provide both the forum and the instruments for the articulation of public policy and the pursuit of policy goals through implementation. In this chapter, I examine those features of Australia's political culture and institutions that diminish deliberative processes and thereby compromise the capacity of the Australian polity to collectively determine any future nation-building agenda.

Australia's present political system was formed in the early twentieth century. The formal structure emerged roughly from 1909 when Free Trade and Protectionist parliamentary groups merged. The architecture of executive-administrative power that was then constituted persists to this day. At its establishment, this architecture reflected prevailing political narratives and social cleavages. Socio-economic class was then the dominant political fault-line. Socialism and social liberalism were the dominant narratives. Present Australian cleavages and narratives bear little relation to those of the early twentieth century. Australian society is more differentiated at every level: ethnically, economically and in citizen aspirations. Socio-economic class has ceased to be the only, or indeed — depending on the issue — the primary, determinant of political orientation. There are no comprehensive political narratives. Think of alignments on WorkChoices, climate change, indigenous reconciliation, refugees, same sex marriage, education and a host of other issues. The first theme of this chapter concerns the need to better align the formal structure of politics to a more pluralised social base. The formal system no longer sufficiently engages this base in the national conversation about policy choices and options. But how might this outcome be achieved? What form might an amended structure take?

A second theme concerns the likelihood of change actually happening. Several scenarios can be imagined. Some involve a turn away from the major parties on the part of electors. But another scenario, albeit perhaps more remote, involves action by political elites themselves. They might yet come to see moves down this path as being in their own political interest. The seven policy U-turns of the Howard government from early 2007 provide powerful evidence of the profound gap between the present formal system and the surrounding society. This gap is a threat to any government with an ambitious policy agenda.

The discussion proceeds as follows. The first section discusses the importance of an informed public from the specific perspective of the policy choices that are available to the executive. It also discusses recent changes in the dynamics of opinion formation. This summarises and extends arguments that I have developed at greater length elsewhere (1985, 1995, 2006, 2007, Marsh and Yencken, 2004). A second section reviews three underlying symptoms of 'dysfunctionality' in the present formal policy-making structure. Drawing on Australia's experience pre-1909, the third section discusses the possible form of an amended system. The formal structure of policy-making would be augmented by what Michael Keating has termed a 'contemplative phase'. In this phase two key tasks would be initiated: on an analytic plane, the issue would be introduced to the public agenda and its broad scope defined; in parallel, on a political plane, the engagement and mobilisation of interests would commence. Neither of these tasks is routinely part of existing processes. A concluding section briefly reviews some scenarios that might be associated with such structural change.

The changing dynamics of opinion formation

Public opinion underwrites executive choices and action. While they must sometimes confront their publics, political leaders mostly need to work with the grain of public opinion. Public opinion plays a role in the political system roughly analogous to that of money in the market system. It is the unit of exchange. But opinion does not spring into life spontaneously or ready formed. Rather, public opinion develops reciprocally in the context of issues, institutions and, perhaps most importantly, ideas. It develops like a snowball. It starts in the belief of a few people that action is required on a particular issue. The protagonists could be community activists, business leaders, university experts, ministers or MPs. Through persuasion and argument the number of people who share a concern progressively expands. If this does not occur the issue dies. But if a concern is to grow in significance, more organised actors need to become involved. This can happen as particular individuals or groups give cues to others or as coalitions take shape (e.g. Yankelovich, 1992; Zaller, 1992).

There are numerous practical examples of these abstract propositions. Take the literature on the rise of the social movements (e.g. McAdam, McCarty and Zald, 1996; Braithwaite and Drahos, 2000) or the emergence of neo-liberal politics in the US and Sweden (Blyth, 2002). Or consider the impact of the abortion debate in the Australian Parliament (Hansard, 9 February 2006), or the *Get-Up* campaign on behalf of David Hicks.[1] Perhaps the most recent vivid example, yet to be fully documented, concerns the development of public opinion on climate change to which protracted drought, Al Gore's film '*An Inconvenient Truth*' and the *Stern Report* presumably all made major contributions.

In any polity, the formal political system is the principal stage for this process. It constitutes a kind of artificial theatre. Its succeeding acts and scenes and its cameo dramas can be the settings from which, and through which, views are transmitted from one group to another. By these means, public attention is mobilised. The distinctive role of Parliament is apparent in the fundamental split between this setting and the administration. Cabinet and ministers provide the link. They are the only actors with standing in both sub-systems. Meanwhile, political exchanges occur mostly in and around parliamentary rituals or parliamentary settings. Question Time, confidence motions, urgency motions, ministerial statements, legislation and (to a lesser degree) committee hearings are the settings in which agendas are established and through which arguments are developed and priorities communicated. These settings provide raw material for the daily media.

Bernard Crick once described parliamentary rituals as tantamount to a continuing election campaign. Reflecting this spirit, they are almost wholly adversarial in character. But in the process of regulating the struggle for power in a developed and civilised democracy, these processes are also supposed to foster social learning. Indeed this is their ultimate rationale. In democratic theory, as the political conversation unfolds, the public becomes better informed (e.g. March and Olsen, 1995; Pettit, 1997; Dryzek, 2000). Public opinion should be refined and distilled as more views are accommodated, more questions answered, more uncertainties dispelled and more consequences recognised. This is the path to effective and adaptive governance.

The premise that social learning is best fostered through adversarial rituals involves a number of assumptions. First, it assumes that there is a fundamental programmatic difference between the major parties. This was indeed broadly the case when the Labor Party was formed. It could be plausibly argued that this persisted until roughly the early 1970s, when both major parties adopted a catch-all stance (e.g. Mair, 1997; Marsh, 2006b). This marked the beginning of convergence on policy between the major parties, a process that is now virtually complete (e.g. Blyth and Katz, 2005). Second, adversarialism assumed that party difference derives from underlying normative orientations that are reflected in whole agendas and programs. Debate does not need to focus on particular issues or on the detail of proposed measures because measures and instruments are assumed to be almost wholly implicit in the competing party programs. We will want to revisit the continuing relevance of these basic assumptions.

In recent decades, the media have come to play increasingly critical transmission and brokerage roles between the formal system and the citizens that it (ostensibly) serves. Media roles have waxed as those of other political institutions (notably the major party organisations) have waned. The media often determine which issues and which voices will be given prominence. However, they rarely set the agenda. This usually involves either top-down announcements by the political leadership or sustained bottom-up campaigning (e.g. *Get-Up* and David Hicks). The media mostly disseminate or re-package messages that others have originated. Key commentators transmit opinions and influence the views of others. They can be very important cue givers. But the media rarely determine the options that enter public debate.

In step with the rise of the media, there have been other changes in the approach of party leaders to informing and influencing public opinion. Perhaps unintentionally, they have largely turned from leading to following the community. With some qualifications (noted in a moment), party leaders now often take their cues from focus groups or talkback radio. This outcome is a consequence of developments from the 1970s. Around that time, the major parties changed their approach to the development of public opinion. The appointment of a new style of party manager was symptomatic of this change. Professionals in public opinion polling and marketing replaced party loyalists (e.g. Mills, 1986). They promised a new outcome. Direct marketing, polling, media advertising and packaging promised to render dispensable organisational policy development and a large party membership base. Clever marketing, focused on the parliamentary leadership, could, it was imagined, sufficiently compensate for weakened party identifications among electors. Indeed conferences, large memberships and internal policy development processes came to be seen as constraints on the political leadership. Liberation from them allowed the parliamentary leadership to reach out directly to the electorate. Sophisticated marketing techniques seemed capable of delivering the required outcomes in mass opinion formation.

A direct approach to the electorate via the media is clearly one viable option for building public opinion but there are many constraints. Media requirements for a punchy 'grab' distort presentations. The media have difficulty maintaining attention on an issue without sensationalising developments. The media have commercial interests, which are not necessarily consistent with the development of an informed public opinion. In sum, media requirements for a punchy grab and their short attention spans have, arguably, significantly diminished public understanding of policy issues and choices (e.g. Lloyd, 2004 ; Henry, 2007). In addition, the focus of public debate on party leaders limits the development of an informed public opinion in fundamental ways. Most major policy announcements are made by the Leaders of the major parties. This means that the leader's prestige is implicated in the successful implementation of whatever has been proposed. A focus on the party Leaders foreshortens the time available for reciprocal exchanges between protagonists and limits the scope for developing public and interest group opinion. It also turns many issues into futile jousts between governments and Oppositions.

Further, market practices are now in common use for policy development: increasing attention is given to focus-group and opinion surveys by ministers, departments and political parties. A reliance on focus groups and talk back radio means knee-jerk public responses and unformed opinion are given inappropriate standing. Finally, policy has been merchandised by the use of commercial advertising to project messages to the general public. Look no further than the recent campaigns associated with WorkChoices, domestic violence or the tax system. Fred Argy has estimated the Howard governments together spent some two billion dollars on advertising and policy promotion — an astonishing sum (Argy, 2007). These developments deflect attention from actions that might be taken to develop better-defined strategies and public opinion about them. There is limited scope for actions that might refine and deepen public opinion and, hence, limited attention to such possibilities.

Three symptoms of a corrupted policy-making system

There are at least three symptoms of a policy-making system that has become corrupted in its capacity to build an informed public opinion. These are public views about the system, contemporary representational patterns and the experience of the Howard governments.

Public trust and confidence

What does the public think about the system? There is an extensive international literature which includes data on Australia that documents the decline in citizen trust (e.g. Dalton, 2004; Stoker, 2006). Recent data also shows that Australians maintain high levels of 'satisfaction with the democracy' with Australian results only second to those of Denmark (McAlister, 2007). Of course it is unclear whether this reflects an underlying faith in government, (for example a primarily normative orientation broadly consistent with a utilitarian political culture) or a judgment about the current structure. I have always been attracted by Peter Bowers (thoroughly utilitarian) reading of our national psyche: 'There is an ephemeral timelessness about the desire of Australians for the ideal party that will govern Australia fairly and wisely for all Australians. Australian politics are driven by a perverse romanticism that few Australians are willing to admit because it runs counter to the preferred national persona of treating all things political with an arid cynicism better suited to a race that has lived in a hard dry country for two hundred years' (*Sydney Morning Herald*, 10 March 1990). In the same spirit perhaps, Greg Craven is credited with proposing that Australians are radical about only one thing: that their politicians be moderate (cited by Ross Gittins, *Sydney Morning Herald,* 28 November 2007, p. 15).

When it comes to politicians, public distrust and cynicism is plain. Federal members of Parliament rank twenty-first and State members twenty-second on the Morgan list of 29 professions as ranked by trustworthiness. Split ticket voting is an indicator of caution amongst electors. While the numbers fluctuate, in recent years up to 25% of the electorate has voted for different parties in the Senate and the House of Representatives. In other words, many Australians like divided government. Further, political parties are themselves increasingly unpopular. In 2001, 76% of Australians indicated they did not think parties care about what people think and in 2004, 70%. In 1993 only 56% held this view. In 1998, 67% of respondents indicated that they think that people in government look after themselves. In 2001 this increased to 68% but declined to 61% in 2004. Similarly, in 1998, 82% said government was run for a few big groups. This declined to 74% in 2001 and 67% in 2004.

The collapse of visceral voter loyalty to one or other of the major parties is also evident. Between 1967 and 1997, the number of Australians without a party identification increased from roughly two percent to around 17%. Further, the number acknowledging only weak identification has increased from 23% in 1967 to around 36% in 1996, 34% in 2001 and 32% in 2004. Thus, between 50 and 60% of the electorate have no — or only weak — identification with one or other of the major parties. High levels of party identification were formerly regarded as the sheet anchor of the Australian political system (e.g. Aitkin, 1977). The erosion in party identification has also diminished the symbolic power of party names. The collapse of party identification means the party 'brand' is no longer sufficient by itself to evoke a loyal response from most voters. This is a particularly significant trend if party names are relied on as a primary cue for citizen attitudes.

Representational patterns

A deeper symptom of misalignment between the formal system and the surrounding community is associated with representational patterns. The formal political system is based on two major parties. For many years these two parties effectively reflected a social reality. Some locate the sources of citizen party identifications in economic circumstances (e.g. Gollan, 1960) and some in cultural and religious orientations (e.g. Brett, 2003). Whatever its source, the notion that a broad cleavage divided Australian society and that this was reflected in the two major parties was widely accepted. As I have argued elsewhere, the contemporary diversity of Australian society, reflected in the proliferation of interest groups and social movements, is arguably the single most important change in the character of post war domestic politics (Marsh 1995, Chapter 2).

Nine major social movements emerged in the 1970s. These championed the environment and rights for women, gays, indigenous Australians, consumers, ethnic Australians and animals. They promoted peace and third world issues. Finally, advocates for the 'new right' have also exerted a powerful influence on political, business and media elites. This has been based on think tanks rather than mass mobilisation. They have generally championed atomised individuals as the only salient political unit.

These diverse groups variously encouraged the formation of other groups, whether in imitation (e.g. the republican movement) or to defend the status quo (anti-abortion movement; monarchists) or to further liberalise the policy agenda (e.g. euthanasia, drugs). Together these developments signify a new diversity in citizen identities (e.g. gender, ethnicity, environmentalism). They mostly augment, and sometimes displace, older class-based cleavages. A linear, left–right continuum was once an apt image of the electoral spectrum. In contemporary Australian society, a kaleidoscope seems a more apt metaphor. This image conveys the diversity and fluidity of political attachments that now characterises the Australian community.

Indeed, it is hard to overstate the degree to which Australia has become a group-based community. The array of organised actors on any issue is legion. These groups vary enormously in size, budgets, political skills, organisational sophistication and campaigning capacities. But the major ones are as effectively organised as the major political parties.

As a consequence, activists no longer have strong allegiance to one or other party and the way that issues are introduced onto the national stage has shifted. It has largely ceased to be an internal process dominated by major party organisations. Party forums are not the principal arenas for activists. Internal processes do not provide the medium for testing the acceptability of proposals or for seeding opinion formation. The initiative has moved elsewhere. Public opinion has been influenced through public campaigns by activists and through the resultant media attention. This has been used to pressure the parliamentary leadership of the major parties to adopt new agendas. The success of these campaigns has significantly widened the national political debate and raised the importance of public opinion formation.

The emergence of an array of interest groups and social movements in the post-1960s period is important because these organisations are durable. They both represent and sustain particular interests and positions — and they seek to persuade the undecided. The space between the major parties and the community is now filled by organisations with political *nous* and media skills and with a demonstrated capacity to shape opinion on particular issues.

Some commentators have decried or downplayed this development. They have claimed there is a mute but underlying 'silent majority'. Or they claim a minority has established a code of 'political correctness' that has staunched the expression of dissent. Or they claim public debate has been taken over by a 'new class' of self-interested individuals in the pay of the state. But the image of the Australian community as a vast silent majority with a noisy fringe of pressure groups is wrong. Talk of a 'new class' as some alien sectional minority who have subverted the public interest in favour of their selfish and unrepresentative concern is wrong. The idea that Australian society has been taken over by a politically correct discourse to the exclusion of a more authentic and unified Australian voice is wrong.

These images may be useful rhetorical ploys in the political game but they do not reflect reality. The pluralisation of Australian society is the fundamental fact — and unless political leaders can persuade us to jettison some of our varied aspirations, it is here to stay. It is evident in values and social attitudes, between regions and community groupings and at the level of organised political action.

Yet these groups lack access to the formal policy-making system. There is no institutional machinery that allows the system to routinely reach out to groups and assess their views. Further, on any issue some will be opposed (the immediate 'losers'), some will gain and others will be undecided depending on how the issue is framed. The formal system lacks routine capacities to bring these last two groups into the consultative process, to create space for redefining the issue, for initiating the formation of coalitions and for engaging in other actions that might better integrate the social base and the formal policy-making system. Let us explore some of the consequences.

The policy-making structure in practice

To understand the way the policy-making system actually works, recall some of its formal premises. One fundamental premise concerns the role of elections. These are assumed to deliver an unqualified mandate to the winning party. The doctrine of ministerial responsibility and the architecture of political-bureaucratic relations derive from this premise. The political authority gathered through an election victory is generally assumed to be sufficient to underwrite executive decision-making. This is also the premise behind Bernard Crick's description of the adversarial political system as tantamount to a continuing election campaign. Of course, in practice, this is less than absolute. For example, many years ago Robert McKenzie described the actual role of interest groups in words that continue to be relevant:

> I have suggested that any explanation of the democratic process, which ignores the role of organised interests, is grossly misleading. I would add that it is hopelessly inadequate and sterile in that it leaves out of account the principal channels through which the mass of the citizenry brings influence to bear on the decision-makers whom they have elected. In practice, in every democratic society, the voters undertake to do far more than select their elected representatives; they also insist on their right to advise, cajole and warn them regarding the policies they should adopt. This they do for the most part, through the pressure group system (1958, p. 9).

Indeed, as discussed in the previous section, interests have multiplied in recent years, far beyond their incidence when these words were penned. In the process, they have fractured the former almost absolute mobilising role of the major parties. However, assumptions about executive authority have not assimilated this development. They remain unchanged as the examples we will shortly review attest. In brief, the incentive structure in the formal system implies that any need to build power for a particular decision can be sufficiently handled by a prime minister or individual ministers on an ad hoc basis (e.g. gun control, GST).[2] There is no need for an additional phase in the policy system that would oblige ministers to routinely engage with affected interests before final decisions are taken by Cabinet. There is no need for a phase that would routinely engage the broader public without committing the government's prestige. There is no need for the addition of a routine process that would allow governments to trial arguments and evidence and gain intelligence about community and interest group views. There is no need for a phase where processes of coalition-building might be initiated. There is no need for what Michael Keating has elsewhere described as a contemplative phase (Keating, 2004, p. 154).

How does the experience of the Howard government illuminate this need? Its defeat challenges a variety of assumptions about the way the system works. One concerns the relationship between policy-making and political strategies. Prime Minister Howard gained a reputation for his tactical cunning and shrewdness. Surely victory in four election campaigns attests to high political skills? But these victories were often based on populist tactics and opportunism or on the spending that good times allowed. Only one election was fought on a contested policy agenda — that involving the GST in 1998. All the others substantially included 'wedge' or 'dog whistle' tactics and played on populist themes, most egregiously in the case of the Tampa episode. Howard was also adept at exploiting leadership weaknesses in his opponents.

Some may wish that politics could occupy a more elevated plane but in the context of a convergence in agendas between the major parties, a populist turn seems inevitable (e.g. Mair, 2002; Marquand, 2004). In this context, the 2007 election is of especial interest. The accession of Kevin Rudd to the Labor leadership in December 2006 was followed by an immediate lift in Opposition standing in the opinion polls. Further, Rudd adopted a very low political profile — carefully avoiding potential wedge issues. Thus many of the tactics that Howard had used so successfully against his earlier opponents were unavailable. And fortune delivered no fresh wedge opportunities.

So policy came into focus. Here the Howard government was forced to acknowledge the considerable gap between the positions that it had championed and public opinion. From late 2006, it backtracked on not one or two but on at least seven quite fundamental issues: education, management of the Murray Darling basin, indigenous reconciliation, refugees, broadband, WorkChoices, and climate change. Of course prime ministers must always be ready to trim for an election. But this represented a wholesale repudiation of announced past positions and attitudes across a wide and fundamental range of issues. This was an unambiguous example of politics driving policy. But what did these U-turns say for the government's previously stated views? Were they wrong? And what is the public to think? Are political leaders' complete chameleons or hypocrites? Do the merits of issues have nothing to do with their determination?

It is instructive to revisit the policy development processes that had been associated with these issues. WorkChoices is the most notable example. This issue was not discussed in the 2004 campaign. Shortly after his election victory, Howard set his department to work canvassing options for change. These were discussed in Cabinet. We now know that there was a considerable divergence amongst ministers about the severity of the measures (*The Australian*, 27/11/2007, p 7). The Workplace Relations Amendment (WorkChoices) Bill 2005 was introduced to the House of Representatives on 2 November, 2005. It was a complex piece of legislation amounting to 762 pages. It went to the Senate on 10 November and was finally passed on 2 December. In sum, 11 days of parliamentary time (House six and Senate five) had been devoted to debate and most of this was grandstanding rather than detailed discussion. At no point were affected interests — business, contractors, trade unions for example — drawn into the conversation. The government lacked a basic understanding of interest group and community views. Interests and the broader community were not engaged in a conversation about needs and options. There was no contemplative phase. There was, rather, only private deliberation and public announcement. Thereafter the policy was 'merchandised' to the electorate through a $55 million advertising campaign (Argy, 2007). The union movement responded with its effective Your Rights at Work' campaign. Notably, this was based on sustained grass roots mobilisation as well as advertisements (*Sydney Morning Herald,* 17-18/11/2007, p30). This forced the government to change ministers (Hockey replaced Andrews in late January 2007) and culminated in a major policy U-turn early in 2007. The former policy was effectively gutted (Wooden, 2007). A further $61 million advertising campaign was launched to merchandise the new approach. Would earlier disclosure of intent and options have produced a different outcome? Of course, the government might have thought such disclosure would have provided ammunition to its opponents. No doubt it also assumed that its right of decision was licensed by the 2004 election. In the event this proved to be a false assumption, with (from its perspective) disastrous consequences.

The other examples of policy U-turns involve issues that were perhaps not so profoundly damaging politically. But they do involve policy development processes that parallel those we have just reviewed. Take indigenous affairs. The government's intervention in the Northern Territory in July 2007 involved land rights and the permit system for communities as well as domestic violence, access to alcohol and sexual abuse. But these measures were introduced with no advance consultation with indigenous leaders and without the preparation of broader public opinion. Yet, as far back as 1999 a report entitled *Violence in Indigenous Communities* had been prepared for the Department by Dr Paul Memmott. This was not released by the then minister (Vanstone) until 2001. The government did not seek to seed a wider discussion about policy options. Meanwhile, ATSIC had been addressing these questions, although how effectively is unclear. In the event, ATSIC's funding was cut by $460 million in the first Howard budget. Thereafter funding was progressively cut until its abolition was announced in April 2004. Prime Minister Howard's position on indigenous issues was publicly clear. He condemned the so-called 'black arm band' view of indigenous history in Parliament on October 30, 1996, and again in the *Sir Robert Menzies Lecture*, which he delivered on 18 November of the same year. On May

26, 1997, Prime Minister Howard repeated this argument at the Reconciliation Convention marking the thirtieth anniversary of the referendum. This theme continued to dominate his public remarks until his adoption of the new narrative of practical reconciliation in March 2000 (*Sydney Morning Herald*, 30 March 2000).

In 2003, the indigenous leader Mick Dodson spoke forcefully at the National Press Club about violence, alcoholism and sexual abuse (*Sydney Morning Herald*, 30 June 2007, p. 35). Nothing happened. An inter-governmental summit on violence and child abuse was held in 2006. This pointed to the cost and blame shifting that characterised federal-territory and state relations. Nothing happened again. There had thus been discussion of the problem of alcohol and sexual abuse at a technical level for at least eight years. The *Little Children are Sacred* report supervened. It was tabled in the Northern Territory legislature in June 2007. The federal government's response was announced in August 2007 as a national emergency, three months prior to the election. Whilst firm evidence is unavailable, it is hard to believe there would not have been some community scepticism about the government's motives.

Climate change reflects a similar pattern of announcements without any prior contemplative phase. Two key events here involved the government's response to the Kyoto decision and the publication of an energy *White Paper* in 2004. The preparation of this document commenced in 2003 and followed the familiar pattern. The government called for submissions and attracted 33 responses. These were considered in private — then a report went to Cabinet and the *White Paper* was announced in Parliament on 15 June 2004. On this occasion there was a parliamentary committee hearing which had no apparent influence. But we know from other accounts that industry representatives enjoyed privileged access to the policy-making process and met with ministers in private (Pearse, 2005, cited in Hamilton, 2007). The government's position was projected through ministerial statements and policy announcements.

Meanwhile, the States had progressively moved to develop emissions trading schemes. Perhaps responding to the *Stern Report* and *An Inconvenient Truth* and the change in public mood that they seemingly stimulated, Prime Minister Howard appointed a Task Force on 30 November 2006 to look at a national scheme. This group took submissions in private from affected interests. Its conclusions provided the basis for a Cabinet submission. This was considered in mid 2007 and the government decision endorsing a scheme (but postponing any decision about targets) was announced in June 2007 (*Sydney Morning Herald*, 5 June 2007). In September 2007, with an election campaign pending this decision was reversed. At the same time the pronouncement against mandatory renewable energy targets in the 2004 White Paper, *Securing Australia's Energy Future*, was also reversed. Again, the government seemingly lacked early intelligence about the development of public opinion and lacked any detailed capacity to communicate its views to a wider public during its earlier years in office.

Two other illustrations of broadly similar policy development processes are provided by policy announcements on the Murray Darling Basin and education. In relation to the Murray Darling Basin this policy issue first entered the agenda around 1992 when the Murray-Darling Basin Agreement was established. Implementation was in the hands of the Murray Darling Basin Commission. Not surprisingly, this 25 member body proved incapable of coming to grips with the issue. It was subsequently joined by a host of special purpose authorities: Riverbank, the National Water Commission, Water for Rivers, catchments management authorities, The Living Murray. At least two other programs were announced: the Achieving Sustainable Groundwater Entitlement program and the National Water Initiative. Another consultative round between the Commonwealth and the States occurred in 2002. According to Ross Gittins, National Party pressure meant one key option was never considered — that is allowing city buyers into the market for Murray water (*Sydney Morning Herald*, 30 May 2007). Another issue that was proved too politically contentious was the over-allocation of water rights by New South Wales compared to the under-allocation by Victoria. It is worth noting no official enquiry ever directly addressed these issues and no distinctively political enquiry mechanism existed for addressing the federal-state and state-state issues in a sustained way. Grandstanding between the States and the Commonwealth dominated the public conversation.

Education is the only policy area that slightly qualifies the above picture. The government cut funding in its first budget in 1996. In January 1997 it established the *West Review*. This was a standard approach to policy investigation. Consultations amounted to soliciting the views of affected interests. The enquiry reported. The department and the Cabinet decided. The resulting ministerial statement was a squib. In the second Howard government, Minister Kemp sought to introduce a voucher like system in higher education. But his Cabinet submission was leaked in 1999 and the idea never got off the ground. Note Kemp's approach. He assumed the right way to introduce a radical initiative was to take a paper to Cabinet and if successful announce a change. This conforms to the formal norms of the system. But no part of that process involved the engagement of public and interest group opinion. Yet how could such a change be contemplated without intelligence about reactions and about the compromises that might have been necessary to gain support for the proposal. In the third Howard government, Minister Nelson went some way down this path in the consultations he lead in the development of the review *Higher Education at the Crossroads*. In April 2002 a discussion paper was released. It attracted 355 responses. Between June and September six papers on key issues were released. This elicited a further 373 submissions. Nelson also held directly or commissioned

48 forums covering all States. The government's response was announced 13 May 2003 as part of the Budget. Thereafter Nelson engaged the Democrats and modified some proposals to ensure their support. This exercise moved policy development closer to the 'contemplative phase' envisaged by Keating. But it involved the minister directly. It was a very time consuming process. The results of the review were not publicly available for comment before final decisions were taken and there was barely any reach beyond immediate stakeholders into broader public views.

The foregoing examples illustrate the very deep failings in present policy-making arrangements. There were failings of intelligence, communication and mobilisation. These were not the result of lapses by individual ministers. They reflect the false assumptions about political authority that are embedded in current policy-making processes. They reflect the enhanced political power of organised interests and the absence of effective integrating infrastructure. Effective in this context refers to the ability to develop and/or accommodate views, to construct coalitions and, if necessary jettison, adapt or build institutions. They also reflect the acute limitations of the media as a primary link between the government and the broader community.

Of course in the recent past public understanding of government policy stances has mostly not been a primary factor in political strategies or campaigns. Tacit bipartisanship has been an important, albeit top-down, driver of policy change. But general public perceptions of competence in relation to the economy and national security have been primary. Wedge tactics, populism and leadership appeal have also featured prominently. But when these ephemera were unavailable policy issues came into focus. When this occurred, the dysfunctional character of present policy-making arrangements can be clearly seen.

An augmented system?

How might a contemplative phase be introduced to the present policy-making structure? For guidance we might turn to the political architecture that characterised the first decade of the twentieth century. Between 1901 and 1909 three parties, Protectionist, Free Traders and Labor, competed for public support. No party won an outright parliamentary majority. Elections produced a Parliament composed of members whose aspirations and attitudes diverged widely. Without a majority party in Parliament, governments were created and unmade according to their ability to gather majority support for their programs and for particular measures. They were also required to obtain majorities in two chambers. This brought into focus the political mechanisms available for building backbench and inter-house support both for governments and for individual measures.

This more fluid political context required a contemplative phase in the policy-making process. This involved parliamentary capacity for an initial assessment of strategic issues. This offers perhaps the most vivid contrast between the pattern of policy-making in the two-party period, and that in the more plural political world that preceded it. In the two-party period, the primary task of strategic political inquiry has been intellectual 'expert' investigation of a complex new issue to recommend what should be done. Examples are the *Campbell Report* on financial deregulation, or the *McClure Report* on the welfare system or the *Hogan Report* on nursing home financing. The government, having established these inquiries, assumed its prior electoral victory gave it sufficient authority to implement the findings, should it agree with them.

The situation was different in the more plural world of 1901 to 1909. The diversity of the Australian community was then mirrored in the existence of three parties. Contested strategic issues were introduced in Parliament before the parties had announced their firm policy stances. This allowed a process of intellectual analysis, political and public exchange and learning. Through this process, political authority sufficient to permit their resolution was mobilised. Indeed, the two tasks of refining analysis and mobilising consent overlapped. Parliamentary inquiries represented a key step. We can see this in operation in the parliamentary enquiries that occurred. Over this nine-year period, 17 select committees and royal commissions were established. MPs dominated most of these inquiries. Fourteen of the 17 inquiries began as parliamentary select committees and were later converted to royal commissions. This was only because the life of a select committee was limited to the parliamentary session in which it was established.

Of the 14 parliamentary inquiries, eleven offer the remarkable spectacle of MPs engaged on major strategic investigations that went to the heart of policy-making and administration. The first major category of enquiries involved those concerned with the strategic agenda. Enquiries occurred at key stages from the point that an issue emerged on the political agenda to the determination of legislation. Seven of the eleven inquiries concerned issues at the frontier of the political agenda: the tariff, the desirability of nationalisation of the tobacco cartel, the need for Australian control of shipping services, federal old age pensions, access to press cable services, Papua, and the future of 'New Protection' following the High Court rejection of the arrangement proposed in 1907.

By far the most significant inquiry in scale, duration and impact was that into the tariff. This was first suggested by the radical Protectionist, Sir Isaac Isaacs, in October 1904 and was established by the Free Trade Prime Minister George Reid in December 1904. The group of eight MPs consisted of three Free Traders, three Protectionists and two Labor members, with two representatives each from New South Wales and Victoria and one from each other state. The inquiry commenced in 1905 and concluded in the middle of 1907. At the outset, it surveyed virtually all significant Australian manufacturers and importers to identify tariff anomalies, local capacity, cost obstacles, special factors and so forth. This covered 2801 establishments. Evidence was gathered over the two years 1905 and 1906. The inquiry held sittings in all capital cities and major provincial centres. In total 211 sittings were held and 618 witnesses examined. Over 3,000 pages of oral evidence were printed. The oral and written evidence offers a unique and comprehensive account of Australian industrial capacity and of the barriers and vicissitudes to which it was subject on account of the scale of domestic markets and the vigour of international competition. The Commission produced 46 individual reports on the various tariff heads. The significance of this inquiry lies not so much in the findings, perhaps predictable given the rival ideologies, but in the immense research, outreach and mobilisation effort that the inquiry represented.

Contested legislation was the second major area of strategic policy-making to which parliamentary inquiries made a particular contribution. The *Bonus for Manufactures Bill 1904* was a Protectionist initiative resisted by a strong faction of their erstwhile Labor supporters on the grounds that local iron production would prohibitively boost upstream costs. By contrast, the *Navigation Bill 1906*, sponsored by the Reid–McLean government stumbled on Labor insistence on Australian crews and special conditions for coastal trade. These were both extensive inquiries that produced divided reports. Neither issue was finally resolved before 1909. Parliamentary inquiries as a vehicle for investigating contested legislation represented a role for Parliament and MPs that has only recently been revived (e.g. GST inquiries).

Finally, two inquiries involved oversight of major government activities: review of electoral administration in 1904 and the Post Office review in 1908–1909. The Post Office review was almost on the scale of the tariff inquiry. It involved a comprehensive assessment of this key federal agency. A minority (Labor) report opposed the restriction of female occupations to typing, telegraphy and monitoring!

To discount these inquiries because their recommendations were not wholly bipartisan or not accepted by the government is to misperceive the role and contribution of parliamentary inquiries in a pluralised political environment. In this more fluid political context, parliamentarians played much more prominent roles in agenda setting and issue refinement.[3] Their judgements were critical to advance of these issues through the policy development process. Parliamentary inquiries brought interested and expert opinion, including departmental opinion, before MPs and a wider public. The inquiries acted as a 'forcing device' engaging stakeholders in a process of advocacy and (reciprocal) social learning. At the outset, different groups might have perceived themselves to be winners or losers or just interested parties. Through a process of public inquiry, all participants gained understanding about other perspectives and concerns and the opportunity thus opened up to develop more encompassing approaches.

The fact that Parliament was the setting for this process, that parliamentary opinion influenced the outcome and that votes on the floor of Parliament counted, was vital for its impact on interest groups, departments and ministers. Further, parliamentary inquiries on strategic issues, matters that were more or less outside the immediate partisan contest, required MPs to seek common ground and, where this proved elusive, at least to isolate points of difference. The whole process occurred in the public domain with evidence sessions published and available for scrutiny and review. Particularly on strategic issues, such inquiries provided opportunities for departmental officers to be cross-examined in public and departmental opinion to be disclosed.

In sum, in renewing the link between the Australian community and the formal policy-making system, there is only one institution in the political structure with the necessary formal standing and authority. This is the Parliament. It is the only institution capable of playing a pivotal or keystone role. It is the only institution capable of achieving an immediate, comprehensive and direct impact on interest-group and official opinion and through this development, broader public opinion. It provides the only institutional setting where the scope for explicit consensus between partisans can could be explored and expressed. Committees are the right institutions to introduce new strategic issues to the political agenda and to engage interest groups and the broader community in the consideration of these issues. This is for example, the role they can play in the United States Senate, the Chamber on which our own Senate was modelled. The House of Commons has also considerably strengthened its Select Committee system in recent years. Whilst not matching fully the 'contemplative' role envisaged here, enquires have become an important adjunct to official policy-making processes. Committee roles are far more developed than those of their counterparts in Australia.

The proposal I advocate would involve parliamentary arrangements specially focused on the long term. These would be outside the immediate direct authority of the government and the immediate influence of the major policy departments such as Treasury, Defence, and Prime Minister and Cabinet. This would be a virtue. Deliberation could occur without commitment of the government. Yet committees with standing in the policy development process would attract interest, media and public attention. They can provide a forum where official, novel, sectional and deviant or marginal opinions can be voiced. Bureaucrats, ministers, interest groups and independent experts can appear on an equal footing. Finally, through its varied processes and deliberations, Parliament can seed the formation of broader public opinion. The theatre of Parliament creates the cameo dramas that communicate the significance of issues to a broader public. This is now mainly fostered through rituals such as Question Time and Urgency Motions that have lost their original purpose. The political drama needs to be refashioned to contribute positively to the development of sectional and public opinion.

To amplify Parliament's standing in the broader political structure, its committees need to have enhanced roles and powers. The present parliamentary committee system is inappropriately structured; committees are insufficiently focused. The committee system would need to be reworked. The present committees work on a shoestring. The incentives for committee work are weak; those with ministerial ambitions may be fearful of taking an independent line. Finally, the use of latent parliamentary powers, particularly in the Senate, to gain attention for committee findings and recommendations is hugely underdeveloped.

Why might committees, working as routine participants in policy-making processes, make the contributions foreshadowed in this chapter? The theoretical base for these proposals can only be mentioned in passing. Recent scholarly work has accorded critically important roles to ideas. These are the foundation for policy adaptation and change. Institutional theory provides the relevant theoretical paradigm. One strand of institutional theory, historical institutionalism, focuses on continuities and a more recent branch, constructivist institutionalism, focuses on policy change and adaptation (e.g. Hay, 2006; Blyth, 2002; Crouch, 2005; D. Marsh et al, 1999). Some noted scholars might qualify this rough summary (e.g. Hall, 2007; Streeck and Thelen, 2005). These arguments continue. In a constructivist perspective however, ideas function as political solvents and catalysts in a number of specific ways. In a medium term perspective, ideas can mediate adaptive institutional development. Mark Blyth has enumerated the five ways that ideas facilitate this outcome (2002, pp. 36-40). First, in periods of crisis ideas reduce uncertainty. Second, following uncertainty reduction, ideas make collective action and coalition building possible. Third, in the struggle over existing institutions, ideas are weapons. Fourth, following the de-legitimation of existing institutions, new ideas act as institutional blueprints. Fifth, following institutional construction, ideas make institutional stability possible.

Elsewhere, and building on Lindblom's work on partisan mutual adjustment, I have discussed the ways ideas also facilitate more immediate accommodation between protagonists (1995, pp. 217-219). Agreement is of course one possibility, but in politics often a rare ground for accommodation. A second ground might involve issue redefinition as a concern is re-framed in more encompassing terms. Third, accommodation may be achieved through commitment to a later review to check that promised outcomes have been realised. Fourth, accommodation might be based on procedural acceptance — I do not agree with the result but

I accept that the process is fair. Finally, consent might be elicited through compensation or log rolling. The formal political and policy-making system to provides the setting in which ideas perform these integrative tasks. The present Australian policy-making structure needs to be developed to allow ideas to do their work of accommodation and integration. They can mediate policy adaptation and change and — what is the same thing — they can create a better alignment between the social base of the policy-making system and the formal structure.

Conclusion: is political change likely?

In line with other commentators (notably Hay, 2006; Marquand, 2004), this paper has argued that the central political problem concerns the gap between the formal system and the people whom it purportedly represents. This is a systemic problem, the result of a failure to adapt the formal structure to profound change in its social base. It has been compounded by the primary basis for policy development post-1983: tacit bipartisanship. This top-down process facilitated rapid policy change with minimal attention to public consent. Meanwhile, in their (public) struggle for office, the major parties have adopted populist and opportunist approaches and they have manufactured or suppressed difference. Citizens may not know what is wrong, but they recognise that much of this political drama is a charade. They see that media events dominate political communications. They see that parliamentary rituals and debates are mostly irrelevant. They see that the major party organisations no longer exercise linkage and communication roles. Memberships are tiny. Conferences are wholly stage managed. These outcomes are a consequence of the incentive structure implicit in adversarial politics. Indeed, there is other evidence that Australian's engagement in politics is undiminished. Citizen energies are now channelled in unconventional activities — for example, the enormous success of the *Get-Up* organisation and its campaigns, the numbers who have participated in anti-war and pro-reconciliation activity, or the new role of Christian and pro-family organisations.

Yet at first blush, it may seem far fetched to anticipate amendment of the formal structure of politics and policy-making. After all, this architecture is firmly rooted in habits and expectations not just of elites but of the public more generally. Quite properly, the inertial forces are formidable. Change in the formal structure of power is rightly no casual development. As many recent democratic transitions illustrate, such developments are often associated with crisis, turbulence and physical force. Yet with the adoption of MMP New Zealand has recently initiated a peaceful formal change in the structure of power. Through changes in party strength and alignments in Parliament, Australia had a similar experience in 1909. A capacity for peaceful regime adaptation has, since the seventeenth century, made British politics exemplary for others (Beer, 1965). So, although rightly rare, such developments are not unheard of. Further,

Australia's Constitution allows such possibilities. The structure of executive power is not constitutionally determined as for example in the case of the United States. It is rather based on three conventions — ministerial responsibility, confidence and collective cabinet responsibility. These conventions are determined by vote on the floor of Parliament, not by constitutional fiat.

Short of a referendum on the voting system (as occurred in New Zealand), there would seem to be at least two broad paths to structural amendment. One would involve a bottom up movement against the established parties. The other might involve executive action. An executive might recognise that its electoral vulnerability ultimately merits an effort to engage the community more effectively in policy development processes. These possibilities are reviewed in turn.

New parties

If minor party support grew sufficiently, the minor parties could take the initiative in proposing change. There are many ways in which they could negotiate with the government or the Opposition. Perhaps above all, they could trade a preference deal for the support of a major party in House of Representatives elections for a real change in the committee structure in the Senate. As I have argued elsewhere, the capacity of minor parties to show their supporters that they are not clones of the government that they are sustaining is critical (1990). Yet backdoor negotiations with the executive run this risk. My earlier study concerned the fate of the Liberals in the UK after the Steel-Callaghan pact was established in the 1970s. The Liberal leader, David Steel, was unable to convince his followers outside Parliament that he had advanced party interests whilst also sustaining the government. In Australia, the Democrats succumbed to analogous problems in their approach to the GST. The Australian Greens face the same difficulty if they become a balance of power party. Yet the experience of the Democrats is also salutary. They were only able to wield a balance of power when supported by one or other of the major parties. Stanley Bach has shown the extent to which in practice the two major parties vote together in the Senate, thus undercutting the influence of minor parties (2003). Adversarial rituals prevail in the House. Shared major party self-interest has mostly prevailed in the Senate.

In any case, to negotiate a deal with a major party as significant as that envisaged here, a minor party would need t be able to demonstrate control of a tranche of votes far beyond that which the Democrats mustered in the past or the Greens do now. Finally, given the parlous state of the Liberal Party, a split along Free Trade and Protectionist lines cannot be ruled out. Electoral incentives are a powerful inertial force. But before its reconstitution by Sir Robert Menzies, splits were a regular feature. At this stage such a scenario is wholly speculative but perhaps also not to be wholly discounted.

Executive initiative

At first blush it may seem unlikely that any executive would freely encourage the development of a new transparent phase in the policy-making process. After all this would be based on structures over which, at best, it would only have indirect influence. Yet the case studies of policy-making by the Howard Government pointed to the serious gaps in present arrangements, gaps which severely constrain the governments' political strategy, indeed bias it towards wedge, opportunist and populist tactics.

There are two reasons to believe structural change may not be wholly unacceptable to an enlightened/ambitious executive. One involves looking backward to the experience of the Howard governments. The other involves looking forward to the emerging policy agenda. Both major parties broadly agreed with the deregulatory and liberalising agenda introduced by Labor in 1983 and continued by the Howard governments from 1996. This micro-economic and deregulatory agenda has now just about run its course. It involved actions by government that liberalised market structures. Assessments were required at the level of the whole economy. Discriminatory or sectoral policies were disfavoured as was the engagement of affected interests. Indeed as public choice theory demonstrated, engagement of affected interests would more likely have corrupted the policy process. Thus the past received wisdom has been to discredit interest groups as selfish and self-serving and distance them as much as possible from policy-making processes.

Emerging policy issues are wholly different in character. Let us take just three: innovation and the knowledge economy; the environment and climate change; and public services such as health, education, hospitals and welfare. In relation to innovation, whilst unfettered markets are absolutely necessary in promoting this outcome, they are not sufficient. The knowledge system that surrounds any particular sector or region is no less important than the market structure in driving continuous improvement. This is the essential conclusion of innovation theory (e.g. West, 2006; Lipsey, Carlaw and Bekar, 2005). This introduces considerations quite other than those pertinent to the deregulating and liberalising agenda that has dominated in the past two decades. Now capacities to mobilise interests and to engage them at sectoral levels become much more critical. Capacities for analysis at sectional and regional levels are also required. In passing, we might note that a strategy based around innovation and the knowledge economy would, if fully developed, be tantamount to the renewal (in another key) of Deakin's protectionist-arbitration strategy. This is because it would unite the most basic social and economic strategies. Access to life long learning would require new educational arrangements matched by support over periods of reskilling. General social security arrangements would need to be consistent with these developments. Meanwhile, federal and state economic strategies would be designed to encourage innovation and continuous improvement at sectoral and regional levels and to aid global engagement. A similar unification was the keystone of the 'Australian settlement' and the crowning achievement of social liberalism. In passing, we might also note that the argument developed in this paper in effect applies innovation theory to the national policy system. This foundational knowledge infrastructure also needs to be mapped and developed.

Climate change introduces an even greater imperative for interest and community mobilisation. If the scientific prognosis is only half right, the politics of adaptation promises to be fraught. The need to build deep understanding of implications and options is surely clear. It is equally clear that this process has barely begun. What infrastructure will underwrite these processes? We have clear evidence of deficient capacity in present arrangements. What else is possible? Finally, in relation to health and community services, federal-state relations are primarily involved. But even here, the COAG structure mobilises affected elites. Even in a developed form, it is unlikely to provide sustained access to broader public opinion or affected interests.

A strengthened parliamentary committee system is not of course a panacea for all issues of policy-making. A host of specialist and sectoral research, enquiry and mobilisation mechanisms will doubtless be required. These can augment the technical and mobilising capacities of the policy-making system. But none can match the parliamentary theatre in terms of formal standing and ability to engage interest groups, media and public attention. In an augmented architecture of policy-making, a reconfigured parliamentary committee system, focussed on the Senate, and drawing on the latent powers of that Chamber, offers the best capstone. Such a structure would introduce a contemplative phase to policy development. To avoid the fate of the Howard Government, moves down this path are clearly in the interest of an ambitious executive. Will it be willing to learn from the experience of its predecessors? Will it be sufficiently prudent to recognise its best interests?

References

Aitkin, D. 1977. *Stability and Change in Australian Politics*. Canberra: Australian National University Press.

Argy, F. 2007. 'Government advertising on industrial relations', *Democratic Audit of Australia*. Canberra: Australian National University.

Bach, S. 2003. *Platypus and Parliament: The Australian Senate in theory and Practice*. Canberra: Dept. of the Senate.

Beer, S. 1965. *British Politics in the Collectivist Age* , New York: Vintage Books.

Blyth, M. 2002. *Great Transformations: Economic Ideas and Institutional Change in the Twentieth Century*. New York, Cambridge University Press.

Blyth, M. and R. Katz. 2005. 'From Catch-all Politics to Centralisation: The political economy of the cartel party.' *West European Politics*, 28(1): 33-60.

Braithwaite, J. and P. Drahos, 2000. *Global Business Regulation*. Melbourne: Cambridge University Press.

Brett, J. 2003. *Australian Liberals and the moral middle class: from Alfred Deakin to John Howard*. Cambridge: Cambridge University Press.

Crouch, C. 2005. *Capitalist diversity and change: Recombinant governance and institutional entrepreneurs*. Oxford: Oxford University Press.

Dalton, R. 2004. *Democratic challenges, democratic choices: The erosion of political support in advanced industrial democracies*. Oxford: Oxford University Press.

Dryzek, J. 2000. *Deliberative democracy and beyond: liberals, critics and contestations*. Oxford: Oxford University Press.

Gollan, R. 1960. *Radical and working class politics: A study of Eastern Australia, 1850-1910*. Melbourne: Melbourne University Press.

Hall, P. 2007. *The Evolution of Varieties of Capitalism in Europe*. Minda de Gunzburg Centre for European Studies, Harvard University.

Hamilton, C. 2007. *Scorcher: The Dirty Politics of Climate Change*. Melbourne: Black Inc. Agenda.

Hay, C. 2006. 'Constructivist institutionalism', in *The Oxford Handbook of Political Institutions*, R. Rhodes, S. Binder and B. Rockman (eds). Cambridge: Cambridge University Press.

Hay C. 2007. *Why we hate politics*. Cambridge: Polity Press.

Henry, K. 2007. *Address to the International Project Managers Symposium*, Canberra, 9 February.

Keating, M. 2004. *Who Rules: How Government Retains Control of a Privatised Economy*. Sydney: Federation Press.

Lindblom, 1965. *The Intelligence of Democracy: Decisionmaking through Mutual Adjustment*. New York: The Free Press.

Lipsey, R., K. Carlaw, and C. Bekar. 2005. *Economic transformaions: General purpose technologies and long term economic growth*. Oxford: Oxford University Press.

Lloyd, J. 2004. *What the media are doping to our politics?* London: Constable.

Mair, P. 1997. *Party system change: Approaches and interpretations*. Oxford: Clarendon Press.

Marquand, D. 2004. *Decline of the Public: The Hollowing-out of Citizenship*. Cambridge: Polity Press.

Marsh, D., J. Buller, C. Hay, J. Johnston, P. Kerr, S. McAnulla and M. Watson. 1999. *Postwar British Politics in Perspective*. Cambridge: Polity Press.

Marsh, I. and D. Yencken. 2005. *Into the Future: The Neglect of the Long Term in Australian Politics*, Melbourne: Black Inc.

Marsh I. 1985. *Policy-making in a Three Party System*, London: Methuen.

—— 1990. 'Liberal Priorities, the Lib-Lab Pact and the Requirements for Policy Influence.' *Parliamentary Affairs* 43(3): 292-321.

—— 1995. *Beyond the Two Party System*. Melbourne: Cambridge University Press.

—— 2006. 'Neo-liberalism and the decline of democratic governance in Australia: A problem of Institutional Design?' *Political Studies*, 53, 1, pp. 22-43.

—— 2006b (ed.) *Political parties in Transition?* Sydney: Federation Press.

—— 2007. 'Political institutions and the corruption of political opinion.' *Australian Journal of Public Administration* 66(3): 329-341.

McAdam, D., J. McCarthy and M. Zald (eds). 1996. *Comparative Perspectives on Social Movements: Political opportunities, mobilizing structures and cultural framings*. Cambridge: Cambridge University Press.

McKenzie, R. 1958. 'Parties, Pressure Groups and the British Political Proces', *The Political Quarterly* 29 (1) , 5–16.

Mills, S. 1986. *The New Machine Men: Polls and Persuasion in Australian Politics*. Ringwood: Penguin Books.

Pettit, P. 1997. *Republicanism: A theory of freedom and government*. Oxford: Clarendon Press.

Stoker, G. 2006. *Why Politics Matters, Making Democracy Work*. Basingstoke: Palgrave Macmillan.

Streeck, W. and K. Thelen (eds) 2005. *Beyond Continuity: Institutional change in advanced political Economies*. New York: Oxford University Press.

West, J. 2006. *An Economic Strategy for NSW*. Hobart: Australian Innovation Research Centre.

Wooden, M. 2007. 'Wage pressure danger lurks on both roads', On Line Opinion. URL: <www.onlineopinion.com.au/view.asp?article=6607>. Accessed November 2007.

Yankelovitch, D. 1992. *Coming to Public Judgement*. New York: Syracuse University Press.

Zaller, J. 1992. *The Nature and Origins of Mass Opinion*. Cambridge: Cambridge University Press.

ENDNOTES

[1] 'Bring David Hicks Home'. Accessed 19 February, 2008, at http://www.getup.org.au/campaign/BringDavidHicksHome

[2] This is not to overlook what has proved the most powerful source of policy change in the past two or three decades, namely tacit bipartisanship. The major parties tacitly accepted all the major policy changes proposed after 1983 save for the GST and Telstra privatisation. Both of these measures were subsequently introduced by the Howard governments.

[3] Oliver MacDonagh describes analogous dynamics in his account of policy-making processes in the nineteenth century in the UK, before the development of mass parties: 'After 1820 ... Select Committees were used with a regularity and purpose quite without precedent. It is difficult to overestimate the importance of this development. Through session after session, through hundreds of inquiries and the examination of many thousands of witnesses a vast mass of information and statistics was being assembled. Even where (as was uncommonly the case) the official enquiry was in the hands of unscrupulous partisans, a sort of informal adversary system usually led to the enlargement of true knowledge in the end. A session or two later the counter-partisans would secure a counter exposition of their own. All this enabled the administration to act with a confidence, a perspective and a breadth of vision which had never hitherto existed. It had also a profound secular effect on public opinion generally and upon parliamentary public opinion in particular. For the exposure of the actual state of things in particular fields was in the ling run probably the most fruitful source of reform in nineteenth century England.' Oliver MacDonagh, *Early Victorian Government, 1830-1870*, Holmes and Meir, New York, 1977, p. 6.

www.ingramcontent.com/pod-product-compliance
Lightning Source LLC
Chambersburg PA
CBHW061240270326

41927CB00035B/3453